A Place to Live

KOREAN CLASSICS LIBRARY: PHILOSOPHY AND RELIGION

A Place to Live

A New Translation of Yi Chung-hwan's T'aengniji,
the Korean Classic for Choosing Settlements

translated, annotated, and with an introduction by
Inshil Choe Yoon

University of Hawai'i Press/Honolulu
Korean Classics Library

Library of Congress Cataloging-in-Publication Data

Names: Yi, Chung-hwan, 1690-1756, author. | Yoon, Inshil Choe, translator,
  writer of added commentary, writer of introduction.
Title: A place to live : a new translation of Yi Chung-hwan's T'aengniji, the
  Korean classic for choosing settlements / translated, annotated, and with
  an introduction by Inshil Choe Yoon.
Other titles: T'aengniji. English | Korean classics library. Philosophy and
  religion
Description: Honolulu : University of Hawaii Press, [2018] | Series: Korean
  classics library: Philosophy and religion | Includes bibliographical
  references and index.
Identifiers: LCCN 2018009982 | ISBN 9780824877606 (cloth ; alk. paper)
Subjects: LCSH: Korea — Description and travel — Early works to 1800. |
  China — Description and travel — Early works to 1800. |
  Homesites — Korea — Early works to 1800.
Classification: LCC DS902.2 .Y513 2018 | DDC 915.1904/2 — dc23
LC record available at https://lccn.loc.gov/2018009982

This work was supported by the English Translation of 100 Korean Classics program through the Ministry of Education of the Republic of Korea and the Korean Studies Promotion Service of the Academy of Korean Studies (AKS-2010-AAA-2101).

University of Hawai'i Press books are printed on acid-free paper and meet the guidelines for permanence and durability of the Council on Library Resources.

Design and composition by Wanda China

For all the mothers and fathers

Have you consulted the *T'aengniji*?
It is the best discussion on the conditions of living.
— *Chǒng Yag-yong (1762–1836)*

Contents

Color plates follow page 86

Maps

Acknowledgments

I was introduced to the *T'aengniji* in primary school and knew it then only by name as a Korean classic. I later studied it at university and came to appreciate it as an exemplary work of Korean human geography. It was not until I left Korea for the United States and then New Zealand, however, that I came to have a better understanding of the *T'aengniji* and its author. Once a public official, Yi Chung-hwan was removed from office early in his career and banished, enduring periods of exile in remote places. As a fellow-itinerant, he has been my greatest inspiration in carrying out my studies of the *T'aengniji*. Living in faraway New Zealand, I've given much thought to places in my homeland.

I am honored to present my recent studies of the *T'aengniji* and its full translation twenty years after my partial translation was first published. My work was made possible by financial assistance from the Korea Foundation, the University of Auckland, and the Academy of Korean Studies. I am most grateful for their support. For his gentle and reassuring guidance and valuable comments, I would like to express my deep gratitude to Robert Buswell, University of California, Los Angeles. I extend my gratitude as well to Jennifer Jung-Kim, Center for Buddhist Studies, UCLA, for her prompt and willing assistance. I would also like to thank Kyung Moon Hwang and the manuscript's anonymous reviewer for helpful comments and suggestions, which greatly enhanced my ability to introduce the *T'aengniji* to English-language readers. I am grateful to Bingjun Pang for his numerous suggestions on my previous translation. Advice from Paul Clark, Kyung-soo Chun, Patrick Hanan, and Richard Phillips is also appreciated. I would also like to thank the School of Cultures, Languages, and Linguistics of the University of Auckland for its generous financial support of the publication of this book.

My sincerest thanks go to Young-jin Kim and Hae-jun Lee for allowing me access to the *T'aengniji* manuscripts in their private collection and to Yong-hun Jun, Tschung-Sun Kim, and Young-ho Lee for helping me acquire copies of the manuscripts. While in Korea, I made numerous trips to libraries over several months to read and make copies of *T'aengniji* manuscripts. I thank the staff of these libraries, especially the library in Kyujanggak, for their kindness. I am indebted to Kyu-won Hwang, Chie Emslie, and Masako Takagaki at the library of the University of Auckland for their help in my search for library sources. I remain grateful to Young-jun Choe, Iware Matsuda, and Song-won Yoon for providing me with articles that were difficult to acquire at the earliest stage of my work.

My heartfelt appreciation goes to Patricia Crosby for her thorough and thoughtful copy editing, Frances Moon for her generous and consistent willingness to help in editing the final manuscript, Caroline Yoon for her magnificent contribution to enhancing its readability, Louise Cotterall for drawing the maps, and Stephanie Chun for overseeing the process to publication. I must also offer my gratitude to Yvonne Brill, Kaaren Hiyama, Rudd Hughes, and Melvyn Galbraith for proofreading. I thank Margaret Lee, Lawrence Marceau, and colleagues in Asian studies at the School of Cultures, Languages, and Linguistics for supporting me in various ways.

The time spent in Korea for this research is memorable in many ways, not least of which is that it was the longest period I had lived with my parents since I left Korea decades ago. I am indebted to my parents for their love and sacrifice and to my grandparents, uncles, aunts, sisters-in-law, and brothers for their support and understanding. I am grateful to my husband, Hong-key, for sharing his views and for his enormous support at the initial stage of the study. My love and gratitude go to my children, Albert, Caroline, Frances, Annabelle, and ReneeMarie, and their spouses, Hilary, Peter, Sam, and Mike, for their care and support, and to my grandchildren, Liam, Emily, Annabelle, Sienna, Sophie, Xanthe, and Ari, whose birth and robust growth have been an enormous joy. Without being aware that their *halmŏni* has been working on the *T'aengniji* all through their lives, they have replenished my spirit along the journey toward the publication of this work.

Conventions

Romanization

Transcriptions of Asian languages follow the systems commonly used in Western scholarship, including Pinyin for Chinese and revised Hepburn for Japanese. I romanize Korean following the McCune-Reischauer system prescribed by G. M. McCune and E. O. Reischauer in "The Romanization of the Korean Language: Based upon Its Phonetic Structure" (*Transactions of the Korea Branch of the Royal Asiatic Society* 29 [1939]: 1–55). To make Korean romanizations easier to parse and interpret for Western readers, I have adopted the following conventions throughout the book.

Personal names are hyphenated to show the boundaries of syllables, for example, Yi Sun-sin.

In transcribing geographic and architectural names, either English- or Korean-language designations are retained, but not both.

Korean geographical suffixes widely used throughout the book — such as *san* (mountain), *kang/-gang* or *ha* (river), *to/-do* (province), *kun/-gun* or *hyŏn* (county) — are given in their English equivalencies: for example, Mount Nam for Nam-san, Han River for Han'gang, Hwanghae Province for Hwanghae-do.

Korean suffixes are retained for less frequently mentioned geographical suffixes, such as mountain pass (*lyŏng, nyŏng,* or *ryŏng*), streams (*kye/-gye*), islands (*to/-do*), lake (*tam/-dam* or *ho*), port (*p'o*), village (*ch'on*), valley (*tong/-dong*), cliff (*am*), and hill (*hyŏn*): for example, Ch'ŏllyŏng, Choryŏng, Kuryonggye, Kado, Todam, Sijungho, Sŭngch'ŏnp'o, Sahyŏn, Karhyŏn.

Korean suffixes are retained for architectural terms such as monastery (*sa*), palace (*kung/-gung*), hall (*hŏn, chŏn/-jŏn*), station (*yŏk*), mountain fortress (*sansŏng*), bridge (*kyo/-gyo*), pavilion (*chŏng/-jŏng, tae/-dae, lu, nu,* or *ru*), and so on: for example, Pusŏksa, Kyŏngbokkung, Un'gyoyŏk, Namhansansŏng, Mansegyo, P'algwaejŏng, Ch'ongsŏkchŏng, Sijungdae, Hwanjŏktae, Chuksŏru, Pubyŏngnu.

Measurements

Equivalents for terms of measurement used throughout the book are as follows:

> *ch'i* — the equivalent of approximately 3 centimeters
> *kan* — the length between two columns, usually 2.4 meters a unit of both length and area, originated from the use of tree trunks as a building unit
> *myo* — 260 square meters
> *ri* — 400 meters
> *chong* — 2,160 or 2,880 liters

I. Translator's Introduction

Translator's Introduction

The *T'aengniji* (Treatise on choosing settlements) begins with a seemingly innocuous statement: "In ancient times there was no scholar-gentry (*sa-daebu*) class.[1] All members of society were common folk." At the time of its writing in the early 1750s Korean society was rigidly stratified, with the *yangban* class, which was composed of scholar-gentry, at the highest level.[2] The opening sentence would therefore have come across as a shocking taunt to its contemporary readership, who were likely members of the scholar-gentry class. On account of this statement, its author, Yi Chung-hwan (1690–1756), is said to have "favored the common people"[3] or even to have advocated for a class-free society.[4] Yi, however, makes no such claims for himself in the text. The statement serves only to open his introduction to the origin and development of the scholar-gentry class.[5] Yi ostensibly concerned himself with "issues concerning the scholar-gentry class," most explicitly the question of identifying places where the scholar-gentry could lead an honorable life.[6]

Yet this very question was itself radical for its time. For most of the Chosŏn dynasty (1392–1910), which was characterized by a patrilocal society, scholar-gentry generally lived within extended families in the hometowns that their ancestors had inhabited for generations, often without ever moving abodes. Male *yangban* sought to enter government office through civil service examinations, after which they would usually move to the capital for an initial government position and later might be posted to another province. When they quit or retired from their posts, they would return to their hometowns.

This typical profile did not, however, apply to many scholar-gentry households in Yi Chung-hwan's day. At the time of the *T'aengniji*'s writing, Yi was a ruined scholar-gentleman, his successful career having come to an abrupt and premature end due to his suspected involvement in the *sinim* (1721–1722) scholar's purge. His banishment would have left Yi in need of a place of residence where he could live with his family, fulfilling his duties as a scholar-gentleman. Mok Hoe-gyŏng's (1698–?) postscript to the *T'aengniji* gives a rare glimpse of Yi's forlorn life: "Yi Chung-hwan wandered around without having a house of his own."[7] The *T'aengniji* concerned the economic survival of a disgraced scholar, which was radical because the upper class of the Chosŏn dynasty shunned discussions of material well-being in favor of the reading of Neo-Confucian metaphysical cannons and cultivation of Confucian moral standing.

Yi's unconventional pursuit of sites suitable for scholar-gentry habitation resulted in a book that has become one of Korea's most enduring and widely read classics.[8] Modern Korean scholars have referred to it as "the finest and most essential book of regional geography and also the first book of human geography in Korea,"[9] "the most prominent work of Practical Learning on geography in Korea,"[10] "a masterpiece in the human geography of the late Chosŏn dynasty and an extremely important source of information for understanding the political and economic history of that time,"[11] and "not only a book of geography but also of philosophy and thought."[12] In order to appreciate the historical context of the *T'aengniji*, we will first look into the literati factional politics that, together with other factors, created unstable living conditions for Yi Chung-hwan and other scholar-gentry.

Literati Factional Politics

One of the most distinctive and long-lasting characteristics of Chosŏn society was the factional politics among the literati that started toward the end of the sixteenth century. Neo-Confucianism was adopted as the official state ideology at the beginning of Chosŏn in the late fourteenth century.[13] Scholars thereafter accepted it as the guiding principle of society and expected governance of the country to be guided by virtue and propriety. They expected that codes of conduct would uphold proper human relationships based on Confucian teaching and believed that righteousness had to be pursued above all else, even to the detriment of one's own life.[14] Such expectations caused some among the scholars to challenge the "meritorious elite," who were involved in King Sejo's usurpation of the throne. The result was the purges that first occurred in 1498.[15]

Literati factional politics began in 1575 when disputes over the appointment of a selection secretary caused the Neo-Confucian scholar-gentry to divide into two factions, the Easterner (Tongin) and Westerner (Sŏin).[16] Each faction claimed exclusive righteousness in its interpretation and application of Neo-Confucian doctrines to important decisions. This sometimes resulted in purges of members of one or more factions, often accompanied by mass confiscation of property, exile, or application of the death penalty. Soon after the initial split into two factions, Easterners came to dominate the political scene. Northerners, who had split from the Easterners, then gained political dominance as their supported prince rose to the throne to become King Kwanghae (r. 1608–1623). Having succeeded in staging a coup backing King Injo (r. 1623–1649), the Westerners enjoyed a long reign of dominance interrupted only by the occasional brief tenure of the Southerners. After the Westerners' division into Old Doctrine and Young Doctrine factions, Old Doctrine continuously dominated the court until the end of the dynasty, even after T'angpyŏngch'aek (Policy of Impartiality) was implemented.

In consequence, the literati factional politics caused elements of upper-class society to become segregated one from another, a segmentation not limited to those who aligned themselves with certain factions but to their descendants and those who worked for them as well. This segregation and any one faction's dominance of official posts naturally affected one's government employment and promotions: substantial numbers of scholar-gentry of the non-dominant factions, unable to secure employment, were often left without the means to make a living. Some had to do the work of a peasant, tilling land that belonged to others and returning a portion of the harvest to their landlords.

In these circumstances, Yi Chung-hwan's investigation of habitable places where scholar-gentry could preserve their former dignity was not simply a personal quest but a search on behalf of many.

Intellectual Influences and Context

By referring to a Confucian saying that "teaching comes after material well-being," Yi Chung-hwan justified the scholar-gentry's search for livable places that could provide them with material well-being.[17] This line of thought, however, had been overlooked by most of the upper class since the establishment of the Chosŏn dynasty. The focus of the scholar-gentry was on cultivating Confucian moral stature, and male offspring aspired to pass civil service examinations and thereby secure employment in government. Those who were not successful in the examinations or who left their government posts would then be reliant on family income such as inheritance, slave holdings, and rent from tenant cultivators. They did not themselves physically engage in securing material goods.

Having experienced hardship, however, mainly caused by a series of foreign invasions between 1592 and early 1637, ideas for reforming practical aspects of political, economic, and social systems started formulating among scholars who were not employed in government. Most noteworthy is the suggestion of Yu Hyŏng-wŏn (1622–1673) for land reform and centralized administration with stronger authority for kings. Realizing the decline of commoners' wealth and inspired by Yu's *Pan'gye surok* (Pan'gye's occasional notes), Yi Ik (1681–1763) wrote extensively on proposed policy changes for enriching the material well-being of the country. He suggested a frugal lifestyle and suppression of purchasing lavish items. He proposed reducing the number of periodic markets in the interest of curtailing spending on extravagant goods. He furthermore suggested introducing high-value currencies, if the practice of using money had to remain.

Being a great-uncle of Yi Chung-hwan and a recognized scholar, Yi Ik was one of the first people to read Yi Chung-hwan's manuscript, and his foreword to it is one of the earliest extant writings in reference to the *T'aengniji*. Yi Ik expressed his great surprise and delight that "every word is focused on acquiring desirable places to live for scholar-gentry, and [that] features of mountain ranges and water flows, social characteristics, and land are presented in an excellent and orderly manner." He also revealed that he had never come across such fine writing.[18] Was Yi Chung-hwan influenced by Yi Ik? On account of the *T'aengniji* also dealing in practical matters and being a great-nephew of Yi Ik of the same Southerner (Namin) political faction, it is easily assumed Yi Chung-hwan was influenced by Yi Ik. Although Yi Chung-hwan is not recognized as one of Yi Ik's core pupils, he could have benefited from Yi Ik's own writings and vast book collection. With an age difference of nine years, informal academic discussions between the two could also be easily imagined. There are, however, unique features in the *T'aengniji* that are in stark contrast to the works of Yi Ik.

Unlike the works of Yu Hyŏng-wŏn or Yi Ik, which are collections of their thoughts on various themes, the *T'aengniji* is one integrated discussion focused on finding desirable habitations for scholar-gentry. The *T'aengniji* makes no suggestions for improving existing social or economic conditions. In traditional Korea, when most people lived off the land, agriculture was the main and most desirable economic activity. Yi Chung-hwan simply pointed out as the most valuable those places on the Korean peninsula with high harvest yields. He also mentioned as desirable those places offering good land or water transportation. It is worth noting in this connection that Yi Chung-hwan considered it acceptable for scholar-gentry to engage in transporting sea products by keeping and utilizing boats in busy water channels. The suggestion of scholar-gentry engaging in commercial activity was revolutionary because an occupation in commerce was traditionally considered to be the least desirable of occupations. Moreover, discussing ways to improve the income of one's own scholar-gentry class would have been extremely unusual; no scholars, including Yi Ik, ever discussed scholar-gentry accumulating wealth.

Apart from the revolutionary content of the *T'aengniji* mentioned so far, the work's structure, which allowed the thematic development to unfold, was also remarkable for its time. Before we go any further, we should have a closer look at the content and structure that make up the *T'aengniji*.

Different Parts of the Text

The *T'aengniji* consists of four parts entitled "The Four Classes of People," "Discourse on the Eight Provinces," "Discourse on the Selection of Habitable Places," and "Conclusion." The first part, which begins with a discussion of the emergence of the scholar-gentry class, strongly emphasizes the dignity and prerogatives of the class. The text here makes the point that, in order to maintain their status and dignity, it was necessary that scholar-gentry have a source of material goods. This part concludes by justifying the unavoidable task of selecting an abode that would afford a class-appropriate life. The importance of material wealth for the scholar-gentry serves as the starting point in Yi's writing the *T'aengniji*.[19]

The second part, "Discourse on the Eight Provinces," makes up nearly half of the book. It begins with a review of Korean geography, introducing the Korean peninsula as an extension of Mount Paektu that is connected to the Kunlun Mountains in China.[20] There follows a brief discussion of the eight provinces of Chosŏn Korea with reference to the territory of preceding kingdoms, geographical and historical descriptions of Korea, and the origins of the Korean scholar-gentry class.

Each of the eight provinces is then discussed in order of geographic location, more or less clockwise beginning with the peripheral northern provinces of P'yŏngan, Hamgyŏng, and Hwanghae, continuing through Kangwŏn Province, and then proceeding to the southern provinces of Kyŏngsang, Chŏlla, and Ch'ungch'ŏng before ending with the central district, Kyŏnggi Province, which encompasses the capital (Seoul). Discussing the eight provinces in this order was an abrupt contrast to court-initiated multivolume geography books, which were arranged in order from the central to peripheral provinces.[21]

An explanation of the physical geography of each province usually begins with its relationship to the mountain ranges that stretch from Mount Paektu. The provinces themselves are usually divided into regions, demarcated by mountain ranges and rivers. Each region is described and

evaluated based on its natural characteristics and human aspects, including physical landscape, suitability as a refuge in time of war, availabil-
ity of produce, economic conditions, lifestyle, and prominent residents,
including those who have held high government posts. Historic events,
legends, and poems related to the area are also often cited. Certain locations are referred to as "livable places," either suitable for the short term
for such circumstances as avoiding war or for long-term settlement for
generations. Finally, comments on the general socio-cultural traits and the
distance of the province from the capital provide assessments on the hab-
itability of the province for a scholar.

The remainder of the book is devoted almost entirely to the third
part, the discussion of the four criteria for selecting a desirable habitation,
namely, geomancy,[22] economic potential, social characteristics, and natural scenery. The first of these criteria, geomancy, is introduced as a way
of ascertaining an ideal site for a household. Six geomantic elements are
listed as essential for determining the auspiciousness of a site: the outlet
of the water course, the terrain, the shape of the mountains, the color of
the soil, the nature of watercourses, and, finally, the existence of a homage
mountain[23] and homage water flow.[24] These six are constituents of what
was thought necessary to maintain the prosperity of a family.

The second criterion is economic potential. Yi Chung-hwan describes
as economically desirable places with rich soil; second most desirable are
places that have the advantage of commercial activity thanks to good land
or water transport. After listing various profitable activities, including
trade with China and Japan, he concludes that scholars should not engage
in large-scale commercial activities but rather should profit by keeping
boats in busy channels and utilizing them to transport sea products.

Yi Chung-hwan explains the importance of social atmosphere by
quoting Confucius that "the wise select good neighbors." After a brief discussion of the regional characteristics of the common people of each province, Yi analyzes at length the customs of scholars since the founding of the
dynasty. He attributes the general mistrust and declining socio-political
situation of the scholar-gentry to century-long factional strife. The implementation of the Policy of Impartiality by the then-king results in the loss
of senses of justice and propriety. After initially suggesting the desirability
of finding a place in proximity to members of the same faction when one
lives in the countryside, he then rebuffs this recommendation in favor of
living alone, without any association with scholars. He concludes that one
would then find happiness even if one takes up the profession of farmer,
artisan, or merchant.

The final criterion for siting an appropriate residence is the locale's natural scenery. The discussion here centers on groups of mountains, mountain forms, islands, scenic spots in Kangwǒn and Ch'ungch'ǒng Provinces, and riverside and streamside settlements. In the first part of the "Conclusion," Yi Chung-hwan discusses the history of Korean surnames as well as the history of the scholar-gentry class in Korea. In the second part, he laments the social decline caused by the ill effects of factional politics among the literati and ends with the conclusion that, in the end, there is no place suitable for scholars to live. After a thorough examination of places employing the criteria he has established, the author comes to a rather startling conclusion. It is not so much that he humbly admits to his failure to accomplish the task he set for himself at the beginning of the book as it is to declare the unacceptability of the then-prevalent ill effects of factional politics, from which scholar-gentry could not escape.

Reception, Historical and Scholarly Significance, and Long-Term Influence

The *T'aengniji* was received from its first appearance with great enthusiasm. Being a great-uncle of Yi Chung-hwan and a recognized scholar, Yi Ik was one of the first people to read Yi Chung-hwan's manuscript.[25] Once circulated beyond the inner circles of his friends and relations, the reception among those readers without knowledge of the author's identity was more mixed: some found it a challenge, while for others it was an eye-opening experience. A few records on the *T'aengniji* allow an insight into the appreciation of its readers. Hong Chung-in (1677–1752), a member of the Southerners, hand copied the *T'aengniji* in an abridged form in the last years of his life. In an apparent challenge to the *T'aengniji*'s suggestion of keeping to oneself when it comes to finding a residence in the countryside, Hong wrote a lengthy justification of his comfortable rural life in the company of other people.[26]

A half century later Sim No-sung (1762–1837), the compiler of *Taedong p'aerim* (Miscellaneous collection of the great east),[27] wrote of his amazement at encountering *Pokkǒsǒl* (Theories on selecting livable places), another name for the *T'aengniji*. Sim commended the writing's easy flow and clarity of discussion. He also commented on the work's fairness and unbiased discussion of the origin and consequences of the stance and arguments of literati political factions. He then concluded that the work encompassed all of the distinctive writings that he had read.[28] This is an echo of Yi Ik's praise placing the *T'aengniji* beyond comparison among any of the other works he had come across.

Writers of forewords or postscripts to the *T'aengniji* commonly agreed it to be an excellent work, but their perception of the purpose of the book varied.[29] Some regarded it as either a "book on choosing suitable living places" or a "diverse writing containing history, geography, and philosophy."[30] In their interpretations of the author's message of the absence of livable places, some postscript writers focused on the author's intent to contribute to society or his motivation in writing the text.[31] It could be argued that the work's most significant effect on the scholar-gentry was as a catalyst for a re-evaluation of their living conditions. The *T'aengniji* prompted them to examine the various regions of Korea and to look into the conditions of their own existence—even of those who like Hong Chung-in decided to maintain their old way of living—and to prioritize the necessities of life. Both Yi Ik and Chŏng Yag-yong (1762–1836), prominent Practical Learning scholars, formulated their own criteria for leading their lives in accord with the *T'aengniji* with a brief evaluation of the regions. In his foreword to the *T'aengniji*, Yi Ik stated as undesirable places with low economic potential, those lacking in spirit, those with a high degree of military conflict, those where extravagance or jealousy prevailed.[32] Chŏng Yag-yong put forward four requirements for livable places: easy access to water and firewood, the ability to grow grains, social customs, and scenery.[33] Chŏng's appreciation of the *T'aengniji* is also revealed in his "Poem Drafted upon Returning Home in Retirement," written on his journey in a small boat along a river toward Ch'ungju. Among often-reminiscent portraits of natural scenery and descriptions of people engaged in fishing or sitting in boats laden with timber, rice wine, or food, Chŏng Yag-yong wrote, "Have you consulted the *T'aengniji*? / It is the best discussion on the conditions of living."[34] This statement demonstrates the huge impact of the text on scholars' traditional Confucian views on economic activity. The *T'aengniji* provided scholars in the late Chosŏn a rationale for why searching for profit was not a shameful act, especially in the case of ruined scholars.

While Chŏng Yag-yong regarded highly the way the *T'aengniji* discussed the conditions for living, Yi Kyu-gyŏng (1788–1856) criticized what he saw as the text's harmful effects on scholars. Quoting the *Analects of Confucius* as the original source for selecting settlements, he lamented the unprecedented trend of scholars' searching for places from which profit could be made.[35] His negative perception of the *T'aengniji*'s influence on the scholar-gentry notwithstanding, Yi Kyu-gyŏng acknowledged it as a valuable geographical survey.[36] Writers and editors of encyclopaedic and other works likewise understood the significance of the *T'aengniji* and included its content in their works. Substantial parts of the "Discourse on the

Selection of Habitable Places" appear as a separate chapter in manuscripts of *Chŭngbo sallim kyŏngje* (Revised and enlarged farm management), written by Yu Chung-nim in 1766. In the entry "Sangt'aekchi" (Writings on selecting abodes) in *Imwŏn kyŏngjeji* (Writings on rural life management), the content of the *T'aengniji* is the most often quoted source.[37] *Imwŏn kyŏngjeji* being the most comprehensive encyclopaedia of the Chosŏn dynasty and edited in the nineteenth century, an entry there favoring quotes from the *T'aengniji* affirms the high esteem in which the latter text was held in the field of site selection.

The *T'aengniji* was also valued for its treatment of literati factional politics. Select parts of the *T'aengniji* were anthologized in collections of the history of politics such as *P'aerim* (Miscellaneous collection),[38] *Aju chamnok* (Assorted records of Hong Chung-in),[39] and *Chosŏn tangjaeng kwan'gye charyojip* (Collection of sourcebooks on factional strife during the Chosŏn dynasty). The "Social Atmosphere" section of the *T'aengniji* is entered in the appendix of *Choya sinp'il* (Trustworthy writings of scholars both in government office and out of office).[40] In *Hwahae hwip'yŏn* (Collection of books on China and Korea), entered before the editor's postscript that appears at the very end, is "an abstract from the writings by Ch'ŏnghwa sanin," Ch'ŏnghwa sanin being a pseudonym used by Yi Chung-hwan. *Hwahae hwip'yŏn*, also known as *Hwahae tangwŏn* (Origins of factionalism in China and Korea), was edited by Yi Wŏn-sun in 1805.[41] In Yi Kŭng-ik's (1736–1806) "Pyŏljip" (Separate collection) of *Yŏllŏsil kisul* (Narratives of Yŏllŏsil), "P'aryŏk pokkŏji" (Writings on selecting livable places in the eight provinces), another commonly used title for the *T'aengniji*, is listed as a work of unofficial history.[42]

The above survey verifies that the *T'aengniji* was not only popularly received by lay scholars but also highly recognized by authors of the late Chosŏn dynasty, who referenced it in their works. This kind of impact and acceptance was not the case with works dealing with practical matters by other scholars, no matter how prominent. Multivolume works such as *Pan'gye surok* (Pan'gye's occasional notes) by Yu Hyŏng-wŏn, the forefather of Practical Learning, were hardly accessible to lay scholars. Neither Yi Ik's *Sŏngho sasŏl*, which further developed Yu's thought, nor Chŏng Yagyong's extensive works containing practical ideas and policies had any but the most limited readership and virtually no chance of being implemented.

The *T'aengniji* helped Koreans maintain their national pride when the country was colonized by Japan. In an effort to preserve Korean tradition, Choe Nam-sŏn established Chosŏn Kwanmunhoe in 1910 and published Korean classics, starting with books on Korean history and geography. When the *T'aengniji* was printed in 1912, Choe Nam-sŏn introduced it as "the finest and most essential book of regional geography and the first book of human geography in Korea."[43]

The importance of the *T'aengniji* was recognized by non-Koreans as well. *Chosen hachiikichi* (The eight provinces of Korea), an abridged Japanese translation of the *T'aengniji*, was published in 1882, and its Chinese version, *Chaoxian dili xiaozhi* (Abridged geography of Korea), was published in 1885.[44] An unabridged version, entitled *P'aryŏkchi*, was first issued by a Japanese publisher in Seoul soon after the Japanese Government General of Korea was established in 1910. Hermann Lautensach acknowledges the existence of "a respectable number of important historical works" in Korea beginning in the twelfth century but notes that there was "much less geographical literature."[45] After a survey of modern scholars' work on geographical writings in Korea, he concludes that, apart from Yi Chung-hwan's, geographical works are "confined basically to enumerations of mountains, rivers, prefectural cities of grades one to four and their curiosities."[46]

The *T'aengniji* is unique in many ways. Unlike other geographical works in Korea, places are not merely described but also interpreted and evaluated. Yi Chung-hwan carried out historical and spatial analyses and evaluated the relationship between humans and the physical and social environment. The following quotation, which comments on a four-day walk he took in his youth (see Plate 1), provides us with a fine example of his scholarly ability to perceive the physical environmental changes of his time.

> When my now-deceased father[47] traveled to his new appointment as governor of Kangnŭng, in the *kyemi* year (1703), I was fourteen years old. Following his palanquin from Un'gyo[yŏk] to Taegwallyŏng, to the west of Kangnŭng City, I found that the roads, regardless of whether they were on flat land or high hills, all stretched through thick forests. I could not see the sky for about four days of the journey.
>
> Over the course of a few decades, the mountains and fields were all turned into farmland and villages sprawled and joined each other.... Because of the landslides that occur every rainy season, the soil flows into the Han River and the riverbed gradually becomes shallow.[48]

It should be noted that Yi Chung-hwan's work was completed before the publications of Karl Ritter (1779–1859) and Alexander von Humboldt (1769–1859), the founding fathers of the modern discipline of geography, who explored the relationship between humanity and the environment within a scientific framework. Furthermore, the discussion of several locational factors, set out as requirements for livable sites, is Yi Chung-hwan's innovative contribution to Korean geographical writings.[49] Yi's geographic locational analysis predates by more than one hundred years the most well-known locational analysis initiated by the economists Johann von Thünen and Alfred Weber.[50] Unlike their models, which focused solely on human economic activities, Yi Chung-hwan's treatment has been acclaimed for considering multiple conditions for living, including physical, economic, and social aspects, as well as many of what are today's geographical approaches such as historical, regional, and topical analysis, and environmental perception.[51] Through the few brief quotations from the *T'aengniji* introduced so far, we can glimpse Yi Chung-hwan's empirical and multi-perspective approach based on his observations and experience accumulated over several decades, whether they be of significant transformation in human behavior due to policy changes in the court or wide-scale environmental damage resulting from the expansion of human habitation and land cultivation. He admits to not visiting either P'yŏngan or Chŏlla Provinces,[52] but he did visit the other six provinces and thus made keen-eyed observations concerning large swaths of Korea.

T'aengniji has also received considerable attention from modern scholars beyond the field of geography. This is mainly because Yi Chung-hwan explored in a neutral manner and from multiple perspectives the causes of the century-long power struggles among court officials and bravely evaluated the effect of the T'angpyŏngch'aek (Policy of Impartiality), implemented by the then-king, Yŏngjo (r. 1724–1776). Among several important opinions offered by modern scholars is that of Yi Hong-ryŏl, who cites Yi Chung-hwan's *T'aengniji* as foremost on the "relationship between *taegan* (the censorial officials)[53] and factional strife."[54] Hong I-sŏp claims that Yi Chung-hwan tried to "identify the factors leading to political unrest from various angles" but expressed his intention indirectly by presenting places for leading a secure life without such unrest because "direct criticism of the government was not allowed" at the time.[55] He suggests that the *T'aengniji* should not be read solely as a book on geography but "must be recognized as a book of history, geography, and political psychology."[56] Based on Yi Chung-hwan's postscript, Chŏng Tu-hi suggests that Yi's real motive for writing the *T'aengniji* was to write a history.[57]

Yi Chung-hwan was a victim of factional politics at the beginning of his time as a selection secretary. Even so, he is presumed to have maintained an objective political standing, as seen earlier in Sim No-sung's remarks. Suematsu Yasukazu concurs, writing that he could not find in the *T'aengniji* a trace of any effort to justify Yi's own position or the faction to which he belonged.[58] Yi Chung-hwan did not support views of the Southerners (Namin) alone, but instead acknowledged contributions by members of other factions, such as Yi I, a member of the Westerner Faction.[59] Yi Chung-hwan's neutral viewpoint is well demonstrated also in his evaluations of his contemporary era. Although he considered the implementation of the Policy of Impartiality to have resulted in the lamentable decay of the scholarly spirit in Korea, he seems to have regarded the reign of Yŏngjo as generally laudable, describing it as a "glorious era under the reign of the benevolent king" with noticeable growth in population.[60]

The greatest contribution of the *T'aengniji* as a book of history, in my opinion, is in opening up a new approach for understanding the nature of politics during the mid-to-late Chosŏn dynasty by illuminating the overall power dynamics of the court. This line of thinking can be illustrated by referring to related quotations from the "Social Characteristics" section of the *T'aengniji*.

> Present-day government organization in Korea is different from earlier times. Even though three chancellors[61] and six ministers[62] are appointed to supervise and control various government offices,[63] great importance is attached to the Office of Inspector General and the Office of Censor General. These offices were given the exclusive right, after discussion, to execute the investigation of officials' alleged wrongdoings based on hearsay, [to oversee] the resignation of officials to avoid conflict of interest, and to implement appropriate measures [for restitution on behalf of] wronged officials.

As guardians of public opinion and critics, the voices of the Offices of Inspector General and Censor-General were strong and were expected to be heeded by officials and kings alike.[64] Unlike the preceding Koryŏ dynasty (918–1392), the Office of Censor General at the Chosŏn court was an independent entity.[65] These two offices also held a much stronger position than their equivalent body in neighboring China, where the admonishing activities were weak and often ignored by emperors. The following quotation touches upon the way the members of the Three Remonstrative Offices[66] were appointed and the logic behind that process.

> Generally, the power to appoint central and local government officials does not belong to the three chancellors but to the Ministry of Personnel. Fearing that this ministry would rival the three chancellors, the right to recommend officials to the Three Remonstrative Offices was not given to the minister of personnel but was instead assigned to the selection secretaries, the senior fifth- and senior sixth-rank officials of the ministry.[67]

This refers to the fact that the selection secretaries recommended officials below senior third rank in the three offices. This special provision gave great privilege and power to the selection secretaries, with all nine posts below inspector general and censor general in the hands of selection secretaries. Their exercise of power was not limited to these appointments.

> Although the positions of the three chancellors and six ministers are most prestigious, if their conduct is even slightly disagreeable, selection secretaries can have the officials of the Three Remonstrative Offices debate the matter and bring about an immediate impeachment. Since the court esteems a sense of honor and takes personal reputation and integrity seriously, once an official is faced with impeachment he has no option but to resign from his post.
>
> The power of the selection secretaries is therefore similar to that of the three chancellors. It is arranged so that superior and inferior posts are interrelated and hold each other in check.... The selection secretaries have the right to recommend their own successors.[68]

This fresh revelation, which had not previously been recorded elsewhere, brought into the open the distinctive nature of political practice in the Chosŏn dynasty. The closest record to this would be found in the *Annals of King Sŏngjong*,[69] which mentions the appointment of a low-ranking official of the Office of Special Advisors to selection secretary. Based on the above and related contents of the *T'aengniji*, Song Ch'an-sik illuminated the political status of selection secretaries and the Three Remonstrative Offices and coined the term *sarim chŏngch'i* (literati politics) for a better understanding of the Chosŏn power structure.[70] Song Ch'an-sik praised the *T'aengniji* as having "extremely lucidly explained the essence of the actual power structure of the court in the Chosŏn dynasty."[71]

After Song's study, serious examinations of political operations in Chosŏn were carried out under the rubric of "literati politics." The key areas of study were the ways in which the Neo-Confucian scholar-gentry achieved their common goals through strengthening the voices of the Three Remonstrative Offices and through exercising the right to recommend one's own successor not only for selection secretary but also for other ministries and offices of equivalent rank. These endeavors are considered to have made a great contribution to the understanding of Korean history from the middle of the Chosŏn dynasty.[72]

The most provocative and even dangerous statements in the *T'aengniji* might be the author's disapproval of the aftermath of implementing a Policy of Impartiality. King Yŏngjo introduced the policy from the start of his reign and appointed government officials from factions that were not in power, expelling those who opposed the policy. In the *T'aengniji* Yi Chung-hwan offers an unreservedly critical assessment of the policy's execution.

> In recent years, as members of all four factions are eligible for promotion, they are interested only in a position at court.... They do not take official life seriously and regard official buildings as taverns. Ministers are called capable and benevolent when they show mediocrity disguised as moderation. The Three Remonstrative Offices (*Samsa*)[73] are highly respected when they keep silent and provincial officials regard integrity and frugality as sheer idiocy. If this continues, will not the present mad stampede soon end in a total disaster?[74]

Yi Chung-hwan's audacity in criticizing the inefficacy of the policy implemented at the order of the reigning king could have been the most compelling reason why the *T'aengniji* manuscripts were initially, and for quite some time, circulated anonymously. In this vein, while recognizing the *T'aengniji* as being primarily focused on geographic writing, its "Social Characteristics" section has been evaluated as offering a superb history of factional strife.

The activities and effects of the Inspector General and Censor General officials are well documented in the records of the Chosŏn dynasty, including *Chosŏn wangjo sillok* (Veritable record of the Chosŏn dynasty). Instances where selection secretaries were involved in and helped guide public opinion against the wrongdoings of officials and kings are rarely recorded in writing, however. How, then, was Yi Chung-hwan able to document this crucially important information? This again must have come from his time as a selection secretary.

Yi Chung-Hwan's Life

Yi Chung-hwan, also known by his pseudonyms Ch'ŏnghwa sanin and Ch'ŏngdam, had a turbulent life. He had a successful public career before being purged and exiled in his early thirties. In the period between holding office and writing the *T'aengniji*, it seems that he was an itinerant. His life can therefore be divided into three distinct stages: youth, life in public service, and life after public service.

Yi was born in 1690 into a well-known *yangban* family of the Yŏju Yi clan, which had a significant scholarly heritage. His father, Yi Chin-hyu, was a governor of Ch'ungch'ŏng and Hamgyŏng Provinces, a local district governor of Andong, and a vice-minister of the Ministry of Rites (Yejo). His great-uncle, Yi Ik, became a major scholar of the Sirhak, or Practical Learning, School. His grandfather, Yi Yŏng (1634–1677), and his great-great-grandfather, Yi Chi-jŏng (1588–1642), were both county magistrates, while his great-great-great-grandfather, Yi Sang-ŭi (1560–1624), had been a minister of the Ministry of Punishment and the Ministry of Personnel and an inspector general. Yi Chung-hwan was related to Yi Kyu-bo (1168–1241),[75] a famous writer of the Koryŏ dynasty, and Yi Ŏn-jŏk (1491–1553),[76] one of the best-known Neo-Confucian scholars of the early Chosŏn dynasty.

Yi Ik described his great-nephew as a diligent and intelligent boy who excelled at writing.[77] Although the *T'aengniji* is his only extant book, Yi Chung-hwan must have demonstrated his literary talent from a young age. He married a daughter of Mok Im-il, a grand auditor;[78] he passed the special civil service examination[79] in 1713 and became a government official of the senior ninth rank.[80] He appears to have progressed well in his career, moving up from a position as second copyist in the Office of Diplomatic Correspondence, to director of the Horse Station of Kimch'ŏn, then recorder of the Royal Secretariat in 1719, then a junior secretary of the Ministry of Military Affairs in 1721, until in 1723 he was promoted to be a senior secretary of the Ministry of Military Affairs. Soon after that last promotion, he was divested of his office and arrested, suffering a series of violent interrogations and eventual banishment in 1726.

The political upheaval resulting in Yi Chung-hwan's banishment can be summarized as follows.[81] At the end of the reign of King Sukchong (1674–1720), the Southerners and the Young Doctrine Faction (Soron) supported the crown prince (later King Kyŏngjong), while the Old Doctrine Faction (Noron) favored his half-brother Prince Yŏning (later King Yŏngjo) to become king.[82] When the sickly crown prince ascended the throne in 1720 without an heir, the ruling Old Doctrine Faction led by Prime Minister Kim Ch'ang-jip quickly sought and succeeded in making Prince Yŏning the crown prince the following year. They then went further and requested that King Kyŏngjong allow Prince Yŏning to rule the country in place of the king himself. Kyŏngjong initially agreed but then revoked the agreement in the face of the Young Doctrine's growing protests against Prince Yŏning conducting affairs of state by proxy. Due to sustained pressure from the two parties, Kim Ch'ang-jip and three other ministers who advocated for Prince Yŏning's rule were banished in 1721 and the Young Doctrine Faction dominated the court.

Mok Ho-ryong, a geomancer and relation of Yi Chung-hwan's father-in-law, Mok Im-il, initially sided with the younger generation members of the Old Doctrine Faction such as Yi Ch'ŏn-gi in protecting Prince Yŏning. Having joined the Young Doctrine Faction in 1722, however, Mok informed King Kyŏngjong of the plot, which dated from the end of King Sukchong's reign, hatched by offspring of the core members of the Old Doctrine Faction, to remove Kyŏngjong either by sending a swordsman to the palace to depose him or by poisoning him. The king reacted to this report by sanctioning the mass killing of Old Doctrine Faction members, including the four ministers who had been banished the previous year.

In 1723, Royal Secretary Transmitter O Myŏng-hang asked King Kyŏngjong to alert the Ministry of Personnel to the misconduct of a newly appointed senior secretary, Yi Chung-hwan, while Yi was director of the Horse Station of Kimch'ŏn. It was alleged that while serving in that post Yi had lent a horse to the same Mok Ho-ryong who later instigated the massive purge of the Old Doctrine Faction plotters by reporting their treason to the king.[83] Yi had earlier reported that he had lost the horse, but it was later found at the house of Yi Ch'ŏn-gi, one of the officials whom Mok had named as a traitor.

After the arrest of Yi Chung-hwan, a member of the Office of the Censor General reported Mok Ho-ryong's petition to the king wherein Mok argued for Yi's innocence in lending him a station horse. Mok's petition went on to praise Yi's contribution in safeguarding the court and even stated that Yi encouraged him with righteous loyalty and advised him on how to control many traitors and subvert plans to remove the crown prince. Mok also said that, although he reported Yi's contributions to the state tribunal, they were not discussed and no reward was bestowed on Yi.[84] Mok himself was soon arrested and investigated. It was later reported that during the investigations Yi denied performing the actions that Mok Ho-ryong had praised. About three months after Yi Chung-hwan's arrest, both Yi and Mok were granted amnesty and released.[85] After Yŏngjo ascended the throne in 1724, petitions claiming the falsity of Mok's 1722 appeal against the Old Doctrine Faction reached the king. Mok Ho-ryong and then Yi Chung-hwan were again arrested and cross-examined. Intimations of Yi Chung-hwan's involvement in Mok Ho-ryong's false accusation in 1722 repeatedly surfaced.[86]

Interrogation in the Chosŏn court was an extremely harsh activity. Interrogation sessions were often accompanied by the flogging of suspects thirty times with a long, wide plank. After one such session, Mok Ho-ryong died suddenly in prison.[87] Yi Chung-hwan was cross-examined twice with Mok Si-ryong, the elder brother of Mok Ho-ryong. Thinking that Yi was the cause of his younger brother's arrest and eventual death,

Mok Si-yong depicted Yi as having sought to meet with his brother to hatch a conspiracy and that the two had traveled together for a long time. Yi Chung-hwan did in fact travel for several months with Mok Ho-ryong to find suitable burial sites in places, including Kŭmch'ŏn in Hwanghae Province, where family graves of the Yŏju Yi clan were located.

During Yi Chung-hwan's second interrogation, after the seventeenth beating, he was found to be having trouble breathing and the beating had to be halted.[88] It was decided that the beatings should be postponed due to Yi's serious physical and mental deterioration.[89] Yi Chung-hwan denied the allegations during the cross-examinations and interrogations. He admitted, however, that he praised Yi Cham, one of his great-uncles and Yi Ik's second older brother, to Mok Ho-ryong. Yi Cham had written a petition to Sukchong asking the king to protect the crown prince and banish Yi I-myŏng, a leading supporter of Prince Yŏning. The writing of this petition was not an easy thing to do, since senior officials of the court were members of the Old Doctrine Faction, who supported Prince Yŏning. Yi Cham was beaten to death in 1706. When the inquisitors and the king questioned why Yi Chung-hwan had praised Yi Cham, he replied that he had done it out of personal affection, as Yi Cham was a relative and had been recently awarded a posthumous government position.[90] There is no way to clarify how deeply, if at all, Yi Chung-hwan was involved in Mok Ho-ryong's report leading to the purge of the members of the Old Doctrine Faction. It is possible that Mok Ho-ryong praised Yi, after Yi's initial arrest, as compensation for the predicament initiated by Mok's use of a station horse in 1717. This is similar to what Yi Chung-hwan stated during his interrogations: Mok's praise was to conceal the fact he, Mok, had stolen the horse.[91]

Yi Chung-hwan was finally exiled to a remote island in 1726.[92] He escaped the death penalty thanks to King Yŏngjo. On the king's decision to spare Yi's life, an official of the Office of the Censor General requested the king revoke the decision, which the king declined. Two days later that same official, along with an official of the Office of the Inspector General, requested it again be revoked.[93] Yi Chung-hwan was released the following year under newly appointed moderate Young Doctrine chancellors. That same year, however, an official of the Office of the Censor General repeatedly requested that the king have Yi Chung-hwan investigated.[94] In response, Kang Hyŏn, the chief of the Correction Tribunal, sent a petition to the king pointing out that Yi Chung-hwan was not to be investigated again because Kang himself had sentenced Yi.[95] The king ordered that Yi Chung-hwan be freed, there being no evidence of his involvement in Mok's report, and he was pardoned.[96] The Office of Inspector General then requested that the king exile Yi Chung-hwan to a remote border area because of Yi's undesirable and unprofessional behavior and his collusion with Mok Ho-ryong. The king accepted the request, and Yi Chung-hwan was banished yet again.[97]

There are no records of the places where Yi Chung-hwan spent his time in exile. As King Yŏngjo acceded to the last request to exile him to a remote border area and it is stated in the *T'aengniji* that he himself had not visited the Chŏlla and P'yŏngan Provinces,[98] we can assume that Yi was most likely sent to someplace in the province of Hamgyŏng, the border area most remote from the capital. It is not clear when Yi Chung-hwan's second exile ended. We know that in 1740 he went to Ch'ŏngp'unggye,[99] where he participated in a meeting of descendants of seven scholars, which included his ancestor Yi Sang-ŭi. This suggests that the banishment was likely to have been lifted by then. After his release from exile, Yi Chung-hwan was said to have refused the court's offer of a government post.[100] In 1753 Yi Chung-hwan received Royal Edicts, which made him a senior third-rank civil official and senior third-rank military official.[101] Officially these edicts were bestowed on him on the basis of his ancestors' service to the court. It, however, could also have been the court's gesture acknowledging his innocence and restoring his honor after his thirty years of suffering. The award may not have had anything to do with the *T'aengniji*, as it is most unlikely that the court was aware that he had written the book. Three years later, in 1756, Yi Chung-hwan passed away.

Korean Society of Yi Chung-Hwan's Time

The Chosŏn dynasty adopted Neo-Confucianism as the official state ideology. Scholars accepted it as the guiding principle of society and expected the country be governed with virtue according to the teachings of Zhu Xi. The Chŏson government bureaucracy was set out in order to balance power between the king and the officialdom.[102] The main administrative organ in the central government consisted of the State Council,[103] Six Ministries,[104] and the Three Remonstrative Offices consisting of the offices of the Inspector General, the Censor General, and the Special Advisers.[105] Having been the central figures in overseeing officials and superintending kings, the duty and the right of the censorial officials were paramount.[106] In reality, however, the balance of power between the throne and the officials was difficult to maintain.[107]

In line with the dictates of the rigid social class structure and distinctive class divisions, the members of *yangban* families were mandated to study literary Chinese and read Confucian classics from an early age. Their choice of jobs was limited to government employment, which in most cases required passing the civil service examinations.[108] Those who did not sit or who failed the examinations would read Confucian classics and compose poems, abjuring activities that created wealth, which were regarded as suitable only for farmers, artisans, and merchants. This social structure was of a hereditary nature, maintained through intermarriage. Exceptions nonetheless existed. For example, a family of the highest class could become slaves if its members committed treason or other severe wrongdoings.[109]

Korean society during the late sixteenth and seventeenth centuries had suffered greatly from the invasions of Toyotomi Hideyoshi in the years between 1592 and 1598 and the Manchus in 1627 and 1636, both of which drastically depleted the workforce and had a devastating effect nationwide on agriculture and living conditions. Even *yangban* families whose members were not employed in government service suffered from lack of even a subsistence level of food due to the destruction of their crops and the loss of slaves, who escaped from villages during the wars. The numbers of people wandering to other regions increased during this time.

It was the view of scholars, many of whom were also government officials, that the state should guide itself by more vigorously implementing the Neo-Confucian ideology so as to prevent and combat calamities such as foreign invasions. In this way, Neo-Confucianism, which was earlier employed mainly in the public domain of the *yangban* class, came to be utilized in detailed private matters and in rural areas, for example, calling for practicing filial piety by performing rituals in accordance with Neo-Confucian manuals. Most Neo-Confucian scholars viewed large-scale foreign invasions in terms of righteousness as defined by Neo-Confucian ideology, accusing the invaders of injustices and emphasizing the importance of confronting the enemy with courage rather than actively working out strategies to resist their better equipped and organized enemies.[110] Under these circumstances there were some scholars who felt the need to rehabilitate war-damaged Korean society and sought solutions to important practical problems facing the Korean people. They are called scholars of "Practical Learning," or Sirhak, by modern scholars. This group emphasized the practicality of technological, agricultural, and geographical knowledge in enhancing the people's welfare. Being mainly members of the Southerner Faction who were largely excluded from political power, their deserving works rarely attracted the attention of the court and their progressive ideas were seldom put into practice.

During Yi Chung-hwan's lifetime, many political and social changes occurred at a relatively fast pace. The literati purges in the years of *sinch'uk* (1722) and *imin* (1723), which deeply affected Yi Chung-hwan, took place at the height of literati factional politics. After King Kyŏngjong's sudden death, King Yŏngjo, supported by the Old Doctrine Faction, proclaimed a Policy of Impartiality and appointed high government officials from both the Young and Old Doctrine factions. After the revolt in 1728, however, high government posts in the court came to be dominated by the members of the Old Doctrine Faction.[111] The Policy of Impartiality was intended to ensure the appointment without prejudice of members of all four factions to government posts. From this point of view, King Yŏngjo's attempt cannot be considered a success.

King Yŏngjo's reformation in civil and economic areas meant that commoners benefited from elevated civil rights and an alleviation of the tax burden related to their military duties.[112] Many *yangban* families, unless they were core members of the Old Doctrine Faction, on the other hand, were unemployed and consequently did not have a regular income. Some of these ruined families could not afford to keep private slaves and so had to live like commoners, sometimes forced to leave their hometowns for economic reasons. With its main theme of identifying desirable residences for the scholar-gentry class, the *T'aengniji* could have served ruined *yangban* as a practical guide on finding safe and economically viable places to live. This intriguing and unprecedented work also attracted the attention of considerable numbers of scholar-gentry and middle-class people serving as government bureaucrats. Translated into vernacular Korean under the title Tongguk chirihae (Notes on the geography of Korea), the *T'aengniji* may also have struck a chord with commoners.

T'aengniji Manuscripts and Bibliographical Notes

From antiquity, popular writings have been copied by hand, inevitably resulting in copyist errors and revisions. While some changes occurred inadvertently, others, whether at the level of word or discourse, were made intentionally. Numerous changes occurred in a manner similar to the way edits are made in Wikipedia articles today. *T'aengniji* manuscripts are no exception. Touching on various aspects of scholar-gentry life, the *T'aengniji* was an unprecedentedly popular yet challenging treatise. That it was initially circulated without any attribution of authorship invited a wide range of readers to engage in copying or editing the original content and form at various levels. Even after its authorship was established, changes not only in the content but also in the form and title continually occurred until the first half of the twentieth century. The result is that there exist *T'aengniji* manuscripts of varying length and structure, some lacking a part or two, some missing certain sections or with differing arrangements of parts.

While study of its content was widespread, mostly based on the Chosŏn Kwangmunhoe version printed in 1912, bibliographical knowledge of the *T'aengniji* was scarce until the beginning of the twenty-first century. The fact that no compiled works of Yi Chung-hwan have been found could have contributed to the dearth of biographical information.[113] A total of two forewords and six postscripts are known to have been written by reviewers during the late Chosŏn. The forewords were written by Yi Ik in 1751 and Chŏng Ŏn-yu (1687–1764) in 1753 and the postscripts by Yi Chung-hwan in 1751, Mok Sŏng-gwan in 1752, Mok Hoe-gyŏng in 1752, Yi Pong-wan in 1753, and Yi Ik and Chŏng Yag-yong.[114] Essential information relating to the *T'aengniji,* such as its original title and content, remain undefined, although recent bibliographical studies have begun to provide clarity on some of these points. Its original structure has been certified to be in the order laid out in this translation.[115]

Most challenging in my study of the work was a lack of or inaccurate copy dates for many *T'aengniji* manuscripts, verification of form and content of earlier and later manuscripts being impossible without a sound knowledge of copy dates. Amid this uncertainty, *Tongguk chirihae,* verified by Huh Woong to have been copied at the end of the eighteenth century, provided a solid guide. The date was established through a linguistic analysis of the manuscript, the only extant *T'aengniji* manuscript written in the Korean alphabet.[116] By selecting and re-examining bibliographical data, I identified copy dates of three "early *T'aengniji* manuscripts"[117]: 1751 or 1752 for the *T'aengniji* in *P'aerim,* 1792 for the *Tongguk p'aryŏkchi* (Treatise on eight districts of Korea) held by Yonsei University, and 1796 for the *T'aengniji* in the Dongguk University collection.[118] Through the cross-examination of contents, I found features shared by these "early *T'aengniji* manuscripts," which are: absence of the story of Pak Sun, an agent to Hamhŭng who was on a mission to plead for retired King T'aejo's return to the capital when he was beheaded by the king's soldier; lack of the statement "this is not discussed here in detail because there are geomancers' books on the subject" in explaining the nature of watercourses in the "Geomancy" section; and, finally, the same arrangement of four parts as in the Chosŏn Kwangmunhoe version.[119]

Identifying the copier of the *T'aengniji* in *P'aerim* to be Hong Chung-in and consequent identification of the manuscript's copy date ended the debate on the time frame for the composition of the *T'aengniji*. Earlier, Koishi Akiko had posited that Yi Chung-hwan might have commenced writing sometime after the fourth month of 1749, based on the latest event mentioned in the text of the *T'aengniji*. The *kyŏngo* year (1750) is given in the *T'aengniji* as the date of King Yŏngjo's order to offer a sacrificial ceremony to the Chongzhen Emperor (r. 1628–1644),[120] among other emperors. But Koishi ultimately rejected this date because the actual date the order was given was at end of the third month of 1749.[121] I have argued that Yi Chung-hwan may have incorrectly recorded the year of the event but that what is crucial is his perception of the king's order being given in 1750. His reference to this date suggests that he wrote the *T'aengniji* not before the time he mentioned, but afterward.[122] According to Yi Chung-hwan's postscript to the *T'aengniji*, writing started in summer, as is noted in the following passage.

> Once when I was staying on the Hwangsan River in summer, there was nothing for me to do. I would climb up to the P'algwaejŏng (Eight-Trigram Pavilion) and spend my days there enjoying the cool mountain air. Now and then I would write.[123]

I therefore proposed, in 1996, the summer of 1750 as the year he commenced composition of the *T'aengniji*.[124] P'algwaejŏng on the Hwangsan River is evidently the place where he started writing it.[125]

There have been two views on the completion date of the *T'aengniji* based on the author's postscript. At its end, before the phrase "*Ch'ŏnghwa sanin-sŏ* 青華山人書" (Ch'ŏnghwa sanin wrote),[126] "*paek-yang-ch'o-ha-sang-wan* 白羊初夏上浣" is entered as the time when he wrote his postscript. Thus it is clear that the postscript was written at the start of early summer (*ch'o-ha-sang-wan*). "*Paek* [白 white] *yang* [羊 sheep]," however, has been interpreted in two ways. Initiated by Suematsu Yasukazu (1939) and subsequently adopted by Kim Yak-sŭl (1968), Nishikawa Takao (1983), and Koishi Akiko (1985), the phrase has been interpreted as the year of the dog and Yi's postscript viewed as having been written in 1754.[127] But most Korean scholars, beginning with Hong I-sŏp (1957), interpret it as the year of the sheep (1751).[128] My verification of *P'aerim* copied by Hong Chung-in definitely confirms that the *T'aengniji* was completed in 1751, before Hong's death in 1752.

Authors' postscripts are normally composed after the completion of the writings to which the postscripts are attached. The only "early summer [初夏]" that falls within the period between the fourth month in 1750 and the start of early summer in 1751 is that of 1750. Therefore, it is appropriate to accept that the writing of the *T'aengniji* started sometime after the early summer of 1750 and continued until sometime before Yi Chung-hwan's postscript was written, which was in the first part of the early summer month in 1751. If we take the date when the postscript was written as the last day of his writing, we can advance the view that it took nearly one year to write the book.[129]

One of the puzzling features of the *T'aengniji* is its great number of titles. Modern scholars often attribute this to the book's popularity. It might also have something to do with the distinctive features of the book, which has several separate parts and sections.[130] Readers who copied it by hand may have given their copy a new title in order to highlight a part that particularly impressed them. Another reason could be that the book circulated as handwritten manuscripts before its first printing at the end of the Chosŏn dynasty; had it been printed earlier for wide circulation, there would have been fewer variations of the title.[131] Another reason for the variation in the book's title may have been that the initial lack of information on authorship of manuscripts encouraged readers to take liberties in that regard. The most intriguing theory for the variety of titles, however, is that the practice may have been initiated by Yi Chung-hwan himself.[132] Given the existence of the two forewords to his work, it is thought that when he showed Yi Ik and Chŏng Ŏn-yu his manuscript and asked them to write a foreword he also asked them to suggest a new title. This hypothesis is based, first, on a letter written by Yi Ik in 1752 that is thought to refer to Yi Chung-hwan's work and reveals that the title of the book became "T'aengniji."[133] Unlike a postscript, a foreword is written by someone other than the author upon request and can be a rather formal and substantial introduction to a book. Foreword writers would not normally change the original title unless they were asked to recommend an alternative.[134]

What, then, was the original title? Although several academics put forward opinions, Koishi's conjecture is the most convincing. She postulates that "Sadaebu kagŏch'ŏ-gi 士大夫可居處記" (Book on habitable places for the scholar-gentry) was the original title based on the phrases "*siijak sadaebu kagŏch'ŏ* 是以作士大夫可居處" (therefore I am writing the habitable places for scholar-gentry) and "*ŏsihojak sadaebu kagŏch'ŏ-gi* 於是乎作士大夫可居處記" (thereupon I wrote a book on the habitable places for the scholar-gentry) at the end of the *T'aengniji*'s introduction and conclusion, respectively. She regards these phrases as expressions of the author's main points.[135] Her interpolation of the Chinese character 記 (K. *ki/gi*, meaning "record" or "book") in her conjectured title is understandable in that this character appears in many book titles written in classical Chinese. While I agree with Koishi that the two phrases are important in speculating about the title of the book, I conjecture that "Sadaebu kagŏch'ŏ 士大夫可居處" (Habitable places for the scholar-gentry), not "Sadaebu kagŏch'ŏ-gi 士大夫可居處記," was the original title.[136] That is because *Sadaebu kagŏch'ŏ*, not *Sadaebu kagŏch'ŏ-gi*, commonly appears in both the introduction and conclusion, and the title "Sadaebu kagŏch'ŏ 士大夫可居處" was entered as the so-called inner title[137] in two out of ten manuscripts that I examined; it furthermore occurred with an explanatory sentence saying that it was the true name of the *T'aengniji*. In recent examination of more than one hundred handwritten manuscripts, twelve have "Sadaebu kagŏch'ŏ 士大夫可居處" as the inner title even though the cover title of most of them is *T'aengniji*.[138] No manuscript is found to have "Sadaebu kagŏch'ŏ-gi 士大夫可居處記" as either its inner or cover title.

There is support for the conjecture of "Sadaebu kagŏch'ŏ" as the original title in the most recently discovered *T'aengniji* manuscript, which is in *Wayurok* (Records for scenic travel), a collection of works written by various scholars and compiled by Nam Ha-haeng (1697–1781).[139] The manuscript was introduced as "T'aengniji" with many omissions.[140] But when the manuscript is carefully examined, it becomes obvious that the title should instead be recognized as "Sadaebu kagŏch'ŏ 士大夫可居處." This is because the text of the *T'aengniji* is entered under the title of "Sadaebu kagŏch'ŏ 士大夫可居處" preceded by Yi Ik's "T'aengnijisŏ" (Foreword to the *T'aengniji*) and followed by Yi Chung-hwan's postscript, which begins with the phrase "T'aengniji hubalwal 擇里志後跋曰" (The postscript to the *T'aengniji* reads). There are no other titles anywhere in the body of the work; no titles are given to any other parts or sections, also suggesting "Sadaebu kagŏch'ŏ 士大夫可居處" as the original title of the *T'aengniji*. The compilation date of *Wayurok* is thought to have been around 1766.[141] It is therefore acceptable to consider the copy date of the manuscript to be about the same time, that is, fourteen years after Yi Ik revealed in his 1752 letter that the title "became 'T'aengniji.'" I will henceforth use "Sadaebu kagŏch'ŏ 士大夫可居處" as the sole title of Yi Chung-hwan's work as it appears in *Wayurok* in order to be faithful to the title given in that collection and to reduce further confusion.

The discovery of *Sadaebu kagŏch'ŏ* in *Wayurok* commands us also to ponder what Yi Chung-hwan originally wrote. If we accept that both *T'aengniji* in *P'aerim* and *Sadaebu kagŏch'ŏ* 士大夫可居處 in *Aju chamnok* were copied by 1752, *Sadaebu kagŏch'ŏ* in *Wayurok*, thought to be hand copied around 1766, is the second oldest copy among the manuscripts with copy dates that have thus far been identified. With copy dates around thirty years or more earlier than other "early" *T'aengniji* manuscripts, these three — *Sadaebu kagŏch'ŏ* in *Wayurok, T'aengniji* in *P'aerim,* and *Sadaebu kagŏch'ŏ* in *Aju chamnok* — should be grouped separately from *Tongguk p'aryŏkchi* (1792, held by Yonsei University), *T'aengniji* (1796, at Dongguk University), and *Tongguk chirihae* (substantiated to have been copied toward the end of eighteenth century).

Among the over ninety manuscripts that I examined, I found that the most common length of *T'aengniji* manuscripts that include all four parts is more than forty thousand Chinese characters.[142] The content of *Sadaebu kagŏch'ŏ* in *Wayurok* is around thirty thousand Chinese characters in length and arranged, in order, as "The Four Classes of People," "Discourse on the Eight Provinces," "Discourse on the Selection of Habitable Places," and "Conclusion." Being shorter in length by approximately ten thousand characters than is commonly found in manuscripts with these four parts, some might view *Sadaebu kagŏch'ŏ* in *Wayurok* as a heavily abridged manuscript. After cross-examining its content, however, and aligning the dates of Yi Ik's foreword and letter and Yi Chung-hwan's epilogue, I have come to consider it to be the closest to and the most revealing about the original manuscript among all the manuscripts I have thus far examined. *T'aengniji* in *P'aerim* and *Sadaebu kagŏch'ŏ* in *Aju chamnok* reveal aspects in form and content of Yi Chung-hwan's early work. But starting with Kyŏngsang Province rather than the four northern provinces and without an introduction to all eight provinces, these manuscripts are heavily abstracted and missing parts and several sections and thus reveal earlier work at a very limited level.[143]

Why did Nam Ha-haeng entitle Yi Chung-hwan's work *Sadaebu kagŏch'ŏ* and enter it in his *Wayurok* while giving the title "T'aengniji" to Yi Ik's foreword and Yi Chung-hwan's epilogue? As one of the recognized pupils of Yi Ik, Nam would have read the original or near-original work of Yi Chung-hwan. Nam could also have heard of or noticed its various derivations from the original work by the time he compiled *Wayurok,* around fifteen years after Yi Chung-hwan completed the work, according to the date attached to Yi's epilogue. Nam aligned Yi Ik's foreword written in the second month in 1751, followed by *Sadaebu kagŏch'ŏ,* and Yi Chung-hwan's epilogue written in the fourth month of 1751. It is unreasonable to posit that Nam reduced the content to thirty thousand Chinese characters and entitled it "Sadaebu kagŏch'ŏ." It makes more sense to accept that the entire work, including and related to *Sadaebu kagŏch'ŏ,* was the most original as far as he could attain. I suggest he could have wanted to preserve the authentic writings of Yi Chung-hwan including the title. The fact that he retained "Sadaebu kagŏch'ŏ" as the title of Yi Chung-hwan's work demonstrates Nam Ha-haeng's commitment to authenticity, although "T'aengniji" would have been recognized as the new title by the time Nam compiled the collection. Accepting this line of reasoning led me to re-examine the aforementioned letter by Yi Ik revealing that the title of Yi Chung-hwan's work had been made into "T'aengniji."[144] In his letter Yi Ik also ponders whether Yi Chung-hwan would accept the indicated errors in more than ten places and their corrections.[145] When and how much Yi Chung-hwan worked on revising his original work is another puzzle to be solved.

Yi Chung-hwan admitted that he had not visited P'yŏngan and Chŏlla Provinces.[146] To find possible sources for the discussions on these unvisited provinces I have compared their descriptions with those of the places he did visit. I have also reviewed the references that he cited for describing provinces, which include official history books and other sources. I noted many statements on regional and social characteristics not supported by reference materials. It is therefore not surprising to see few references cited for these two provinces. But interestingly I found the scenery and activities of these provinces to be just as vividly described as for the provinces that he had visited. For example, in the description of P'yŏngyang Oesŏng (Outer City Wall of P'yŏngyang), readers would feel that they were "actual[ly] there hearing the noises made by seagulls, laundry paddles and people in the shops."[147] I have reviewed some of the other existing records that describe the area, such as *Sinjŭng tongguk yŏji sŭngnam* and *Sejong sillock chiriji*, but did not find similar descriptions. It is therefore likely that these vibrant and colorful descriptions were based on those transmitted verbally by others.

The engaging writing style of *T'aengniji* manuscripts and the eccentricity in storytelling often found there could have been what attracted readers and copiers. Among the numerous stories contained in the *T'aengniji* manuscripts, the majority tell of historical events. Legends harboring supernatural elements are mostly related to Buddhist monasteries, but other supernatural phenomena, such as Ch'oe Ch'i-wŏn becoming an immortal, are also found.[148] An incident involving Okinawans drifting to Chejudo is found in official records, such as *Kwanghaegun ilgi* (Diary of King Kwanghae) and *Injo sillok* (Veritable records of King Injo).[149] There is, on the other hand, a dramatized and detailed retelling of the unfortunate death of an Okinawan crown prince who, having drifted to the island bearing supernatural treasures, composed a poem during his last moments; the poem appeared first in the *T'aengniji* and later in several collections of narratives.[150]

The most vividly described from among several stories related to the Hideyoshi invasion is the dramatic unfolding of a strategic victory by the

Ming force led by Yang Hao at Sosa River. Waiting until the Japanese force neared, hundreds of monkeys hiding under a bridge got on horseback and charged toward the invading army. While the Japanese camp was in chaos, Xie Sheng and other Tartar generals commanded the cavalry to attack. It is claimed that this story involving monkeys was first recorded in the *T'aengniji*.[151] Admiral Yi Sun-sin, who blocked the supply route of the Japanese army by holding a firm grip on the southern sea, is portrayed to have used with great success metal chains strung across a narrow strait to capsize Japanese warships. Prior to this entry in the *T'aengniji* only one record on the use of metal chains has been found,[152] but in this instance there is no detailed explanation of how the chains were used and to what effect. Yi Sun-sin's alleged strategy therefore became an elaborated and fascinating record thanks to the *T'aengniji*. Several other orally transmitted local legends are reported to have been recorded for the first time in the *T'aengniji*;[153] it is also the case that it served as the vehicle by which many historical and folk narratives were handed down.

Modern Influence and Appropriation of the *T'aengniji*

The *T'aengniji* was translated into premodern vernacular Korean during the Chosŏn dynasty. Written in the Korean alphabet, *Tongguk chirihae* is verified to have been copied at the end of the eighteenth century. The existence of *Tongguk chirihae*, the only extant *T'aengniji* manuscript in premodern Korean, testifies that readers of the *T'aengniji* were not confined to upper- or learned middle-class people in Korea but also included those who could not read classical Chinese.

The first translation and publication of the *T'aengniji* into modern Korean was carried out by Yun Sŏk-wŏn in 1964 in North Korea.[154] In South Korea, a translation by Rho Do-Yang (No To-yang), completed in 1968, was published in 1969. He revealed that his translation was based both on "*P'aryŏkchi*, the metal-type print, and a *T'aengniji* manuscript stored in the library of Seoul National University."[155] The *P'aryŏkchi* mentioned by Rho would be the one printed in 1910.[156] Subsequent translations and publications into modern Korean include the versions by Yi Ik-sŏng (1971), Yi Yŏng-t'aek (1975), Chŏng Yŏn-t'ak (1977), Ch'a Ch'ang-yong (1994), Hur Gyeong-jin (Hŏ Kyŏng-jin) (1996), Yi Min-su (2005), and Kim Hŭng-sik (2006). Some of these translations have been revised and published several times.[157] All printed modern Korean-language translations, except for Rho Do-Yang's first translation, were based solely on the text of the Chosŏn Kwangmunhoe edition with the title T'aengniji. The present-day acceptance of T'aengniji as the proper title could be due to Ch'oe Nam-sŏn's use of it when he reviewed *T'aengniji* manuscripts and printed the book in 1912.

The popularity of *T'aengniji* in contemporary Korean society is clear, evidenced for reasons beyond the frequency of its translations. Soon after Yi Chung-hwan died, his life, including his journey for writing the *T'aengniji*, was made into a novel,[158] and *T'aengniji* started to be used as a common noun meaning "regional geography" or "travelogue." The commonization of the work's title is seen in book titles and names of project teams: *Tasi ssŭnŭn T'aengniji*; *Taegu sin T'aengniji: Taegu ŭi chaebalgyŏn*; *Ul-san T'aengniji*; *Saero ssŭnŭn T'aengniji*; *Seoul T'aengniji*; Seoul sin *T'aengniji* P'ŭrojekt'ŭt'im; and *Sŏm T'aengniji*.[159] The *T'aengniji* has also been substantially edited to cater to a wide spectrum of readers, from elementary to secondary school students, accompanied by illustrations and cartoons. *Manhwa Yi Chung-hwan, T'aengniji* (Yi Chung-hwan's *T'aengniji* as cartoon [2008]) is a cartoon adaptation. Other editions with the title T'aengniji have multiple illustrations.[160]

Outside Korea, part of the *T'aengniji* was translated into Japanese by Kondo Sinsuki and published in 1882 under the title Chosen hachiikichi (The eight provinces of Korea). Based on this Japanese translation, a Chinese version was prepared by Jian Jinggui and published in 1885 as *Chao-xian dili xiaozhi* (Abridged geography of Korea). Parts of the *T'aengniji* were later translated into Japanese again and published under the titles Tokokusansuiroku and Hachiikichi. The *T'aengniji* was also published around 1903 under the title of Chishi (Regional geography) by members of a Japanese research group residing in Seoul as a supplement to their periodicals.[161] It was not until 1983, however, that a full Japanese translation, based on Yi Ik-sŏng's translation of the book into modern Korean, was published.[162] My own English translation of sections of the *T'aengniji*, based on the Chosŏn Kwangmunhoe edition of the text, was published in 1998,[163] but it did not include the sections on the four provinces of Hwang-hae, Kangwŏn, Chungch'ŏng and Kyŏnggi.

The translation included in the present volume is a full and revised edition of my previous translation of the *T'aengniji*. In the translation included here I follow the Chosŏn Kwangmunhoe printed edition, which is the most significant version of the *T'aengniji* for the following reasons. While, since its creation in the mid-eighteenth century, few manuscripts were identified by their copiers and copy dates, the Chosŏn Kwangmun-hoe version provides clear information on the reviewer and the printed date. It has served over a century as the basis for almost all translations into Korean and has made this important text familiar to numerous readers in Korea and abroad. Moreover, the Chosŏn Kwangmunhoe edition has been the most widely quoted and studied version. It is the recension that represents the early-period *T'aengniji* manuscripts in structure and layout and includes all of the parts and sections.[164] At the same time, the Chosŏn Kwangmunhoe edition has its idiosyncratic features[165] and includes parts that have been added to and altered by later copyists.[166] In the annotations to the present translation I have noted and explained the parts that are significantly different from *Tongguk chirihae* or *Tongguk p'aryŏkchi*, two manuscripts of similar length and verified to have been copied by the end of the eighteenth century. As already mentioned above, the other early-period *T'aengniji* manuscripts with identifiable copy dates include *T'aengniji* in *P'aerim*, *Sadaebu kagŏch'ŏ* in *Aju chamnok*, *Sadaebu kagŏch'ŏ* in *Wayurok*,[167] but they are much shorter or lack parts and sections. This new translation is thus not only a complete translation of the Chosŏn Kwangmunhoe edition but also an updated rendering of the text incorporating newly found facts discovered during my years of studying *T'aengniji* manuscripts.

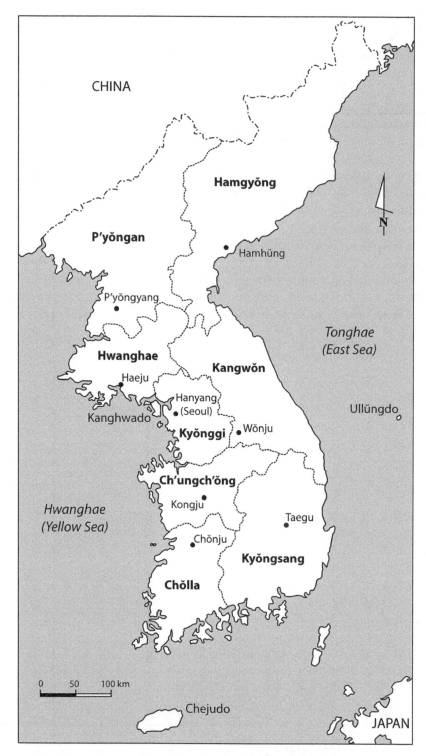

Figure 1: Eight provinces and provincial capitals of the Chosŏn dynasty in the eighteenth century. Map designed by Inshil Choe Yoon and drawn by Louise Cotterall.

II. Translation:
The *T'aengniji*,
by Yi Chung-hwan

Figure 2: Frequently mentioned places in the *T'aengniji*. Map designed by Inshil Choe Yoon and drawn by Louise Cotterall.

The *T'aengniji*,
by Yi Chung-hwan

The Four Classes of People

In ancient times[1] there was no scholar-gentry class. All members of society were common folk, of whom there were four groups. Those of scholarly ability and virtue were made officials by the king of the realm, and those who received no such appointment became either peasants, craftsmen, or traders. Shun[2] was once a tiller of the land at Mount Li, a potter by the Yellow River, and a fisherman and fishmonger by Lake Lei. The general tradition among the ancients was that if [a scholarly person was] not called upon to serve the king, he should naturally return to the class of peasants, craftsmen, or traders. Now Shun, who attained a zenith of harmonious rule, was a paragon for the common people of all times. When both you and I and everyone else are common folk, digging wells and tilling the land happily together, are there differences in ranks and titles?

Ever since the beginning of the civilized world the increasing complexity of rites has given rise to diverse titles, and diverse titles entail diverse ranks and rites. Hence the numerous ritual forms and formalities designed by the sages. During the period of the Three Dynasties[3] there were numerous dukes and princes of hereditary nobility whose hereditary scholar-officials managed wealth and noble titles with ritual propriety. Scholars who were not made officials, although in possession of no hereditary titles, still observed the code of the ancient sages. In handling their family affairs and in their effort to perfect themselves, they emulated the nobility and hereditary scholar-officials to the best of their abilities, without encroaching on the latter's privileges. They studied the *Shijing* (Book of poetry)[4] and the *Shujing* (Book of documents)[5] and practiced benevolence, justice, propriety, and music. From this background emerged the "scholar-gentry," a term that marked the differentiation of lifestyle. Farmers, craftsmen, and merchants were thereafter looked down upon

and the scholar-gentry commanded more and more respect. When the period of feudal princes ended with the conquest by the Qin (221–207 BCE),[6]
anyone, apart from the emperor, who pursued a scholarly life was called
scholar-gentry, no matter whether he served in the imperial court or not.
Thus the scholar-gentry increased in number. But this was not the social
order of ancient times.

One may ask, "In Yao's time,[7] Shun was not ashamed to farm, manu-
facture, or trade, why then should his latter-day counterparts recoil from
such jobs?" Those scholars who despise farmers, craftsmen, and traders
and those farmers, craftsmen, and traders who envy the scholars are all
ignorant of the origins of these occupations. Not only are scholars capable
of following the ancient sages' example, so too are farmers, craftsmen, and
traders. How can there be any difference between them? One must admit,
however, that people of later generations are inferior to the ancients in regard to personal qualities, such as innate characteristics and professional
skills. A scholar may perhaps be capable of farming, manufacturing, and
trading, but a man whose main occupation is as a farmer, craftsman, or
trader may find it impossible to take over a scholar's job. Thus a natural
tendency arose in later times for the scholar to gain more and more social
importance.

Some peripatetic scholars exercised their powers of persuasion to de-
vise interstate balances of power. Others traveled far and wide to challenge commanders of armies of ten thousand chariots. Still others chose to
mix with plowmen, herdsmen, vegetable gardeners, potters, and vendors
of charcoal or herbal medicines and were able to prove themselves well
versed in these trades. In sum, they could move up and down the social
ladder and feel perfectly free to do whatever they liked. Who could stop
them? As a result, the title of scholar became extremely attractive everywhere in the country.

And yet, what is essential to the good name of a scholar is his obser-
vance of the code of the ancient sages. Whether in pursuit of the career
of a scholar, peasant, craftsman, or merchant, he should always perfect
himself as a scholar. This cannot be achieved without practicing appropriate rituals, which again cannot be maintained without material
wealth. A scholar must acquire a house and manage the property. Only
after this can he perform the four rituals,[8] serve his elders, bring up his
young, and conduct the daily routine of the household. Hence, I have
written on desirable abodes for the scholar-gentry. In general, times are
either advantageous or disadvantageous, places are either auspicious or
inauspicious, and scholars' advancement in a career varies from person
to person.[9]

Discourse on the Eight Provinces

A branch range of the Kunlun Mountains[10] extends to the south of the great desert and forms Mount Yiwulu[11] in the east, ending abruptly to form the Liaodong Plain.[12] At the other end of the plain, the mountain range rises again to form Mount Paektu,[13] which is called Mount Buxian in the *Shanhai jing* (Book of mountains and seas).[14] The mountain range runs one thousand *ri* to the north,[15] between the two rivers, and moving toward the south it becomes Ningguta.[16] A mountain range that extends to the south becomes the head of all Korean mountain ranges.

There are eight provinces: P'yŏngan Province, which is close to Shenyang City;[17] Hamgyŏng Province, which borders on Jurchen[18] territory and then Kangwŏn Province, which lies to the south of Hamgyŏng Province; Hwanghae Province, neighboring P'yŏngan Province; Kyŏnggi Province, which lies to the south of Kangwŏn and Hwanghae Provinces; to the south of Kyŏnggi Province lie Ch'ungch'ŏng and Chŏlla Provinces, and to the east of Chŏlla Province is Kyŏngsang Province [see Figure 1].

Kyŏngsang Province is the territory of the ancient states of Pyŏnhan and Chinhan.[19] Kyŏnggi, Ch'ungch'ŏng, and Chŏlla Provinces comprise the territory of [what was once] the ancient state of the Mahan and the kingdom of Paekche.[20] Hamgyŏng, P'yŏngan, and Hwanghae Provinces are territories of [what were] the kingdoms of Kojosŏn (Old Chosŏn)[21] and Koguryŏ.[22] Kangwŏn Province, however, was the territory of the ancient state of Yemaek,[23] whose rise and fall remains little known. Toward the end of the Tang dynasty, the first Koryŏ king, whose surname was Wang, came to power. He unified Samhan (the Three Han States)[24] and founded the Koryŏ dynasty (918–1392), from which the present Chosŏn dynasty (1392–1910) is descended.

Korea is surrounded by the sea to its east, south, and west. Only to the north is the Korean peninsula connected to the Jurchen [territory] and Liaodong [peninsula]. There are many mountains and few plains in Korea, and the people are gentle, cautious, and rather parochial. The land stretches three thousand *ri* in length. Across, from the east coast to the west coast, however, the distance is less than one thousand *ri*. [To the west] across its southern sea, Korea faces the area between Wu and Huiji Counties in the Chinese province of Zhejiang.[25] In the north of P'yŏngan Province is Ŭiju City, the [country's] biggest border town, approximately as big as Qingzhou [in China]. Generally speaking, this country [Korea] lies between Japan and China.

In ancient times while Emperor Yao reigned, a demigod was born in a rock cave under a sandalwood tree on Mount Myohyang in Kaech'ŏn, P'yŏngan Province [in Korea]. His name was Tan'gun and he became chief of the Nine Eastern Tribes.[26] Little is known of the events of his time or his descendants. Afterward, Kija[27] became a feudal lord of Korea and established the capital at P'yŏngyang. Years later during the Qin dynasty, his descendant Ki Chun was expelled by Wiman,[28] who came from the state of Yan. Ki Chun fled by boat and shifted the capital to Iksan County in Chŏlla Province, naming his state Mahan. As there is no clear historical record of the boundary of Mahan being ruled by the Ki family, we only know that Mahan made up a part of the Three Han States along with Chinhan and Pyŏnhan.

Hyŏkkŏse[29] rose to power at the time of Emperor Xuan (r. 74–49 BCE) of the Han dynasty (206 BCE–220 CE) and conquered the whole of present-day Kyŏngsang Province. He subjugated Chinhan and Pyŏnhan, renamed the country Silla (57 BCE–935 CE), and chose Kyŏngju to be its capital. The three families of Pak, Sŏk, and Kim produced kings in turn. The Wi family was defeated during the reign of Emperor Wu of the Han dynasty. When the local inhabitants were moved and the territory abandoned during the Han dynasty, Chumong[30] rose from the Malgal people, occupied P'yŏngyang, and named the country Koguryŏ. When he died, his second son, Onjo, secured the land south of the Han River and destroyed Mahan, naming the country Paekche and choosing Puyŏ as the capital. Both Koguryŏ and Paekche collapsed during the reign of Emperor Gaozong of the Tang dynasty. When the Tang soldiers left the land, the combined area of both countries became known as the territory of the [Unified] Silla kingdom. At the end of the Silla dynasty, the territory was divided by Kungye and Kyŏn Hwŏn,[31] but the Koryŏ dynasty again unified Korea.

The above is a summary of the succession of the Korean kingdoms. Before the [Unified] Silla dynasty the three kingdoms had warred continuously among themselves and left scarcely any historical records. Recorded history therefore begins with [the founding of] the Koryŏ dynasty. During the Koryŏ period the term "scholar-gentry" was not yet well established. Many local clerks became central government ministers or even higher officials and served kings. Once they became high officials their descendants also belonged to the scholar-gentry class and maintained their homes in the capital [Kaesŏng]. The capital therefore became the seedbed of the scholar-gentry. Few from provincial areas became high officials [see Figure 2].

When Shuang Ji[32] introduced the government examination system, people from provincial areas were gradually appointed to high office. Many people from the northern region became military officers, and from the southeast came many civil servants. Toward the later years of the Koryŏ dynasty, literary standards improved greatly, and some people passed the civil service examinations in China as a result of our diplomatic relations with the Yuan dynasty (1271–1368). The celebrated great families nowadays are mostly descendants of high Koyrŏ officials. Thus, the history of the scholar-gentry can be written starting from the Koryŏ dynasty.

P'YŎNGAN PROVINCE

P'yŏngan Province lies to the south of the Amnok (Ch. Yalu) River and to the north of the P'aesu [see Plate 2].[33] This was the land where Kija held his fiefdom. The old boundary extended beyond the Amnok River and reached Qingshi Mountain Pass [in Manchuria]. The so-called Anshi[34] and Baiyan fortresses mentioned in the histories of the Tang are located in this area. At the beginning of the Koryŏ dynasty, however, these places were lost to the Khitan,[35] and the Amnok River became the boundary.

P'yŏngyang is the governor's seat and it lies on the P'aesu [River]. It was the capital of Kija's fiefdom. Thanks to Kija, of all the territories of the Nine Eastern Tribes, this area developed its civilization first. It was the capital for one thousand years under the Ki family and for eight hundred years under the Wi and Ko families. [Up to this day] it has lasted for over a thousand years as one of the most important garrisons in the entire country. There remain traces of the grid-pattern land division system of Kija's state and of Kija's tomb. The Sunginjŏn was erected near the tomb and the Sŏnu family was designated as caretaker of the sacrificial ceremonies from generation to generation. This is similar to the Kong family of Qufu looking after the shrine of Confucius.

The natural scenery is extraordinarily beautiful and there are many historical ruins alleged to be of the Chumong era. Many of the tales are too extravagant to be believed, however. The fortress lies on the river, and on the cliff there is the pavilion of Yŏn'gwangjŏng.[36] The faraway mountains on the other side of the river extend way beyond the broad plains and tall forest; the magnificent beauty of the landscape is indescribable. Kim Hwang-wŏn, a poet of the Koryŏ dynasty, spent a whole day at the pavilion and managed to compose only one couplet.

Flowing around the fortress is the river,
To the east of the great plain are scattered mountains.

Unable to continue without further inspiration, he is said to have wept bitterly and then descended from the pavilion.[37] His effort was ridiculous, and the lines are not good either. When Zhu Zhifan of the Ming dynasty (1368–1644) came here as an envoy he climbed up to the pavilion and admired the beauty of the scenery. He himself wrote the six characters "*ch'ŏn-ha-che-il-kang-san* 天下第一江山" (finest landscape in the world) on a plaque and had it hung. In the year of *chŏngch'uk* (1637) an emperor of Qing[38] saw it on his way back to China and said, "Since there is Jinling and Zhejiang in China, how can one say that this area has the best landscape in the world?" He initially gave orders for [the plaque] to be destroyed, but when he noticed the fine calligraphy, he ordered only that the two characters "*ch'ŏnha*" (in the world) be obliterated.

To the north of the pavilion is the cliff Ch'ŏngnyubyŏk, and where the cliff ends is the pavilion of Pubyŏngnu in front of the monastery of Yŏngmyŏngsa, which is situated in one corner of the city wall [see Plate 2]. During the reign of King Myŏngjong a Confucian student named Hŏ Pong (Hagok)[39] spent some time relaxing with his friend at the pavilion. He also invited the governor's son-in-law to the feast, where they were entertained by good music and the company of *kisaeng*.[40] The governor's wife got angry when she heard of her son-in-law's misbehavior. She asked the governor to send patrolmen to arrest all of the *kisaeng* and lock them up. Hagok returned home in a hurry and composed a poem, called "Spring Festival on the Pubyŏngnu," which ridiculed the governor. The poem immediately became popular and the governor lost his dignity.

Although the land is good for five grains,[41] it produces only a small amount of cotton. People engage only in dry-field agriculture on the hillsides, on the banks of the river, and in the valley. Downstream, however, is Pyŏkchido, in the middle of the river where the water dries out to form silt soil. People make rice paddies here and harvest one *chong* for every one *myo* that is planted.[42] The river starts at Mount Paektu and runs three hundred *ri* to the southwest down to Yŏngwŏn County, where it widens. Upon reaching Kangdong County it is joined by the stream from Yangdŏk and Maengsan; it forms the Taedong River in front of Pubyŏngnu. On the southern bank of the river is a long forest stretching ten *ri*; the [local] government authorities prohibit people from cutting trees or shepherding here. Ever since the Kija era the forest has flourished. In spring and summer, the sun is blocked by the green foliage [of the forest].

Sŏngch'ŏn (成川) City is to the east of P'yŏngyang. It was the ancient state of Songyang[43] and was annexed [to Koguryŏ] by Chumong. The administration center is by the riverbank. During the Hideyoshi invasion (1592–1598), Prince Kwanghae fled to this place carrying the ancestral tablets. When he came to the throne he ordered Pak Yŏp, the mayor, to carry out large-scale renovations of Kangsŏllu, which is next to a guest house. The pavilion measures over three hundred *kan*[44] and its structure is magnificent.[45] It is the best pavilion in the whole country. In front of it are the twelve peaks of Mount Holgol. The color of the rocks, however, is not beautiful; [furthermore] the water is shallow and the plains are narrow and end abruptly. This place is not as attractive as P'yŏngyang.

King Kwanghae (r. 1608–1623), recognizing Pak Yŏp's capacity, appointed him governor [of Sŏngch'ŏn City]. At that time the Manchu were aggressive and there were many incidents on the western border. King Kwanghae trusted Pak Yŏp, who had talent and wisdom. He served as governor continuously for ten years and spent a great deal of money on espionage. One day when Pak Yŏp [was] at Kusŏng Castle, having arrived after inspecting the province, Qing soldiers suddenly besieged the fortress. In the middle of the night, a Manchurian man climbed over the fortress wall, entered the bedroom of Pak Yŏp, and whispered in his ear. The next morning Pak Yŏp ordered his men to serve wine and kebabs to the Qing soldiers. The number of kebabs was exactly the same as the number of soldiers. The Qing general was astonished and presumed that Pak Yŏp possessed supernatural powers. He made an agreement [with Pak Yŏp] and, dismantling the blockade of the fortress, returned [home]. In the *kyehae* year (1623), one of Pak Yŏp's staff said to him secretly, "The court will collapse soon; since you are one of the king's loyal officials, you will definitely be purged. It would be better to make a secret agreement with the Qing. Then if something happens in the court, you can quickly yield this area [to the Qing]. Otherwise it will be difficult to avoid a purge." Pak Yŏp said, "I am a civil officer trained to be loyal. How can I be a traitor?" Since he did not listen, the staff officer left him and fled. Before long, Injo assumed the throne and an envoy was dispatched to assassinate Pak Yŏp, and Pak was killed in his office.

Over one hundred *ri* to the west of P'yŏngyang is Anju, situated on the Ch'ŏngch'ŏn River. The Paeksangnu lies on the riverbank with Ch'ilbulsa (Monastery of Seven Buddhas) beside it. During the Koguryŏ dynasty, when Sui (581–618) soldiers reached the river, they saw seven monks crossing the river in front of them, the water not reaching their knees. The Sui soldiers followed but many drowned, and when the rest of them retreated, the monks who had been crossing the river could no longer be seen. The local people, on hearing this, erected a temple and offered a sacrifice to the monks.

To the northeast of Anju is Yŏngbyŏn, a city erected on the side of the mountain. It is so high and strong that it is called Ch'ŏrongsŏng (Iron Jar Fortress), and in the whole of P'yŏngan Province only this place is protected from any attack. To the north of the city is the pass, Kŏmsallyŏng, where evidence of Hwandosŏng[46] of Koguryŏ still remains. Over two big mountain passes to the north is Kanggye City. It is more than five hundred *ri* from this city to Mount Paektu; here in this area one finds the closed four outposts.[47] In the reign of King Sejong (1418–1450) they were amalgamated with Kanggye City, and the local populace shifted out of the area, leaving it empty of human habitation. It has since become a secluded area with tall trees blocking the sky. Wild ginseng grows in abundance here, and every spring and autumn people are allowed to enter the area to gather it. It is sent to the government as a tribute and a tax; Kanggye is therefore called the land of ginseng.

To the west of the city is the Wiwŏn area, where there are the tombs of the ancestors of Yi Sŏng-nyang, the father of Li Rusong (K. Yi Yŏ-song).[48] The father of Sŏng-nyang was from Wiwŏn. Having killed a man, he fled to Kwangnyŏng and a son, Sŏng-nyang, was born to him there. [That is why] Li Rusong had earlier said that he was Korean.

There are six towns to the west of Wiwŏn. Ŭiju is the biggest city on the border and is connected to Shenyang [City] by road. The town faces the Amnok River. In addition to this this river, two big streams from the barbarian land of northwestern Manchuria flow and meet to become three separate rivers to the north of the town. Whenever the water rises and overflows, these three rivers become one.

In the sea is [the island of] Wihwado. At the end of the Koryŏ dynasty [General] Ch'oe Yŏng advised King U to attack Liao[dong].[49] Ch'oe Yŏng arrived at P'yŏngyang with him. He then ordered Yi Sŏng-gye [founder of the present dynasty] and sixty thousand soldiers to be stationed on this island. It was mid-summer. After consulting with his men, Yi Sŏng-gye petitioned three times for the withdrawal of his army, but [General Ch'oe] Yŏng refused to listen. Yi Sŏng-gye discussed with several generals about the retreat of the army and the killing of [Ch'oe] Yŏng, and the whole army agreed. General Ch'oe heard this news and fled with King U to a fortress. Having besieged the fortress, Yi Sŏng-gye put Ch'oe Yŏng to death and deposed King U and his son.[50] He then arranged for King Kongyang[51] to assume the throne.

In general, the southern part of the Ch'ŏngch'ŏn River is called Ch'ŏngnam, and the width from east to west is narrow. The northern part of the river is called Ch'ŏngbuk and a vast [expanse of] land stretches to the east. Because the east of the province is near the mountain range, it has many mountains but few plains. The lack of streams and ponds that can be used for irrigation minimizes [use of] rice paddies; the plains are all used for dry agriculture. At the height of the Kija and Koguryŏ periods, because the population was too large for the land, mountains were therefore cleared and land reclaimed. Later, having been targeted many times by Qing soldiers,[52] the land became devastated; moreover, after the unification of the country by the Wang family [Koryŏ dynasty], many people migrated down to the three southern provinces. [As a consequence] at present the plains are broad but there are few inhabitants, and mountainous areas are seldom cultivated.

To the west in the various towns close to the sea, dams have been built to block the tidal water from the rice paddies. Compared with the dry fields, there are few rice paddies. Rice in this province, therefore, is always much more expensive than in the three southern provinces. People weave silk and hemp, but fish and salt are extremely rare. Even though they are next to the sea, not much salt is produced; neither are bamboo, persimmons, ramie,[53] and paper mulberry.

Ch'ŏngbuk is even more mountainous and very cold. It is close to the national boundary; no flowers or fruits are seen, and produce is scarce. Many people live in poverty. It is only in the two big cities of P'yŏngyang and Anju that goods from China are abundant in the streets. Every time merchants follow envoys to China they make a profit, and there are therefore many wealthy people. While Ch'ŏngnam is inland and reveres literature, Ch'ŏngbuk has primitive customs and reveres the military. Only Chŏngju produces many scholars who pass the civil examinations.

HAMGYŎNG PROVINCE

To the east of P'yŏngan Province, the great range of Mount Paektu stretches to the south as if it were carving up the sky and then descends to form a mountain pass. To the east of the mountain pass is Hamgyŏng Province, which was once the territory of old Okchŏ.[54] It is bounded by the pass, Ch'ŏllyŏng, to the south and the Tuman (Ch. Tumen) River to the northeast.[55] While the length of the province exceeds two thousand *ri*, its width from west to east is less than one hundred *ri* because it is close to the sea.

In ancient times it belonged to Suksin[56] and then, during the Han dynasty, to Hyŏndo.[57] Later on it became the territory of Chumong [Koguryŏ], and after the collapse of Koguryŏ, the Jurchen occupied it. In the Koryŏ period Chŏngp'yŏng City to the south of Hamhŭng became the boundary.[58] In the middle of the Koryŏ, Yun Kwan and his soldiers chased the Jurchen seven hundred *ri* to the north of the Tuman River and established the boundary at Xianchun Mountain Pass. Later the area was returned to the state of Jin,[59] and the boundary was set up at Hamhŭng. During the present dynasty the Great King of Changhŏn[60] ordered Kim Chong-sŏ to expand the northern territory by one thousand *ri* up to the

Tuman River. Six garrisons and military camps were established on the riverside and the bases of the Jurchen to the southeast of Mount Paektu were all occupied.[61]

In the year of *chŏngyu* (1717), during the reign of King Sukchong, the [Chinese] Kangxi Emperor (1661–1722) had Mu Kedeng climb Mount Paektu to set the boundary between the two countries. Following the course of the Tuman River he arrived at Undusansŏng[62] of Hoeryŏng. On the big hill outside the fortress he saw many tombs, which the local people called imperial tombs. He ordered his men to excavate them and found a small stone epitaph near the tombs on which were inscribed the four Chinese characters *songjejimyo* (Song emperor's tomb). He ordered his men to pile the soil back up into high mounds and left for home. Thus, for the first time it was revealed that the fortress, Wuguocheng (Oguksŏng) as mentioned by the Jin people, was Undusansŏng. Because only the Chinese characters *songje* (Song emperor) were written, it is not clear whether they referred to Emperor Huizong[63] or Emperor Qinzong.[64]

Undusansŏng is only two hundred *ri* from the East Sea (Tonghae)[65] and is very close to the old territory of Koryŏ by the sea route. With a favorable wind it was possible to sail the short sea route from Chŏlla Province to Hangzhou in several days. It would have been wonderful if Emperor Gaozong[66] of the Song dynasty had discreetly allowed Koryŏ to attack the fortress from the East Sea with one thousand men so that he could have taken the remains of Emperor Huizong, as well as Emperor Qinzong and Empress Xing, through the territory of Korea to Chŏlla Province and then back to Hangzhou by sea. It is sad, however, that Emperor Gaozong did not think of his father but instead indulged himself in merriment at Xi Hu (West Lake).[67] It can be said that Emperor Gaozong's lack of filial piety was a crime that was noticed in the heavens. This is a most shameful and regrettable event in history. In less than a hundred years after his death, however, Emperor Gaozong's tomb was excavated by a thieving monk. Although Emperor Huizong died and was buried in a foreign land, his tomb has been preserved until now; the way heaven works is indeed incomprehensible. The locals who till the land on the hill often pick up things like ceremonial vessels, wine bottles, kettles, and fire urns. One of the tombs seems to be Emperor Huizong's, the rest seem to be those of courtiers and officers.[68] According to the locals there is also an emperor's tomb ten *ri* north of the Tuman River, but it is not clear whether this is Qinzong's.

North of Hamhŭng the landforms are rugged and the people not well mannered. The weather is cold and the soil is barren; only millet and barley are produced while rice is scarce and cotton nonexistent. Locals live through the winter wearing dog skins and endure hunger as the Jurchen people do. In the mountains, sables and ginseng are abundant, so people exchange these for cotton cloth with merchants from the south. If one is not rich, however, one cannot afford to exchange such goods. Fish and salt are abundant around the coastal areas. The water is clear and rough with many rocks. The fish and salt here are not as tasty as those of the western sea.

Hamhŭng City is the governor's seat. In earlier days the whole province was illiterate. But during the reign of King Sŏngjong (1469–1494), Governor Yi Kye-son (Kyŏnghŏn'gong)[69] selected clever boys and taught them the classics, history, and the code of conduct. From that time on literary education flourished and a few young men occasionally passed the civil service examinations; people called this "a breakthrough."[70] When the governor died, the local people erected a shrine and offered sacrificial ceremonies. The city [of Hamhŭng] is on the Kunja River, over which the five-*ri*-long bridge Mansegyo lies [see Plate 3].[71] On the southern gate of the city wall is the pavilion of Nangmillu, from which one can see the whole town. It is comparable to Yŏn'gwangjŏng of P'yŏngyang. The wide plain faces the sea, the atmosphere is grand and fierce; this place is, however, not as beautiful or bright as P'yŏngyang. In the middle of the plain there is an old house where our King T'aejo lived in his youth. A portrait of the king hangs in the house and an official is employed as caretaker and to offer sacrificial ceremonies at the correct time. It is the hometown of the king who founded the [present] dynasty.

Queen Sindŏk,[72] whose last name was Kang, died in the year of *chŏngch'uk* (1397), during the reign of King T'aejo. Acting on Ha Ryun's advice, [the king's fifth son, who was given the posthumous title] the Great King of Kongjŏng 恭定[73] gathered soldiers and quelled the rebellion of Chŏng To-jŏn.[74] Crown Prince Pangsŏk yielded his right to the throne but both he and his elder brother, Prince Pangbŏn, were killed. The irascible King T'aejo gave up his throne to [his second son, who was given the posthumous title] the Great King of Kongjŏng 恭靖[75] and went to Hamhŭng with his close followers. Not long afterward, King Chŏngjong [King T'aejo's second son] yielded his throne to King T'aejong [King T'aejo's fifth son]. Upon assuming the throne, King T'aejong sent an envoy to plead with his father to return to the capital. King T'aejo killed all the envoys.

Ten years after the king's envoys were killed, the king sent Pak Sun, a childhood friend of his father's, to Hamhŭng. First [Pak] Sun obtained a mare with a colt. He tied the colt where it could be seen from the gate of the palace. Then he rode the mare to the gate, tied it, and went to meet King T'aejo, who was close to the gate. While they were talking, the colt started neighing loudly for his mother and the mare cried back, jumping up and down. Wondering what was happening, King T'aejo asked why the horses were making so much noise. Sun answered, "I rode here on the mare and I tied the colt in the village. Thinking of his mother, the colt is calling out and the mare is expressing her love for her colt. Even dumb animals show their affection. How can a benevolent person not think of his love for the king [i.e., his son]?" King T'aejo was touched and after awhile agreed to return. He said, "You must leave this place before the cock crows and quickly cross the Yonghŭng River of Yŏnghŭng County tomorrow morning. Otherwise you will be killed." Sun ran away in the night. Because King T'aejo had killed envoys on many occasions, court officials and King T'aejo's personal officers despised one another. At dawn the following day, King T'aejo's officials asked that Sun be killed. King T'aejo refused but they kept urging him. When King T'aejo thought that Sun would have passed Yŏnghŭng, he gave his consent, then said, "If he has crossed the Yonghŭng River, don't kill him and [instead] come back." The officials reached the river just in time to see Sun boarding the boat. They took him down and killed him by the side of the boat. Facing death, Sun left a message for King T'aejo, "Although I'm about to die I ask my lord (King T'aejo) to keep his promise." King T'aejo was moved and ordered his return to the capital.[76] Commending Sun's righteousness and loyalty, he made a special provision by appointing his descendants to public office.[77]

Anbyŏn City lies one hundred *ri* to the south of Yŏnghŭng and north of Ch'ŏllyŏng. To the northwest of the town center is Sŏgwangsa. Before King T'aejo assumed the throne, he dreamt he was carrying three ridgepoles on his back; in the dream there were also flying flowers and a mirror that fell and broke. He asked Monk Muhak to interpret his dream. The monk replied, "Carrying three ridgepoles on one's back represents the Chinese character *wang* (king); flying flowers result in fruition and the breaking of a mirror signifies that a noisy event will occur." King T'aejo was delighted and later had a temple built that he named Sŏgwangsa. For two days a prayer service was performed and five hundred disciples[78] of the Buddha appeared in the air.

To the northwest of Anbyŏn City bordering on Tŏgwŏn County is the coastal village of Wŏnsanch'on. The residents live close to the sea and make a living by fishing and gathering shellfish and seaweed. A sea route connects Wŏnsan with the six garrisons to the northeast and it is here that all the merchant ships of the six garrisons and the ships of many other towns along the coast harbor. Fish, salt, and seaweed are taken from the sea. Fine hemp, switches of hair, sables, ginseng, and timber for making coffins are also products of the area. Many merchants from the provinces of Kangwŏn, Hwanghae, P'yŏngan, and Kyŏngsang therefore gather here and the town has goods piled up high. Many people have become rich middlemen. The government has built a granary here and now transports grain on the water from Kyŏngsang Province and stores it in the granary. Whenever the harvest in the north is poor, grain is taken to various towns in time to succor the starving.

To the southeast of Anbyŏn City is Mount Hwangnyong, on which there is a dragon pit;[79] the springs and rocks [here] are beautiful. This is the boundary between Hamgyŏng and Kangwŏn Provinces. To the south of the mountain lies Hŭpkok County. When, as a general, King T'aejo wrested the throne from the Wang[80] family, there were many other brave generals from the northern region among the officials who assisted him to obtain power. Once he gained the throne, however, he gave the order not to employ in high government positions people from the northwest. Therefore, for three hundred years there were no prominent officials from either P'yŏngan or Hamgyŏng Province. Even those from these regions who passed the civil service examinations did not normally rise in rank above county magistrate. Some became candidates for the offices of inspector general, censor general, royal secretariat, or special advisers, but that was very rare. Only Kim Ni from Chŏngp'yŏng and Yi Chi-on from Anbyŏn managed to attain [to the office of] either vice minister or vice mayor, and Chŏng Pong-su from Ch'ŏlsan and Chŏn Paeng-nok from Kyŏngsŏng served as military commanders-in-chief.

Since Koreans regard prominent families highly, the scholar-gentry from the capital did not marry or associate with the northern people, while the people from the northwest did not dare associate on equal terms with scholars. The scholar-gentry finally ceased to exist in both northern provinces and no new scholar-gentry families cared to move there. Only the Ŏ family of Hamjong County, the Yi family of Ch'ŏnghae,[81] and the Cho family of Anbyŏn, who were originally from P'ungyang County,[82] were prominent at the beginning of the present dynasty. They shifted to the capital and some of them passed the civil service examinations. There are no other prominent families apart from these. The northern provinces of Hamgyŏng and P'yŏngan are not desirable places to live.

HWANGHAE PROVINCE

Hwanghae Province lies between the provinces of Kyŏnggi and P'yŏngan [see Plate 4]. Generally speaking, a branch range of Mount Paektu extends to the south and drops sharply to become Kŏmmullyŏng, extending further to the south to become the pass [known as] Noinch'i. Having divided into two mountain ranges here, one mountain range extends to the south and ends at Sambangch'i but rises again to become the pass [known as] Ch'ŏllyŏng. Another mountain range extends southwest and passes Koksan and becomes Hangnyŏng.

Having divided again into three mountain ranges at Hangnyŏng, one becomes Mount Ogwan and another becomes Mount Songak, both of which are the mountains of the old capital of Koryŏ. Another mountain range passes by Sin'gye and becomes Mount Myŏnak[83] in P'yŏngsan, the ancestor mountain of the whole province. This mountain range extends again to the west to become Mount Ch'anggŭm and Mount Suyang in Haeju. Having descended into a plain, [this mountain range] becomes a flattish hill. Turning northwest, it becomes Mount Ch'u of Sinch'ŏn. Turning again to the north it ends to form Mount Kuwŏl in Munhwa, which Tangun chose as the capital. The other mountain range passes Koksan and Suan and forms high mountains and mountain passes such as Chabiryŏng and Chŏllyŏng and ends to the west in Kŭksŏng of Hwangju.

Hwangju lies to the north of Chŏllyŏng and faces Chunghwa City in P'yŏngan Province. In Hwangju, a military camp led by a commander in chief was stationed to defend the road from the west. A road from Hwangju runs over Chŏllyŏng and passes through the four counties of Pongsan, Sŏhŭng, P'yŏngsan, and Kŭmch'ŏn before reaching Kaesŏng; it is the straight road connecting the south to the north. To the east of the road lie such counties as Suan, Koksan, Sin'gye, and T'osan. They are all situated among remote mountains that have rugged terrains; their people are foolish. The valleys are deep, and robberies are often committed. From olden days, few scholars and high-ranking officials have been produced here. This is the same for the counties through which the major road goes. A number of scholar-gentry have nevertheless migrated from other places and lived in P'yŏngsan and Kŭmch'ŏn.

Kŭmch'ŏn, established through an amalgamation of Kangŭm and Ubong, has harmful vapors and has recently deteriorated, which makes the place unlivable. P'yŏngsan also has harmful vapors. To the west lies Mount Myŏnak; there is Hwachŏndong on the eastern slope. In the valley there is a massive tomb said to be the tomb of the ancestor of Qing Chinese. From [the site of] the tomb, a plain spreads out and the soil is fertile. There are many rich and prosperous settlements that have produced prominent scholar-gentry.

Originally the major road to the north passed through Chabiryŏng. At the end of the Koryŏ dynasty, however, it was closed and trees were planted. Chŏllyŏng was instead opened up as the gate to the south and north. After passing here less than ten *ri* away, the mountain range is disconnected and becomes [a set of] flattish hills that then turn into a plain. This is the Kŭksŏng Plain. During the Koryŏ dynasty, Mongolian soldiers came not through Chŏllyŏng but through the plain. When Qing soldiers invaded Korea during the reign of King Injo (r. 1623–1649), they also came through the Kŭksŏng Plain. The Kŭksŏng Plain extends over ten *ri* from east to west and ends at the Namori River. Downstream the river does not freeze thanks to tidal waves. A long wall stretching from Chabiryŏng to the riverbed on the Kŭksŏng Plain would make a natural fortress disconnecting the south and the north. Facing each other, Chŏllyŏng in the east and Mount Kuwŏl form between them a great outlet of water in the west.

Namori River runs from south to north across the middle of the plain and flows into the P'ae River.[84] To the east of the river are the counties of Hwangju, Pongsan, Sŏhŭng, and P'yŏngsan, and to the west are the counties of Anak, Munhwa, Sinch'ŏn, and Chaeryŏng. All eight counties have generally the same customs and are to the north of Mount Myŏnak and Mount Suyang. The soil is very rich and suitable for growing five grains and cotton. Soft iron is produced from various places in the counties. On both the eastern and western slopes of the river, banks are erected. The area inside the banks consists of rice paddies, which are wide and stretch endlessly just like the Suzhou and Huzhou [plains] in China. Rice produced here is long and glutinous, which is different from that of other areas. The rice used for the cooking for kings and queens is from here.

The mountain range from Mount Suyang and Mount Ch'u up to Mount Kuwŏl consists of high and low parts. In fact it forms a great trunk-mountain range. Outside the mountain range toward the sea is the town of Haeju to the south. Kangnyŏng and Ongjin are to the right of Haeju and Changgyŏnbu is to the west. Songhwa, Ŭnnyul, and P'ungch'ŏn are to the north of Changgyŏnbu. Finally, there is Changnyŏn, which is separated by a small sea from Samhwabu of Pyŏngan Province. A branch of Mount Ch'u circles around Changgyŏn and extends to the southwest and stops at Changsan'got. Changsan'got is surrounded by mountain peaks and the adjacent valley is deep and blocked. In the Koryŏ dynasty, along with Pyŏnsan of the Honam region and Anmyŏndo of the Hosŏ region, pine-growing fields were established to supply pine for building palaces, ships, and carts.

To the north of Changsan'got there is Kŭmsasa temple. All of the seashores are [comprised of] sandy beaches. The golden sand is extremely fine and glitters in the sun for twenty *ri*. Every time the wind blows, sand mounds are formed. Some of them are high and some low. They shift endlessly, sometimes to the east and other times to the west; their movement to the right or left is unpredictable. Pagodas and shrines on the sand are nevertheless grand and are neither buried nor crushed. This is quite strange, and some say that it is the work of the sea dragon. Sea cucumbers are found in the sand. They look like *pangp'ung* grass.[85] When boats from Dengzhou and Laizhou in China arrive here *en masse* every fourth and fifth month, the local government dispatches officials to chase them away. Having dropped anchor, the boats wait, floating on the sea, until no one can see them. Then the fishermen land on the shore, collect sea cucumbers, and sail away.

In the sea below Changsan'got, puffers and sea cucumbers are also caught. A sea cucumber is a boneless, dark cucumber-like [piece of] flesh covered all over with tentacles. Chinese use it for dying clothes black. Puffers are what Wang Mang (45 BCE–23 CE)[86] ate, as described in *Hanshu* (The history of the former Han dynasty), and are also caught in [the sea near] Dengzhou and Laizhou Counties, although [the ones caught there] are not as good as those caught in Korea. [The fishermen] collect puffers when they come to collect sea cucumbers. As their profit is high, the number of boats sailing from Dengzhou and Laizhou Counties has increased every year. This causes quite a lot of damage to the residents on the shore.

Even though the eight towns [of Haeju, Kangnyŏng, Ongjin, Chang-yŏnbu, Songhwa, Ŭnnyul, P'ungch'ŏn and Changnyŏn] have the advantage of the adjacent sea, the soil is infertile. Only the soil of P'ungch'ŏn and Ŭnyul is very rich. There is a man-made field where rice paddies yield several hundred *mal*[87] from every one *mal* seed sown. Even in the years of poor harvest, the yield is never below one hundred *mal*. The harvest from the dry fields is of the same amount; this is rare even in the three southern provinces. The north of Changgyŏn is blocked by Changsan'got to the south and is connected, only in the north, to P'yŏngan Province. Grains and cotton are abundant and peasants and families of low status boast their wealth and call themselves scholars.

In the middle of the sea to the south of Changgyŏn are two islands, Taech'ŏngdo and Soch'ŏngdo. They are quite broad. When Wenzong[88] of the Yuan dynasty banished Shundi (the Shun Emperor)[89] to Taech'ŏngdo, Shundi had a house built and lived there, keeping a statue of the Buddha made of pure gold. Every day at dawn, he prayed to return to his home country, and before long he returned home and was enthroned. He [subsequently] sent over one hundred skilled workers and had them build, under the supervision of a eunuch, a large Buddhist monastery on Mount Suyang in Haeju. This is Sin'gwangsa. The scale and grandeur of the monastery was the greatest in Korea. It later burned down and was rebuilt, but the new monastery is not as grand as the old one. The island is now deserted and the trees have grown tall, covering the sky. Mulberry and lacquer trees, vegetables and the other plants Shundi cultivated grow wild in the bush and dry out. The stairs and cornerstones of the palace remain vivid.

Haeju, the seat of a provincial governor, is to the south of Mount Suyang. The seawater entered between two mountains, swirled around right in front of the mountains and formed a big lake away from them. Locals call it a small-scale Lake Dongting. Clean mountain passes are a good part of this beautiful scenery. When Yi I (Yulgok) was the provincial governor of Haeju, he acquired a place with springs and beautiful rocks at Sŏktam at the foot of Mount Suyang. After his retirement, he built a house there and taught. Many scholars from Seoul and other provinces gathered there. When he died, a shrine was built and sacrificial rites were performed. His students and descendants resided there generation after generation and honor his education. Their level of literature and decorum, and the number of those who passed the civil service examination, was the highest in the province. The vigor of study dwindled later [however,] and the locals divided themselves into groups under the guise of Confucian schools and attacked each other like enemies. People of other areas regarded this place as being nasty.

A branch of Mount Myŏnak turned around and extended to the east and formed Yŏnan and Paekchŏn. They are to the east of Haeju, to the west of the Husŏ River,[90] and to the north of the downstream of the Poryŏn River. Not only are high mountains, wide rivers, broad fields, and long streams intertwined here, but tidal waves also reach here. It is open and cheerful just like the scenery of the Yangzi and Huai Rivers in China. As this area is the most livable of places, scholar clans from Seoul have come here to reside. The soil is barren and prone to dry out, however. It is not suitable for growing cotton. Residents enjoy sailing along the rivers or to the sea and engage in commerce. As the area is connected to two provinces [Hamgyŏng and Kangwŏn] to the east and Honam and Hosŏ to the south, people gain high profit from trading local produce.

This province in general lies to the northwest of the capital and is connected to P'yŏngan and Hamgyŏng Provinces. The people like archery and horseback riding; men of literature are scarce. It is situated between the sea and mountain ranges and it produces lead, iron, cotton, rice, millet, fish, and salt. Although there are many rich residents, scholar-gentry families are scarce. As eight counties on the plain have rich soil and ten counties on the shore have many scenic spots, it is not an undesirable place to live. Because the terrain juts out into the West Sea, it faces the sea on three sides. Only on one side to the east is it connected to the major road running north-south. To the north, there are rugged mountain passes and to the south it is delineated by rivers; it is covered with mountains and rivers. Inland there are many steep castle walls and also fertile fields and wide plains. Therefore, it is really a god-given/naturally endowed place for defense. In case of an emergency, it certainly will become a battleground, a shortcoming for a desirable place to live.

KANGWŎN PROVINCE

Kangwŏn Province lies between P'yŏngan and Kyŏngsang Provinces; [it] joins Koksan and T'osan Counties in Hwanghae Province to the northwest and Kyŏnggi and Ch'ungch'ŏng Provinces to the southwest [see Plate 5]. A mountain range from Ch'ŏllyŏng runing south [looks] as if it touches the cloud at the sky's end and reaches Mount T'aebaek.

There are nine counties to the east of the mountain range: Hŭpkok, which joins Anbyŏn in Hamgyŏng Province to the north; T'ongch'ŏn; Kosŏng (高城); Kansŏng; Yangyang; Kangnŭng, the capital of the old Maek Kingdom; Samch'ŏk; Ulchin; and P'yŏnghae, which joins Yŏnghae in Kyŏngsang Province to the south [see Plate 5]. All of the nine counties abut the East Sea. Although the distance from north to south is about one thousand *ri*, that from east to west is less than one hundred *ri*, as in the case of Hamgyŏng Province. To the northwest, it is blocked by main mountain ranges and to the southeast it is connected to the sea in the distance. Situated below the high mountain [range], the area is narrow. The mountains and fields are nevertheless all low, bright, and excellent.

Since the East Sea is not tidal[91] and the water is not murky, it is called the azure sea. As it is not blocked by ports or islands, it looks vast, being open far and wide, as if facing a big pond or flat banks. There are many famous lakes and strange boulders in the area. When one climbs up high, one can see the blue sea stretch out far in the distance, and when one goes to a valley, its scenery is secluded and quiet. In terms of the landscape, it is really the best in the whole country.

There are many excellent pavilions. Sijungdae in Hŭpkok, Ch'ongsŏkchŏng in T'ongch'ŏn, a pavilion on the lake [called] Samilp'o in Kosŏng, Ch'ŏngganjŏng in Kansŏng, a pavilion on the Ch'ŏngch'oho in Yangyang, Kyŏngp'odae in Kangnŭng, Chuksŏru in Samch'ŏk, and Mangyangjŏng in Ulchin are collectively called the Eight Scenic Beauties of the Kwandong District.[92]

To the west of the nine counties there are mountains such as Mount Kŭmgang (Diamond Mountain), Mount Sŏrak, Mount Tut'a, and Mount T'aebaek. There are many extraordinary, beautiful places between these mountains and the sea. Valleys are secluded and deep, with clean water and rocks. Tales of strange traces of supernatural beings are heard every once in awhile. The locals enjoy having fun. Older people take wine and meat dishes along with *kisaeng* and musicians to the lakes and mountains for a party. These are important occasions for them. Their children are influenced by this behavior; few engage themselves in learning. As the area is far from the two capitals, it has produced few prominent people.[93] Kangnŭng is an exception [in that] quite a few people have passed the civil service examination. The soil consists of very dry gravel; one *mal* sown in rice paddies yields just over ten *tu*.[94] Kosŏng and T'ongch'ŏn have the most rice paddies and the soil is not so barren. Next comes Samch'ŏk, where one *mal* of seed yields forty *mal*. These three counties, however, have produced no prominent persons. In general, all nine counties abut the sea and the residents make a living from fishing and salt making. There are accordingly many rich households, barren soil notwithstanding. The mountain range to the west is so high, however, that it is like a different country. It is a suitable place to visit for an outing but not for living for a long period of time.

There is Taegwallyŏng to the west of Kangnŭng and Mount Odae to the north of the mountain pass. The Ut'ong Stream starts here and becomes the source of the Han River. A branch of the Taegwallyŏng extends to the south and becomes Mount Tut'a over the two mountain passes [called] Ssanggye and Paekpong. On top of the mountain, there is a stone wall that people of olden days built, and below the mountain is Chungbongsa.

Imgyeyŏk in Kangnŭng is immediately to the north of the monastery.[95] Yi Sŭng-hyu from the Koryŏ dynasty lived there in hiding.[96] Lately, Yi Cha, defense inspector, built a house on the mountain and lived there without holding a government office. The mountain accommodates open spaces and rice paddies as well. The rocks in the stream are beautiful. As a place suitable for both agriculture and fishing, it makes a world where supernatural beings live.

Passing Sangdong in Yŏngwŏl County, the stream flows into the town [of Yŏngwŏl], which is in front of the hill to the west of Imgye. To the south is Yŏryangch'on of Chŏngsŏn, through which the Ut'ong Stream from the north runs before flowing south. The banks on both sides are quite open, and tall pines and white sands on the banks are reflected in the clear water. It is truly where hermits would live. The only regrettable thing is that there are no rice paddies. Locals nevertheless make a good living.

When the stream reaches the east of the town of Yŏngwŏl, it joins the Sangdong Stream. After it flows a little further, it joins the Chuch'ŏn

River. Between the two rivers there is Changnŭng, the tomb of King Tan-jong (r. 1452–1455). In the year of *pyŏngja* (1696), Sukchong (r. 1674–1720) restored his status as king, repaired the grave, and bestowed on it [the status of] a royal tomb.[97] Prior to this, a shrine for the illustrious Six Loyal Ministers[98] was erected. This was a splendid act.

Generally speaking, rugged mountains and deep valleys stretch to the south from Hoeyang and Chŏngsŏn in the north, and all of the streams flow west to the Han River. Slash-and-burn cultivation is broadly practiced and rice paddies are scarce. The climate is very cold, the soil is barren, and the residents are slow. As the area is remote [and boasts] extraordinary scenery, it is a good place for avoiding war for a while, [but] it is not suitable for living for generations. Ch'unch'ŏn and Wŏnju are a bit better.

Ch'unch'ŏn is to the west of Inje. Hanyang is over two hundred *ri* to the southwest of Ch'unch'ŏn by land and water. Mount Ch'ŏngp'yŏng lies to the north of the city center of Ch'unch'ŏn. On the mountain is a monastery; next to the monastery, there remains the site of the Kongnanam, where Yi Cha-hyŏn, a recluse, lived in the Koryŏ dynasty. Although he was a relative of the royal family and of a young age, he lived here and concentrated on self-cultivation without marrying and advancing at court.[99] When he died, the monks of the monastery erected a pagoda [where they] kept his ashes. It is still ten *ri* to the south of the mountain.

Ch'unch'ŏn, the capital of the state of Maek for a thousand years, is by the Soyang River. On its outskirts, there is a big village called Udu. This is the very place where Emperor Wu of the Han dynasty had Peng Wu open a road to Usuju.[100] At the base of the mountain, a broad field opens out through which two rivers flow. The place has a pleasant climate, beautiful scenery, and rich soil. Many scholar-gentry have lived here for generations.

Wŏnju, to the west of Yŏngwŏl, is the seat of a provincial governor. Hanyang is two hundred fifty *ri* away to the west. It is close to mountain passes and remote mountain valleys to the east and joins Chip'yŏng County to the west. Raised flat fields open up between mountains and valleys, so it has excellent scenery, neither steep nor blocked. Situated between Kyŏnggi Province and high mountain passes, it became a city for the whole province, where fish, salt, ginseng, coffins, and timber for palaces are gathered. Being close to mountainous areas, it is easy to escape during times of emergency. Being close to the capital, it is easy to advance to the court at a time of peace. Therefore, many members of the scholar-gentry class from Seoul enjoy living here.

Mount Chŏgak is to the east; it is where Wŏn Ch'ŏn-sŏk (Un'gok) taught students while he resided in hiding. In his youth, our Great King of Kongjŏng[101] also came and learned from him. After his study matured, [the king] returned and passed the civil service examination at the age of eighteen. Having seen indications that King T'aejo would succeed the kingdom after he returned from Wihwado, Un'gok wrote a letter of dissuasion. Later, King T'aejong ascended to the throne and came to Mount Chŏgak to visit Un'gok. Un'gok was not to be seen, however; he had gone into hiding. Only the old maid who used to prepare his meals was there. When the king asked her of the teacher's whereabouts the maid replied, "He went to Mount T'aebaek to look for a friend." The king rewarded her abundantly, left an edict in which he appointed Un'gok's son as the magistrate of Kich'ŏn, and returned to the palace. People say that Un'gok's integrity is higher than that of Yan Ling[102] and cannot be compared with such people as Huan Rong, who seek to get on in the world.[103]

To the north is Hoengsŏng County. The town is spread out in a remote valley, and yet it is bright and wide with azure water and flattish mountains. There is a special kind of clear energy that is indescribable. In the area, there are also many scholar-gentry who live for generations. Water flowing to the west from Mount Odae enters to the northeast of this area. Running southwest, it becomes the Sŏm River and enters Hŭngwŏnch'ang and meets the downstream of the Ch'ungju River to the south. There is a township between the two rivers, which act as the blue dragon and the white tiger.[104] They join in front of the town to become a deep pond.

The western branch of Mount Chŏgak, which is to the west of Mount Odae, is completely disconnected here. Mountains beyond the rivers cover the land both to the right and to the left as if they are locked gates. The area has the most favorable benefit from the landform.[105] This is the place where all of the goods heading for Seoul are gathered. There are many scholar-gentry who have lived here for generations. There are also many who became rich by using boats for trading.

During the reign of King Kwanghae, Minister Yi (Paeksa)[106] found it risky to conduct himself politically. Therefore, he asked Chŏng Ch'ung-sin to look for a place to relax in his retirement upstream of the Han River. Ch'ung-sin came here and drew what he saw and presented it to [Paeksa]. Paeksa wanted to secure a site where he could build a house, but he could not implement his plan as he had to go into exile in Pukch'ŏng. When I passed through here earlier I remembered him and composed a poem.

I look up and down the scenery and find it the same as in
    olden days.
The hero's judgement is still dignifying.

Fearing the wind from the west might contaminate the picture of the
  royal offspring,
You desired to shift the whole house to the edge of the upstream.

The place is, however, very close to the two rivers [and is] without rice
paddies [so it] does not have the advantage of cultivating rice. Over a hill
to the southeast of the village is Tŏgŭnch'on. This village is connected
to the village Ch'ŏngnyong of Ch'ungju to the east. Between the valleys
there are many rice paddies. The scenery of springs and rocks is relaxing
and clear. It is also a good place for living in retreat.

Water from Ch'ŏllyŏng and Mount Kŭmgang flows to the south
and becomes the Mojin River in Ch'unch'ŏn and enters the Han River
at Yongjin. Across the river to the west from Ch'unch'ŏn are the seven
towns of Yanggu, Kimhwa, Kŭmsŏng, Ch'ŏrwŏn, P'yŏnggan, Anhyŏp,
and Ich'ŏn (伊川). They are all to the north of Kyŏnggi Province and to the
east of Hwanghae Province.

Ch'ŏrwŏn City is where Kungye, the king of T'aebong, set up the capital. Kungye, as a prince of the Silla dynasty, had been a ruffian since his
youth. As he grew up he became a thief based between Ansŏng and Chuksan. He re-occupied parts of the territories of Koguryŏ and Yemaek and
enthroned himself as king (r. 901–918). Having been very cruel, he was
expelled by his subordinates, who finally crowned Wang Kŏn as T'aejo.
This was the beginning of the Koryŏ dynasty. Ch'ŏrwŏn City belongs to
Kangwŏn but is established on a field. It is connected to Changdan in the
province of Kyŏnggi to the west. Although the soil is barren, it is flattish
and bright, with broad fields and low mountains. Situated between two
rivers, it is a city in a remote mountainous area. In the middle of the field
there runs a river, which is deep and has black rocks with the appearance
of having been gnawed off by insects.

A journey starting from Hanyang to the east, across the port of
Yongjin, past Yanggŭn and Chipyŏng, and over Karhyŏn, will reach the
boundary of Kangwŏn Province. A day's walk from there to the east will
end at Un'gyoyŏk, the western boundary of Kangnŭng City. When my
now-deceased father traveled to his new appointment as governor of
Kangnŭng in the *kyemi* year (1703), I was fourteen years old.[107] Following his palanquin from Un'gyo[yŏk] to Taegwallyŏng, to the west of
Kangnŭng City [see Plate 1], I found that the roads, regardless of whether
they were on flat land or high hills, all stretched through thick forests. I
could not see the sky for about four days of the journey.

Over the course of a few decades, the mountains and fields were all
turned into farmland and villages sprawled and joined each other. This

left no trees thicker than one *ch'i*.[108] Based on this, I can imagine that other cities are the same. During our glorious era under the reign of the benevolent king, the population has gradually expanded, but the land has become severely exhausted. In olden days, ginseng was produced in all the remote areas on the western side of mountain passes. As the residents of the mountain practiced slash-and-burn cultivation, ginseng production decreased. Because of the landslides that occur every rainy season, the soil flows into the Han River and the riverbed gradually becomes shallow.

KYŎNGSANG PROVINCE

Kyŏngsang is the best province in terms of its geomancy [see Plate 6].[109] It lies to the south of Kangwŏn Province and adjoins Ch'ungch'ŏng and Chŏlla Provinces to the west. To the north is Mount T'aebaek, which projects high into the sky and which geomancers[110] classify as a water-type star mountain.[111] A big branch range starting from Mount T'aebaek stretches toward the East Sea on the left and another is formed by Mount Sobaek, Mount Chaksŏng, Mount Chuhol, Mount Hŭiyang, and Mount Ch'ŏnghwa on the right. This range [to the right] also includes Mount Songni, Mount Hwangak, Mount Tŏgyu, Mount Chiri, and ends at the South Sea. Between the two ranges lies a fertile plain one thousand *ri* wide.

Hwangji is a natural lake that lies below the main peak of Mount T'aebaek. The water in the lake flows from north to south to Yean County. Bending first to the east and then to the west, it circles to the south of Andong. At the boundary of Yonggung and Hamch'ang Counties, it turns to the south to become the Naktong River. Naktong means "east of Sangju." [112] The river enters Kimhae, flowing through the middle of Kyŏngsang Province. The eastern side of the river is called the left side of the province,[113] and the western side of the river is called the right side of the province. Two branches join to make a large river at Kimhae. Water from seventy counties flows out through the same channel forming a big, wide plain.

In ancient times there were many small states of one hundred *ri* square in the province, but they were unified by the Silla dynasty. This dynasty, which lasted for one thousand years, had its capital in Kyŏngju. In olden days Kyŏngju was called Kyerim Kunjaguk (State of Gentlemen in the Chicken Forest).[114] It is called Tonggyŏng (Eastern Capital) nowadays and is governed by a mayor. The main administrative center is located in the middle of the left branch of Mount T'aebaek; geomancers named it *hoeryong kojo* (dragon looking back to the ancestors' landform).[115]

To the northwest is a vast open plain. The water from the plain flows to the east to form a large river that empties into the sea. On the plain are old sites of the Silla dynasty such as Panwŏlsŏng, P'osŏkchŏng, and Koerŭng. Silla conquered various states in the Yŏngnam region[116] and later took advantage of the fall of Koguryŏ and Paekche to unify the Three Kingdoms. When a queen assumed the throne toward the end of Silla, the political situation fell into chaos.[117] Buddhism was so excessive that there was a monastery in every valley and many ordinary people became monks. In the meantime, Kungye gained power in the old territory of Koguryŏ and Kyŏn Hwŏn rose against Silla in the old territory of Paekche. When King T'aejo of Koryŏ (Wang Kŏn) unified both Later Koguryŏ and Later Paekche, the Silla kingdom surrendered to Koryŏ, giving up its entire territory. Because the Silla kingdom was blocked to the north by the Great Desert[118] and the Khitan Mountains, its only ties with the Tang dynasty (618–907) were by the sea route. Because the officials of both countries visited each other frequently, Chinese civilization and cultural activities were honored and emulated.

Another thousand years have passed between Koryŏ and the present dynasty. For several thousand years, from ancient times, Kyŏngsang Province produced chancellors and generals, ministers and scholars, who were famous for their scholarship and virtue. Prominent people of great merit and integrity, masters of Taoism, Buddhism, and Confucianism were also produced. Thus, it acquired the name "treasure house of prominent people." Especially during the present dynasty, top administrators in the court of King Sŏnjo (r. 1567–1608) all came from Kyŏngsang Province, and the four great Korean Confucian scholars who are offered memorial services in the National Confucian Shrine were also from this province.[119]

Ever since King Injo brought peace to the country,[120] members of the old families residing in the capital have received preferential appointment, along with the disciples of Yi I (Yulgok), Sŏng Hon (Ugye), and Yi Hang-bok (Paeksa). During the last hundred years, however, only two people from the Yŏngnam region have become ministers, only four or five have been appointed vice ministers, and no one from that district has become a chancellor. The highest rank to which residents from this area have been promoted is the third rank;[121] the lowest ranks are at the county magistrate level.

Because of the legacy of its predecessors, the people of this province honor propriety and rites as well as literary traditions. This province still produces the greatest number of people who pass the civil service examinations. The people of the left side of the province are poor and frugal because of the barren soil [there], but many scholars rise from among them. On the other hand, the people of the right side of the province are better off, thanks to the rich soil. They are lazy, though, and prefer socializing to study. Therefore, few scholars from this area have made their way to high government posts. This is only a sketchy comparison of the two sides of the province. In fact, both sides have both fertile and barren patches of land and have produced prominent people.

The towns of Yean, Andong, Sunhŭng, Yŏngch'ŏn, and Yech'ŏn are south of Mount T'aebaek and Mount Sobaek. It is said that these towns were regarded by a deity as auspicious. The foothills below Mount T'aebaek are bright and beautiful, and the plains are broad. The soil, a mixture of white sand and firm clay, is just like that of Hanyang. Yean is the hometown of Yi Hwang (T'oegye) and Andong is the hometown of Yu Sŏng-nyong (Sŏae). Their shrines are built where they used to live and memorial rites are offered. These five villages are close together, and among them they have produced more scholars than any other villages. These people are either students or descendants of T'oegye or Sŏae. Since people take morality and righteousness seriously, the voices of people reading aloud are heard even in poor remote villages. Even villagers in rags living in crude cottages talk about ethics, human nature and the destiny of human beings. This tradition has weakened in recent years, however. Although discreet and honest, the villagers are now parochial, less earnest, and rather contentious. They are not living up to the standard of past generations. Many villagers on the right side of the province are even worse.

The administrative center of Andong County is located south of Mount Hwasan. The water from Hwangji runs from the northeast through the town of Ch'ŏngsong and on into Imha. The water joins in the southeast, circles around the city wall, and then flows away to the southwest. To the south is the pavilion of Yŏnghoru, where King Kongmin (r. 1351–1374) gave a banquet while taking refuge in the south. The inscription on a hanging board in the pavilion is his calligraphy. To the north of the pavilion is an old temple of the Silla dynasty. It is closed and no monks reside there now. The main building that stands alone in the middle of the ground has not tilted or decayed and people compare it with the Hall of Lingguang[122] of the state of Lu. To the west is the Sŏaksa and in the monastery is a shrine of Guan Wang with a stone statue.[123] The shrine was erected when Ming military officers attacked the Japanese [soldiers] in the year of *imjin* (1592).[124] To the south is Kwiraejŏng, built by former county magistrate Yi Koeng.[125] The building of Imch'ŏnggak is to the east, and the Yi family has lived there for generations. Together with Yŏnghoru these are the only landmarks in the town.

About two hundred *ri* north of the town is Mount T'aebaek, and below the mountain are the villages of Naesŏng, Ch'unyang, Soch'ŏn, and

Chaesan, nestled in deep and remote valleys where the villagers live together in groups. Being connected by a transportation route, they have the advantage of acquiring fish and salt from the coast of the Kwandong region. These places can provide refuge in times of war or turmoil. The two counties of Yŏngyang and Chinbo to the east of the four villages have roughly the same customs. Over the pass of Ŭmnyŏng to the east from Chinbo County is Yŏnghae County, whose northern part joins P'yŏnghae County of the Kwandong region.

To the south of Andong, over the Hwangsu [River], is Mount P'algong. Between the north side of the mountain and the south bank of the Hwangsu [River] are eight or nine towns, such as Ŭisŏng, and to the southeast of these towns lies Kyŏngju. Nine towns, including Yŏnghae to the north and Tongnae to the south, are scattered all over the T'aebaek Mountain Range. This group of towns forms a long, narrow strip from north to south. Because they are close to the sea they enjoy the benefit of fish and salt. Kyŏngju, the biggest of the nine towns and the hometown of Yi Ŏn-jŏk (Hoejae) of the present dynasty, still preserves the customs of the ancient [Silla] capital.

West of the big river and south of Mount P'algong[126] is the town of Ch'ilgok, and southeast of Ch'ilgok are several towns such as Hayang, Kyŏngsan, and Cha'in [see Plate 6]. None of the towns in the whole of Kyŏngsang Province can be protected by walls. Ch'ilgok alone is on top of a mountain as high as ten thousand men,[127] and it faces the main road between the north and south. It is an important strategic defense fortress. Taegu, seat of the provincial government, is situated in the center of a vast plain surrounded by high mountains. In the middle of the plain, the Kŭmho River flows from east to west, where it joins the lower Naktong River. The administrative center lies south of the river. Taegu is situated in the center of the province and has a good landscape.

From the southeast of Taegu City to Tongnae are eight towns. Although the soil is rich these are not desirable places to live because of their proximity to Japan. Miryang is the hometown of Kim Chong-jik (Chŏmp'iljae), and Hyŏnp'ung the hometown of Kim Koeng-p'il (Hanhŏndang). Adjacent to a river and near the sea, they enjoy the advantage of access to fish and salt as well as to water transportation. These places are prosperous and auspicious. Many interpreters come from Hanyang and are stationed here, trading precious goods with the Japanese and making good profits. Tongnae is southeast of Miryang.[128] It is the first port of call after a journey from Japan across the southeast sea. Before the year of *imjin* (1592) a Japanese residential compound (*waegwan*)[129] was established south of the town. A wooden fence tens of *ri* long along the boundary was guarded by soldiers, and people of this country were prohibited from visiting. Each year, men from Tsushima [carrying] letters from the governor of the island brought hundreds of Japanese to stay there. The court gave the Japanese staying in the compound a portion of the tax collected from Kyŏngsang Province, half of which was offered to the governor of the island and the other half of which they used for their expenses. Their only task was to exchange letters and goods [between Korea and Tsushima]. When payment was not made in full and the remainder was promised for the following year, it was termed as "being withheld."

Japan has many miasmal springs that cause endemic diseases. If ginseng is soaked in the water, the pernicious effects disappear straight away. Ginseng is therefore regarded as a very precious item, and the Japanese living far away [from Korea] procure a supply of ginseng from Tsushima. Within Korea the court distributes a certain amount of ginseng each year and prohibits private sale. Since trade in ginseng generates a lot of profit, however, private trading does go on regardless of the threat of execution of any private vendor. In recent years the prohibition has been relaxed a little and many people violate the ban. The price keeps rising and and ginseng becomes scarcer every day.

In the past, the Great King of Changhŏn sent troops to pacify Tsushima, but he did not place officials to keep watch there. Instead, he left a governor in charge of the island. At that time, Japanese would not have been allowed to stay in the residential compound; it is not clear when this practice started [but] it is actually meaningless. This island originally did not belong to Japan, [but] being situated between the two countries [of Japan and Korea], it demands favors from Korea using Japan as a pretext. At the same time, it is considered important by the Japanese because of its proximity to Korea. By acting as "a bat between birds and beasts" it takes advantage of both countries. It is therefore best to conquer the island and subjugate it. An alternative is to let the governor of the island visit [our] court once a year to pay tribute. If the islanders show submission they may be treated courteously as good servants and may be rewarded generously as before. Accommodating the Japanese in the residential compound and providing them with taxed goods is tantamount to paying tribute to them. Such measures therefore should be stopped right away. Tsushima has very barren soil but is densely populated. Those who became pirates on the seas at the end of the Koryŏ dynasty are all from this island. Appeasement and trying to coax them not to rob other countries is futile, serving only as a temporary solution, and there have been no such historical precedents [for appeasement]. Nowadays they stay in our territory wearing Korean dress and learning the Korean language. They even try to spy on our court. During the Hideyoshi invasion in the year of *imjin* (1592) they suddenly retreated. They did not lend us any support during the war but instead caused us harm. The policy has nevertheless been in place for a long time, and it is not wise to switch policy suddenly and cause an abrupt change in the relationship. We must show our military prowess first and bring them to an agreement later.

On the right side of Kyŏngsang Province lies Mun'gyŏng County below Choryŏng. Majestic Mount Chuhol is to the north and Taet'an to the south. Mount Hoeyang and Mount Ch'ŏnghwa lie to the west and Mount Ch'ŏnju and Mount Taewŏn to the east. Therefore, Mun'gyŏng County is on a small plain surrounded by mountains and is the most prominent town on the border of the Yŏngnam region. This town directly faces the main road that connects north and south. At the time of the Hideyoshi invasion, when Japanese soldiers advanced to the north and reached Taet'an they were very afraid of this place. They passed through here only after making sure that the town was not defended. They did the same upon reaching Choryŏng. The town is made up of rocks, however, and is in the middle of very rugged terrain. Geomancers say that the place is less affected by malevolent energy.

To the south is the Hamch'ang Plain and to the south of Hamch'ang is Sangju. Sangju is also called Nagyang and is a big city below Choryŏng. The mountains are majestic and the plain is broad. To the north, Sangju is close to Choryŏng, which connects the city to Ch'ungch'ŏng and Kyŏnggi Provinces, and to the east it meets the Naktong River, which connects it to Kimhae and Tongnae Counties. Connected to both the north and south by road and river, it forms a central point for transportation. Because of its convenience for communication and trading, there are many wealthy people here and also many famous Confucian scholars and high-ranking government officials: Chŏng Kyŏng-se (Ubok) and Yi Chun (Ch'angsŏk) are both from Sangju.

To the west of Sangju is Hwaryŏng and to the west of Hwaryŏng is Poŭn County of Ch'ungch'ŏng Province. Hwaryŏng is the hometown of No Su-sin (Sojae) and Indong County in the east is the hometown of Chang Hyŏn-gwang (Yŏhŏn). To the south is Sŏnsan County, which boasts a landscape clearer and brighter than that of Sangju. It is said that half of the talented people in Korea are from the Yŏngnam region and half of those in Yŏngnam are from Sŏnsan County. Since the olden days, many literary scholars who demonstrated excellence were from here. During the Hideyoshi invasion Ming troops passing through the area had among their commanding officers a geomancer who was jealous of the many talented people that Korea had produced. He had his soldiers scorch the area with fiery charcoals to cut off the mountain range behind the town and drive big metal spikes into the ground to suppress the vital energy of the land. Since then, the area has been depleted as a source of human talent.

To the west of Kŭmsan is Ch'up'ungnyŏng and to the west of the pass is Hwanggan. The water from the east of Mount Hwangak and Mount Tŏgyu converge to become the Kamch'ŏn River, which intersects with the Naktong River to the east. In the basin are villages such as Chirye, Kŭmsan, and Kaeryŏng. Just as in Sŏnsan, the people here enjoy the advantage of irrigation. Thanks to the fertile rice paddies, the villagers are well-off and law abiding and avoid wrongdoing. A number of families have produced many generations of scholars. Kŭmsan is the hometown of the minister Ch'oe Sŏn-mun. Sŏnsan, where Mount Kŭmo lies, is the hometown of Kil Chae, the chief scribe in the Ministry of the Chancellery: Ch'oe Sŏn-mun was loyal to Prince Nosan[130] while Kil Chae was loyal to the Koryŏ dynasty.

South of Kamch'ŏn is Mount Sŏnsŏk, and south of the mountain are the towns of Sŏngju (星州) and Koryŏng. Koryŏng is part of the territory of the ancient state of Kaya. Further to the south is the town of Hapch'ŏn, which together with Koryŏng formed the eastern part of the ancient state of Kaya. The rice paddies of the three towns are the most fertile in the Yŏngnam region and yield the richest crops. The locals are all well-off and nobody begs or migrates. Sŏngju has such a bright and excellent landscape that it helped nourish many celebrities and famous scholars during the Koryŏ dynasty. In the present dynasty, both Kim U-ong (Tonggang) and Chŏng Ku (Han'gang) are from this area.

Samga County, to the south of Hapch'ŏn, is the hometown of Cho Sik (Nammyŏng). Three people—Kim U-ong, Chŏng Ku, and Chŏng In-hong—are disciples of Nammyŏng. Claiming to be a scholar, In-hong supported Nammyŏng, attacked T'oegye (Yi Hwang), and had numerous followers who were later purged. When Tonggang withdrew from his political career he decided to avoid In-hong. Instead of returning to Sŏngju he settled at the foot of Mount Chŏngjwa of Ch'ŏngju and remained there until he died. During the reign of King Kwanghae, as head of the Major North faction,[131] In-hong was promoted to chancellor. After the coup of King Injo, however, he was publicly executed in the marketplace. The people of Sŏngju who honored righteousness preserved his house. This is a credit to the teachings of Han'gang and Tonggang.

To the southeast of Mount Tŏgyu is Anŭm County. It is the hometown of Chŏng On (Tonggye), who was promoted to the post of minister of the Personnel Office. In the year of *pyŏngja*, when Qing troops surrounded Namhansansŏng, Chŏng On deemed it wrong to betray the Ming dynasty and surrender to the Qing. As King Injo went down the mountain to surrender, [Chŏng] On tried to commit suicide by slicing open his abdomen with a knife. His family had the wound stitched up once his intestines were put back, [and] after a while he revived. Later when the Qing soldiers returned, he went back to his hometown and did not return to public duties at the court.

To the east of Anŭm County is Kŏch'ang County and to the south [of Anŭm] is Hamyang County. Anŭm County lies to the north of Mount Chiri. These four counties have fertile soil. Hamyang is also called Sansugul; together with Kŏch'ang and Anŭm [they] make up a renowned area. Anŭm, however, is too much in the shade of a mountain to be habitable. Waters from the four counties form the Yŏng River, which empties itself into the Naktong River to the south of the city of Chinju. Chinju is a big city that lies east of Mount Chiri; it has produced many civil and military officers. It has rich soil and beautiful scenery. The local scholar-gentry are proud of their wealth and enjoy building mansions and pavilions. They do not hold public office but have the title "prince of leisure." During the Imjin War, the town was besieged by the Japanese army, and Kim Ch'ŏn-il, [who was] a ch'ang'ŭisa,[132] and Ch'oe Kyŏng-hoe, a military commander in chief, were killed in action. The residents erected a shrine and observed sacrificial rites. The court commended them by presenting the shrine with a hanging board inscribed with the words "loyal martyrs." During the reign of King Sukchong (r. 1674–1720) a county magistrate intended to repair the shrine. He asked for help [with the repairs] from a military commander in chief but was not granted assistance. He had it repaired and decorated at his own expense, whereby the shrine was totally changed. In a dream, many military officers appeared [before him] and thanked him saying, "Although you are a civil official you were very considerate to us, while the military officer does not look after us. He will be duly punished." At dawn the people found that the commander in chief had died overnight. One cannot say for sure that ghosts and spirits do not exist.

To the east of Chinju are Ŭiryŏng and Ch'ogye, whose social customs are similar to those of Chinju. From olden days the thirteen towns to the south of the Yŏng River have yielded only a few talented people who were promoted to high government posts. The towns are close to the sea and to Japan. Because the waters and springs there have been haunted by morbid spirits, they are not desirable places to live. Hadong, the hometown of Chŏng Yŏ-ch'ang (Iltu), is situated to the south of Mount Chiri, adjoining Kwangyang County of Chŏlla Province. They say that "in the noble province to the left and the wealthy province to the right, there are towns of thousand-year renown." Because this province is far from the capital it is difficult for scholars to settle there unless they are from that area. It is not favorable for habitation, not only in terms of its position but also in terms of present circumstances.

CHŎLLA PROVINCE

Chŏlla Province shares its eastern border with Kyŏngsang Province and its northern border with Ch'ungch'ŏng Province [see Plate 7]. It was originally the territory of Paekche. Kyŏn Hwŏn of the Later Paekche kingdom occupied this land at the end of the Silla dynasty and attacked the first king, King T'aejo of Koryŏ, many times, leaving [the king] in a dangerous position. When the Koryŏ dynasty conquered the Kyŏn family, King T'aejo distrusted the people of Paekche, saying that all the waters to the south of the Ch'aryŏng Range flowed rebelliously. On his deathbed he decreed that people from south of the Ch'aryŏng Range should not be employed as government officials. Toward the middle of the dynasty there were a few who were promoted to the premiership, but these were very rare indeed. This prohibition has been relaxed in our present dynasty.

The whole Honam region[133] has rich soil and the southeastern part is near the sea. It benefits from fishing; making salt and silk; raising crops of rice, cotton, and citrus fruit; and producing ramie, paper mulberry, and bamboo. The customs of this region are sybaritic and extravagant, and the people are superficial and shrewd, and have an aversion to literary study. Fewer people from the Honam region pass the civil service examinations than those from Kyŏngsang Province, for there are not many from this area who are proud of being known as diligent scholars. The Honam region nevertheless still has its share of talented people born under the guardianship of the local spirit. Ki Tae-sŭng (Kobong) from Kwangju, Yi Hang (Iljae) from Puan County, and Kim In-hu (Hasŏ) from Changsŏng County were all renowned for their scholarship. Ko Kyŏng-myŏng (Chaebong) and Kim Ch'ŏn-il (Kŏnjae) were both from Kwangju and both were known for their rectitude and righteousness. Yun Sŏn-do (Kosan) was from Haenam County and Yi Sang-hyŏng (Mukchae) was from Namwŏn County; both established themselves in literature. Chŏng Chi and Chŏng Ch'ung-sin (Kŭmnam) were famous generals from Kwangju; also from Kwangju was O Kyŏm, a chief secretary on the Supreme Council. Yi Sang-jin, a premier from Chŏnju, became famous. Paek Kwang-hun (Okpong) from Kobu County and Ch'oe Kyŏng-ch'ang (Kojuk) from Yŏngam County were also renowned for their literary talent. The scholars who resided in the area are Sin Mal-chu, a county magistrate who lived in Sunch'ang County, and Yi Kye-maeng, a second secretary on the Supreme Council who lived in Kimje County. Minister Yi Hu-baek, who lived in Haenam County, and Minister Im Tam, who resided in Muan County, were also born here. As for Taoists, we have Namgung Tu, a master of Taoism from Hamyŏl County, and Kwŏn Kŭk-chung (Ch'ŏngha) from Kobu County, who was famous for his Taoist learning and training. All were righteous and noble spirited and well known for many generations after their death.

Mount Tŏgyu lies where the three provinces of Ch'ungch'ŏng, Chŏlla, and Kyŏngsang meet and extends westward to join with Chŏnju City. To the east it becomes part of Mount Mai (Horse Ear Mountain), with two rocky peaks towering in the sky. In the past, when the Great King of Kongjŏng[134] was learning martial arts in the Honam region, he called the mountain Mount Mai. One branch range from Mount Mai runs to the southwest between Imsil County and Chŏnju City, and another, which runs to the west to become Mount Moak of Kŭmgu County, meets the rivers of Man'gyŏng and Tongjin. Yet another runs to the southwest and becomes Mount Tŏkhŭng of Sunch'ang County and Noryŏng of Chŏngŭp County; it is a main route connecting north and south. Noryŏng branches in four directions: to the west it stops at Yŏnggwang County, to the southwest it stops at Muan County, to the north it stops at Mount Pyŏnsan in Puan County, and to the southeast it forms various mountains below Tamyang and Kwangju Counties.

Mount Puhŭng is in the middle of Chŏlla Province. An open plain is enclosed by two mountains, forming a valley with a stream flowing eastward. People say the place is good enough for building a walled town. During the reign of King Sukchong, however, people tried unsuccessfully to shift a military camp here.

Mount Mai stretches to the north to become Mount Chujul, which is between Chinan County and Chŏnju City. A branch of Mount Chujul to the west forms the base of Chŏnju, which is the seat of local government. To the east is Wibongsansŏng and a little to the north is the peak of Kirinbong, with a branch reaching to the northwest of Chŏnju and becoming Mount Kŏnji. People say this is where the tomb of Mokcho[135] was. In the year of kyŏngsul (1730), during the reign of the present king, the governor was ordered to have all the tombs moved and to put up signs every ten ri to ban the cutting down of trees. A branch from Mount Kŏnji stretches to the west and forms the lake of Tŏkchi, which is very wide and deep. Beyond the lake, [Kŏnji] becomes a gentle sloping hill surrounded by large fields. This place is extremely desirable for habitation, with water from Manmadong flowing into it.

The water from the valleys west of Mount Chujul passes through Kosan County. Upon crossing the boundary of Chŏnju City they merge into big streams such as the Yuldam, Yangjŏnp'o, and Obaekchu. The land is well irrigated and has good soil; it produces rice, ginger, ramie, bamboo, and persimmon, and people catch fish from the nearby water. The numerous villages are well equipped to make a living in this area and have boats carrying fish and salt westward to the area of Sat'an. Chŏnju City is densely populated and has large accumulations of goods; it is no different from Seoul and is a very big city. All the towns to the north of Noryŏng harbor pernicious miasma. Chŏnju alone is tidy and neat enough to be a highly desirable place to live.

A mountain range north of Mount Chujul stretches to the west and becomes Mount Yonghwa in T'anhyŏn County and stops at Okku County. There are five towns to the northwest of T'anhyŏn, one being Yŏsan. Yŏsan, which adjoins Ch'ungch'ŏng Province, has clay-like soil and miasma. It is not a good place to live. The old capital where Ki Chun ruled was situated on top of Mount Yonghwa. One can still find ruins of the city wall and the palace. A branch of this mountain stretches to the north and becomes Mount Ch'aeun, which is to the northwest of Yŏsan. This mountain stands prominently in the middle of a plain like a lonely peak, and on top of the mountain there is a miraculous spring that, according to legend, is the place where King Ŭija of Paekche enjoyed himself and feasted with his guests.

Passing over Mount Ch'aeun and a small plain, one reaches Hwangsanch'on. A rocky mountain rises abruptly over the river and becomes a cliff. Since there is a little port there, one can reach Kanggyŏngch'on by boat, which makes it a site of scenic beauty. To the west are Yong'an, Hamyŏl, and Imp'i Counties, all of which lie south of the Chin River. Mount Osŏng of Imp'i County is especially beautiful. Up the river is a big village called Sŏsip'o. This is the place where many boats come to moor; this village is as famous as the Hwangsanch'on of Kanggyŏng. Sŏsip'o is said to be so named because Sŏsi was born here in ancient times.[136]

Okku County, which is to the west of Imp'i County, faces the West Sea where one finds Chach'ŏndae. A small slope protrudes to the sea and on top of the hill there are two stone chambers where Ch'oe Ko-un, the county magistrate, stored secret documents. The chambers, set in a gigantic stone, were abandoned on the hillside. No one dared open them, but whenever people tried to move them a storm would suddenly blow in from the sea. The villagers took advantage of the phenomenon, and whenever there was a drought, several hundred of them would gather around to pull the rocks with big ropes in order to bring on an immediate rain [storm] to water the rice paddies and fields. Whenever the king's messengers came to the county, they would all go to look at the rocks, which was a nuisance for the villagers. A pavilion there was demolished one hundred years ago, and the stone cages were also buried. Today nobody goes there to look for them.

To the east of T'anhyŏn is Kosan County and to the south of Mount Yonghwa is Iksan County. Both places are affected by miasma and, although the soil is rich, the topography of Kosan is too rugged to be a desirable place to live. To the west of Mount Myoak are Okku and Man'gyŏng Counties. The water from the spring is very clear and the mountains moreover are void of malevolent energy. As the two rivers that meander across the middle of the plain embrace the fields, the vital energy is not dispersed and there are many desirable places for dwelling sites.

Apart from those mentioned above, villages such as T'aein and Kobu, which are close to mountains, and Puan and Mujang, which are close to the sea, are all afflicted with miasma. Only the areas of Pyŏnsan of Puan County and southern Changji of Hŭngdŏk County have fertile soil and good scenery, including lakes and mountains. Places without miasmic springs make desirable locations to live.

To the west of Noryŏng are the towns of Yŏnggwang, Hamp'yŏng, and Muan, and to the south are the settlements of Changsŏng and Naju. These five towns do not have miasmic springs and are superior to the towns north of Noryŏng. Pŏpsŏngp'o of Yŏnggwang County has a harbor where the tide enters as well as a beautiful lake, mountains, and clusters of villages. People call the lake Sosŏho (West Lake Minor). Towns close to the sea all keep their rice stores in Pŏpsŏngp'o, whence the rice is shipped to the royal palace. Changsŏng also has fertile soil and beautiful scenery. Naju is a city at the foot of Noryŏng backed by Mount Kŭmsŏng and facing the Yŏngsan River to the south. The landform of the township is similar to that of Hanyang. There have been many houses of famous officials there over the years. The Yŏngsan River here flows to the west and reaches Muan County and the Mokp'o settlement. Along the river there are many good villages and scenic spots. Across the river a vast plain extends to Kwangju to the east and connects with Yŏngam to the south. This plain has a bright and free atmosphere and is abundant in produce. It is studded with villages. To the southwest the plain has the advantage of river and sea transportation. The two towns of Kwangju and Mokp'o are famous.

The Ch'ilsan Sea to the west of Naju was deep in the past, but in recent years sand deposits have made the sea at the shore very shallow. When the tide goes out the water is barely knee-high and only the channel in the middle is as deep as the river itself. Ships sail along this middle channel. To the southwest of Naju is Yongam County, which is at the foot of Mount

Wŏlch'ul. The mountain has such fine and beautiful features that it is categorized in geomantic landscapes as "the fire mountain in the morning sky."[137] To the south is Wŏllamch'on and to the west, Kurimch'on, both famous during the Silla period. Because this area is situated at the meeting point of the West Sea and the South Sea, it is from here that all ships bound for Tang China set sail during the Silla dynasty. It is a day's sail to Hŭksando, then from Hŭksando it takes another day by ship to Hongŭido and still another day to Kagado. With a northeasterly wind it takes three days to sail to Dinghai County in Ningbofu of Taizhou, but with a favorable wind it takes only one day. When the Southern Song (1127–1279) traded with Koryŏ, the ships also set sail from Dinghai County and could reach Koryŏ territory and land in seven days. During the Silla dynasty when people traveled to Tang China by sea, their ships crossed this place frequently, as if it were an important ferry crossing. Ch'oe Chi-wŏn, Kim Ka-gi, and Ch'oe Sŭng-u all entered Tang China by merchant ships and passed the Tang civil service examinations. Koun worked for Gao Pian[138] and excelled in four-six style prose.[139] "The Official Pronouncement on the Huang Chao [Rebellion]," written in the *liwen* style,[140] was composed by Koun. Together with Kim Ka-gi and Ch'oe Sŭng-u, Ch'oe Chi-wŏn met Taoist master Shen at the monastery on Mount Zhongnan and acquired a book, *Naedanbigyŏl* (Secret recipe for the elixir of life). Later, after returning to the Eastern Nation [Korea], he continued to practice the art and finally attained immortality.

To the east of Mount Puhŭng lie the counties of Imsil, Sunch'ang, Namwŏn, and Kurye, all of which are mountainous. The water to the southeast of Mount Mai passes through Imsil County and flows southward to reach Namwŏn County. It joins the Yochŏn and flows toward [the ferry crossings of] Chansujin and Amnokchin. To the west of the river are the towns of Okkwa, Tongbok, and Koksŏng. From Amnokchin the river starts bending to the east and becomes the Agyang River. It is connected to the tidal waters of the South Sea and flows around to the south of Mount Chiri to become the Sŏmjin River, which flows into the South Sea. In these areas the Sŏmjin River forms the boundary of Chŏlla and Kyŏngsang Provinces.

The Namwŏn city walls were built by Yang Yuan, the renowned Ming general of the Imjin War, but were destroyed by the Japanese army during the year of *chŏngyu* (1597). A violent military spirit still dwells here. Passing one peak over to the east one comes to Unbong County, which is situated to the north of P'allyangch'i on Mount Chiri. This is the major route connecting Chŏlla and Kyŏngsang Provinces. In front of the township is Mount Hwang (荒山), where our first king [Yi Sŏng-gye] defeated the Jap-

anese marauders toward the end of the Koryŏ dynasty. To the southeast
of Namwŏn City is Sŏngwŏn, where the Ch'oe family lived for generations. It has beautiful scenery. To the south lies Kurye County. Between
the counties of Sŏngwŏn and Kurye a large proportion of the plain yields
good harvests by producing one *chong* per *myo* from its many rice paddies.
Pongdong in the west of Kurye County has good scenic places. In the east
of Kurye County there are scenic spots such as the monasteries Hwaŏmsa
and Yŏngoksa and, in the south, Kumanch'on.

In the basin between the upper and lower streams from Imsil to Kurye County are many famous sites, beautiful spots, and also big villages.
Kumanch'on alone is on the edge of a stream and [so] only this area benefits from shipping, fisheries, and salt making and has become the best
place in the area to live. Namwŏn and Kurye Counties are both situated
to the west of Mount Chiri. Just as the three counties of Yosan, Kosan, and
Iksan to the west of the Sŏmjin River have been afflicted by miasma and
labeled as inauspicious places, so have Namwŏn and Kurye Counties. Recently, however, it has been said that they have become somewhat clear
and clean.

The southern branch of Mount Puhŭng passes through Tamyang and
Ch'angp'yŏng Counties and forms Mount Mudŭng at Kwangju. To the
east of the mountain are three towns, including Okkwa, and to the southwest are the towns of Kwangju, Hwasun, Namp'yŏng, and Nŭngju, which
are all situated to the north of Yŏngam Town. Kwangju is connected to
Naju to the west and has an open atmosphere. Since ancient times it has
had many famous villages from which many people rose to prominence.
Along the coast to the southeast of Yŏngam are eight towns. All have similar customs, except that Haenam and Kangjin are port towns and benefit
from having ferry boats sailing to and from T'amna (present-day Chejudo), and horses, cowhides, pearls, citrus fruit, and bamboo are sold here.
These eight towns, however, are all too far from the capital and too close
to the South Sea. During winter, leaves do not change color, worms do not
hibernate, and the sultry heat vapors from the mountain and the sea are a
source of miasma. Furthermore, the area is very close to Japan. Therefore,
in spite of its rich soil, it is not a desirable place to live.

From Samjuwŏn[141] of Haenam County a rocky outcrop stretches
across the sea and forms Chindo County [see Plate 7]. It is thirty *ri* long
by sea and Pyŏkp'ajŏng is right at its entrance. The rocky stretch from
Samjuwŏn to Pyŏkp'ajŏng forms a stone bridge whose top and bottom
parts are cut off to form a staircase. The tide runs from east to west day
and night and it is like a rapid waterfall. In the year of *imjin* (1592), upon
arriving at P'yŏngyang the Japanese monk Genso brought a letter to the

king's field headquarters in Ŭiju. He said, "Since one hundred thousand sailors will come up from the West Sea and advance together with the army, where will the king go?" At that time the Japanese navy was advancing north. The [Korean] admiral Yi Sun-sin was waiting for them in the South Sea, having fastened a heavy metal chain across the stone bridge. As the Japanese ships reached the bridge they were snagged by the metal chain and capsized. The ships on the other side of the stone bridge could not see the overturned vessels and assumed that the ships in front had passed the bridge and sailed on with the tide. The closer to the bridge, the faster the water ran. The ships sailed into the rapid current and it was useless for them to try to sail back. Not one of the entire fleet of five hundred ships survived.[142]

Around that time Chen Weijing[143] tried to gain time by inviting the Japanese envoy to stay in P'yŏngyang City. As the Japanese army intended to wait for their navy to join them in the north before advancing, the Japanese party accepted Chen Weijing's invitation, apparently wanting to oblige. The Japanese navy did not arrive for a long time, however, and so while both parties were engaged in mutual deception, Li Rusong[144] found the opportunity to quickly destroy the Japanese army. This was clearly an intervention by heaven. If Yi Sun-sin had not destroyed the Japanese navy at sea, in a month or so they would have arrived at P'yŏngyang. And once their navy had arrived, the Japanese would certainly not have kept their promise to Chen Weijing not to unleash the army. It is amusing that the Japanese invaders were pleased that Korea would acknowledge and pay tribute to Japan while not knowing the war situation in the South Sea. The spectacular victory over the Japanese army by Li Rusong at P'yŏngyang should be credited to Yi Sun-sin.

Later on, the famous Ming general Chen Lin stationed Ming troops by the sea. Between the years of pyŏngsin (1596) and chŏngyu (1597) the Japanese navy often attacked the counties along the coast. Each time Yi Sun-sin defeated them at sea he gathered the [decapitated] heads of the defeated and turned them over to Chen Lin so that Chen Lin could claim the credit. Chen Lin was pleased and reported to the court that "the admiral has the ability to rule the world and has contributed immensely to his country." Thanks to Yi Sun-sin, Chen Lin reported more decapitations upon returning home in the year of musul (1598) than any other Ming general and was awarded land. In the Mingshi (The history of the Ming dynasty) there is a commentary on the Ming general's contribution to the eastern expedition. How could the people of China know of the achievement of Yi Sun-sin? Yang Hao[145] was imprisoned despite his contribution [in defending Korea from the Japanese army], but thanks to Yi Sun-sin,

Chen Lin acquired fame and received a generous reward. Such was the reward and punishment meted out by the Ming emperors.

In general, the whole of Chŏlla Province lies to the far south of the country and is abundant in local products. Since the mountainous counties are irrigated with streams, they have frequent rich harvests and few years of bad crops. The coastal counties, on the other hand, are irrigated due to the building of dykes. Because the big embankment built during the Silla dynasty has not been maintained in the present dynasty, this area has had many droughts and few good harvests.

In olden days Sushuigong[146] said that the people of Min[147] were sly and wicked. In the days of Zhuzi (Zhu Xi), however, many sages were born there. If sages dwell there and teach conduct and literature, then Chŏlla Province is not a bad place to live. Although the province has many famous scenic spots, its vital energy has manifested very little from the Koryŏ dynasty to the present dynasty. [That energy] will definitely manifest one day, but at the moment [the province] has undesirable features and is too far [from the capital] to be a good place to live.

CH'UNGCH'ŎNG PROVINCE

Ch'ungch'ŏng Province lies between the provinces of Chŏlla and Kyŏnggi [see Plate 8]. It faces the sea to the west and Kyŏngsang Province to the east. Counties in the northeastern corner, such as Ch'ungju, extend far into the southern part of Kangwŏn Province. Half of this southern part is to the south of the Ch'aryŏng Range and is close to Chŏlla Province; the other half is to the north of the mountain range and is close to Kyŏnggi Province.

Although the number of local products is not as abundant as that of the other two southern provinces, the terrain is gentle and beautiful. Situated close to the south of Seoul, it became a place where many scholar-gentry came to live. No prominent families that have lived for generations in Seoul do not own grain-yielding fields and houses as their primary basis for living. Customs near the capital are not strikingly different from those of Seoul, which makes the province most desirable when selecting a place for residing.

The governor of the province resides in Kongju [see Plate 8].[148] This is the place where Liu Renyuan established a commandery at the end of the Paekche dynasty.[149] It is three hundred *ri* away from Hanyang and lies to the south of the Ch'aryŏng Range and Kŭm River. One can reach Seoul from here by crossing the Kŭm River, climbing the Ch'aryŏng Range, passing Ch'ŏnan and Chiksan, reaching Yangsŏng in Kyŏnggi Province in the north, and passing Chinwi, Suwŏn, and Kwachŏn. Following the road, fields are scattered to the north of Chiksan; the soil is barren and petty thieves thrive. It is not a desirable place to live.

In Ch'ungch'ŏng Province, the Naep'o area is the best place to live. About two hundred *ri* to the northwest from Kongju is Mount Kaya. To the west there is a wide sea and to the north there is, starting from seaside towns in Kyŏnggi Province, a broad marsh. In short, it is where the West Sea protrudes. To the east there is a broad plain, in which there is a big marsh called Yugungjin. Boats can sail only during high tide. The area to the south is blocked by Mount Osŏ, which is a mountain extending from Mount Kaya, but is connected to Kongju only through the southeast of the mountain.

The ten towns in front of and behind Mount Kaya are [what is] called the Naep'o area. As it is positioned away [from the center of the peninsula] at one corner and since no major road goes through it, the area was not affected by either the Hideyoshi invasion from the south or the Manchu invasion from the north.[150] Not only is the land fertile and flat, fish and salt are abundant. Therefore, many rich people and scholar-gentry have resided here for generations. In the area near the sea, however, malaria and leg swelling occur frequently. Although the landscape is low-lying and beautiful with gentle slopes and an open view, [this area] is less spectacular. Only the landscape of Poryŏng is excellent. To the west of the town there is a naval commander in chief's military camp, in which Yŏngbojŏng lies. As the scenery of the lakes and mountains is beautiful and extensive it is called a scenic spot.

To the north are Kyŏlsŏng and Haemi and to the west over a big swamp is Anmyŏndo. These three towns are to the west of Mount Kaya. To the north are T'aean and Sŏsan. These two towns face an island, Kanghwado, to the north over a small sea. To the east of Sŏsan are Myŏnch'ŏn and Tangjin and further to the east over a wide swamp is Asan. Diagonally to the north, Asan faces Hwaryang of Namyang in Kyŏnggi Province over a small sea.[151] The four towns are to the north of Mount Kaya.

To the east of Mount Kaya are Hongju and Tŏksan. They are to the west of Yugungjin. Together with Yesan and Sinch'ang, which are to the east of the water's edge, Hongju and Tŏksan are quickly accessible to Seoul by water. To the southeast of Hongju are Taehŭng and Ch'ŏngyang. Taehŭng was the Imjonsŏng at the time of Paekche. All eleven towns are to the north of Mount Osŏ.

A branch that stretches out to the front from Mount Osŏ extends to the southwest and forms Mount Sŏngju (聖住). To the west of the mountain are [the towns of] Piin and Namp'o. The area has extremely rich soil, and, facing the sea to the west, it also has the advantage of abundant fish, salt, and rice. To the south of the mountain are Sŏch'ŏn, Hansan, and Imch'ŏn, which are on the Chin River.[152] As the land is suitable for growing ramie, the profit from ramie ranks first in the country. Situated between the river and the sea, transportation by boat is not less convenient than that in Hanyang. The southern part of the Chin River borders on Chŏlla Province. To the northeast of the mountain are Hongsan and Chŏngsan. Hongsan is to the north of Imch'ŏn and is connected to Kanggyŏng by a river. Chŏngsan, which is to the east of Ch'ŏngyang, is connected to Mount Kong. These seven towns share similar customs and [are home to] scholar-gentry families who have lived there for generations. The two towns of Ch'ŏngyang and Chŏngsan, however, have harmful vapors [emanating from] their springs and so are not desirable places to live.

Kongju is extensive, covering both the south and north of the Kŭm River. Locals say Yusŏng is the best, Kyŏngch'ŏn the second best, Iin the third best, and Yugu the fourth best.[153] This [ranking] is in regard to the desirability of these places for living. Forty *ri* to the southeast of Kongju is Mount Kyeryong. A branch from the mountain extends to the west, abruptly disconnecting to form P'anchi and then rising again to become Mount Wŏlsŏng.[154] It is the guardian mountain of Kongju. The Kŭm River flows down from the east to the north of Kongju and then turns south. This is the place where it is called the Ungjin. As it flows further, the river is named Paengma, then Kanggyŏng. Turning again to the west before it flows to the sea it is called the Chin River.

Passing around the southern bank of the Kŭm River from the east of Kongju and over the hills behind Mount Kyeryong, the great plain of Yusŏng is spread out. It is in the northeastern direction from Mount Kyeryong. The valley to the south of the mountain was thought to have been chosen as the capital at the beginning of the Chosŏn dynasty. This was not proven, however. The water from the valley runs through the plain from the west and joins with the water of the Okkye in Chinsan and in the east flows into the Kŭm River in the north. The name of the stream is Kapch'ŏn. To the east of Kapch'ŏn is Hoedŏk County and to the west, Yusŏngch'on and Chinjam County. Mountains to the east and the west embrace the plain in the south and meet each other to the north of the plain. The plain is surrounded in all directions by mountains. Flattish hills stretch like a snake and the foothills are clear and excellent. Mounts Kubong and Pomun stand high in the north. Their clear and bright spirit seems better than that in the eastern outskirts of Hanyang. The arable fields are superb and broad. Being a little distant from the sea, however, it is necessary to trade with Kanggyŏng, which is less than one hundred *ri* away.

All four towns to the southwest of Mount Kyeryong are on the broad plain, which borders with the Kanggyŏng jetty to the west and Kongju to the north. From the four summits of Mount Kyeryong, a branch extends to the west and forms Kyŏngch'ŏnch'on. It is to the south of P'anchi. The soil is rich and the mountain is colossal. The residents are rich with abundant product. To the east of Mount Kyeryong is Taejangch'on. To the west is Isan and Sŏksŏng and to the south, Yŏnsan and Ŭnjin. Although Isan and Yŏnsan are close to the mountains, they have rich soil. Ŭnjin and Sŏksŏng are on the plain but have barren soil and experience frequent floods and droughts. The four towns are connected to Kyŏngch'ŏn by the broad plain. As Kanggyŏng is affected by a tidal current, these towns enjoy the advantage of having access to navigable water in the middle of the plain.

Kanggyŏng is to the west of Ŭnjin. In the middle of the plain, a small mountain stands up at the edge of the river, in which two big streams to the right and the left enter from the east. The river that flows around the back of the town is connected to a tidal current, although the water is not that salty. As there are no wells in the town, all the households keep big jars in the ground and fetch water from the river and pour it into them. After a few days, a thick residue sinks to the bottom of the jars and the water above is clear and cool. The taste of the water does not change even after several days; the longer it is kept the cooler it gets. Those who have suffered from harmful vapors will be healed completely if they drink the water for a year. Some say that "the water from the point where river water and tidal water is mixed is half bland and half salty and is the best for healing endemic disease." The water from this river is of the highest quality. Sajech'ŏn, which is to the northeast of Ŭnjin, is connected to the borders of Kosan and Chinsan to the southeast. The water and area along the long valley stretch as far as eighty *ri* and have a harmful vapor. It is not a suitable place to live.

Puyŏ is to the southwest of Kongju. Being on the side of the Paengma River, it was the capital of the Paekche kingdom. Choryongdae, Nakhwaam, Chaondae, and Koransa are all remnants of the Paekche kingdom. Rocks along the river are fantastic and the scenery is splendid; in addition, the soil is fertile. Many wealthy people live here. But when it comes to the site for a capital, the area is small and narrow. It is far inferior to P'yŏngyang and Kyŏngju. Iinyŏk is to the northeast of Puyŏ and to the west of Kongju. It has low mountains and wide plains with fertile rice paddies. It is also a desirable place to live.

The land to the north of Kŭm River and to the south of the Ch'aryŏng Range is fertile. However, the mountains are not void of malevolent energy. Along the rivers are pavilions such as Sasongjŏng, Kŭmbyŏkchŏng,

and Tongnakchŏng. Sasongjŏng is ours, Kŭmbyŏkchŏng belongs to Mr.
Cho, a secretary of a minister, and Tongnakchŏng is the old place of the
Im family. All are situated where it is worth climbing up to appreciate the
scenery.

To the northwest of Kongju is Mount Musŏng. It is at the southern
end of the Ch'aryŏng Range. In the area surrounded by steep-sloped
mountains with flattish tops there is Magoksa and a station, Yuguyŏk.
The valley has many streams and fertile rice paddies and is also suitable
for growing cotton, millet, and Italian millet. Once the scholar-gentry and
commoners settle, they do not worry whether it be a year of good harvest
or not. As many households maintain their wealth and few contemplate
wandering or shifting their residence, it is generally a happy place to live.
The terrain has formed a geomantic landscape at the top of the mountain.
Because hills are low and flat without rugged or sharp shapes and there
are no rocks in the mountains, it has less murderous energy. Nam Sa-go
(1509–1571) therefore wrote in "Sipsŭnggi" that the area between the two
valleys of Yugu and Magoksa is a place worth hiding in during wars.[155]

Over a mountain pass to the west is Naep'o. As the land is not suitable for growing cotton, seaside residents bring fish and salt to Yugu and
swap them for cotton. In Kongju, Yugu alone attains the benefit from the
trade in fish and salt in Naep'o. Therefore, it is a suitable place to live
during both peaceful times and in war. Having formed a geomantic landscape at the top of the mountain, its homage mountain (chosan) is not seen
and it harbors a less clear and excellent spirit. It is for this reason inferior
to Yusŏng.

To the north of the town, a small mountain zigzags along the river
in the shape of the character kong (公). This is the reason why the place
acquired the name Kongju. As the small city wall was built along the line
of the mountain and the river acts as a moat, the area is narrow but solid.
When King Injo retreated here at the time of Yi Kwal's revolt[156] in the year
of kapcha (1624), he saw two trees on the mountain. Leaning against the
trees, he used to view places, like the archery building and its grounds, to
the north every day. One day a man approached him on a horse as if he
was flying. When asked, he presented a report of victory [of government
soldiers over Yi Kwal]. Out of great joy, the king bestowed on the two
trees the title of T'ongjŏng Taebu.[157] Afterward, the local government built
a pavilion on the mountain. The trees are now dead but the pavilion remains. Provisions and arms are stored in the city walls. Along with Kanghwa and Kwangju [in Kyŏnggi Province], this city suddenly became an
important place. Kongbungnu to the north of the city is quite grand and
splendid. Being situated on the river, its scenery is also excellent. After Yu

Kŭn (Sŏgyŏng, 1549–1627) became governor of the province during the reign of King Sŏnjo, he climbed up to the pavilion and composed a poem. There is a stanza that reads, "Su Dongpo[158] had a good time at Red Cliff but I now relax at Blue Cliff. / Yu Liang climbed up on the South Pavilion but I am up here on the North Pavilion."[159]

[The verse reflects the fact that] Ch'angbyŏk (Blue Cliff) is on the upper stream of the Kŭm River and the name of the pavilion is Kongbungnu.[160] Some said that this was from a poorly written poem by Xu Ning,[161] but Sŏgyŏng himself boasted that this was a beautiful stanza.

A branch range of Mount Songni extends to the south and drops sharply to become Ch'up'ungnyŏng and then rises up to become Mount Hwangak in Hwanggan. Having entered Chŏlla Province the branch range becomes Mount Tŏgyu in Muju and then descends sharply between Changsu and Namwŏn. To the west it becomes Mount Mai in Imsil. From here a rocky range turns north to become Mounts Churyu, Unje, and Taedun. In Ch'ungch'ŏng Province, with the Kŭm River running behind it, the range turns again and becomes Mount Kyeryong. This forms a major mountain range facing south with its back to the north.

Streams from all of the towns between Mount Tŏgyu to the east and Mount Mai to the west merge with water from the valleys to become the source of the Kŭm River, called the Chŏktŭng. The Chŏktŭng River runs from south to north and joins the water flowing from Mount Songni to the east of Okchŏn before turning west to become the Kŭm River. To the east of the Chŏktŭng River are the counties of Changsu, Muju, Yŏngdong (永同), Hwanggan, Ch'ŏngsan, and Poŭn. To the west of the river are the counties of Chinan, Yongdam, Kŭmsan, and Okch'ŏn. Changsu, Muju, Kŭmsan, Yongdam, and Chinan belong to Chŏlla Province, and Okch'ŏn, Poŭn, Ch'ŏngsan, Yŏngdong (永同), and Hwanggan belong to Ch'ungch'ŏng Province.

Situated below Mount Tŏgyu, Muju and Changsu are replete with wide forests and deep valleys, which is rather stifling. Yŏngdong (永同) lies between Mount Songni and Mount Tŏgyu. To the east, Ch'up'ungnyŏng is where a branch range extending from Mount Tŏgyu rests its energy. It is known as a mountain pass by name but in reality is a plain. Although there are many mountains in the area, they are neither too rough nor grand, neither too low nor flat. All of the rocks and peaks glow and harbor clear energy, and the valleys and streams are clear and clean. This area is favorable as there are no ugly or surprising features. As the land is fertile with easy access to water for irrigation, there tends to be less drought. The same situation is shared by Ch'ŏngsan, which is connected to Poŭn to the north. Poŭn has very barren soil. Kwandae, which is to the south of

Mount Songni and to the west of Chŭnghang, has broad fields and rich soil. It is the most desirable place to live. These two towns harvest much jujube, on which residents make their living. Hoeinhyŏn, which is to the north of Poŭn, lies in remote mountains. Although the town is small, P'unggyech'on is a livable place.

Chinan, which is below Mount Mai, has soil suitable for growing to-bacco. As it grows well anywhere, even on top of high mountains, many residents make their living on it. Yongdam, which is to the north [of Chinan], has peculiar mountains, a spring called Chujul, and a rock, Panil. It makes a good refuge. To the north [of Yongdam] is Kŭmsan and even further north is Okchŏn. There are many rocky mountains in Kŭmsan and Okchŏn, all lying apart from each other in the middle of flat land. As for Okchŏn, the Kŭm River is its northern boundary and it faces a moun-tain pass to the west, over which is Hoedŏk. The scenery is clean and the color of the soil is clear; the same [is the case with] the eastern suburbs of Hanyang. As the land is very dry, rice paddies produce small yields, so residents rely solely on cotton to make a living. The soil is most suited for cotton. Okchŏn is also known for producing many scholars. Both Nam Su-mun (Haksa) and Song Si-yŏl (Ujae) are from Okchŏn. Kŭmsan is bor-dered by the Chŏk River[162] to the east and Mount Taedun at its western end. Between these areas there are two mountains called Chogye (釣溪) and Chillak. Thanks to many large streams, irrigation in this area is easy. For this reason the land and fields are quite fertile. As the scenery is also splendid it is a place judged to be the most habitable among these ten towns.

Mount Songni lies one hundred *ri* to the east of Ch'ŏngju. Water from the mountain flows to the east and enters the Naktong River in Kyŏngsang Province to the west and the Kŭm River to the north; it be-comes the Talch'ŏn at Ch'ungju and then enters the Han River. A branch of the mountain range runs to the north and becomes Kŏdaeryŏng and then runs along the Talch'ŏn to the northwest to become Mount Ch'ilchang at the boundary of Chuksan in Kyŏnggi Province. The mountain range from Mount Ch'ilchang that runs northwest along the Han River splits into several mountains to the south of the Han River. The mountain range that runs southwest forms a series of mountain passes. These [passes] are known as Taemullyŏng in Chinch'ŏn and Maillyŏng in Mokch'ŏn. To the west of the town of Chŏnŭi the mountain range ends abruptly to form a plain before becoming the pass, [called] Ch'aryŏng, to the north of the Kŭm River and Mount Musŏng and Mount Osŏ to the west. It ends at Imch'ŏn and Hansan to the south and at T'aean and Sŏsan to the north. A big plain spreads out between the eastern Maillyŏng and the western

Kŏdaeryŏng. Watercourses from the two mountains to the east and west join on the plain to become Chakch'ŏn. Chakch'ŏn originates from the east of Ch'ilj'ŏng and Chinch'ŏn and enters the upper stream of the Kŭm River to the south at Puyongjin.

In the mountainous area to the west of Chakch'ŏn are counties known as Mokch'ŏn, Chŏnŭi, and Yŏn'gi. In the mountainous area to the east of Chakch'ŏn are counties known as Ch'ŏngan, Ch'ŏngju, and Munŭi. Ch'ŏngju, the biggest among them, is one hundred *ri* to the northeast of Kongju. The town lies below Kŏdaeryŏng. Its area covers the west of Chakch'ŏn, runs between Mokch'ŏn and Yŏn'gi, and stops at the mountains to the west of Chakch'ŏn. The mountains that swerve down south from those to the west of Chakch'ŏn are made of soil rather than rocks. Having turned around at the west of Chakch'ŏn, from Mokch'ŏn and Chŏnŭi to the north and to Yŏn'gi to the south, the color of the mountains is beautiful, and the terrain is surrounded by folds [of a semicircular range of hills]. Geomancers say that the place is void of murderous energy. Compared with Kŭmch'ŏn and Mokch'ŏn, this area is much flatter and more fertile, which is good for grains and cotton.

The east of Chakch'ŏn is a big field stretching forty *ri* to the southeast in the midst of which is a mountain. As it has eight peaks it is named Mount P'albong (Eight Peaked Mountain). Facing northwest from the south, its hill and foothills are positioned firmly in the middle of the field. To the east, it faces Kŏdaeryŏng. Its white sand, shallow streams, even hills and beautiful foothills are similar to those of Changdan.

The town [of Ch'ŏngju] faces west. As it is low-lying while the bedding of the stream is high, annual flooding is a worry. Chŏng To-jŏn was a councillor at the end of the Koryŏ dynasty. Acting as the adviser to King T'aejo of the Chosŏn dynasty, he disliked good people such as Yi Saek (Mogŭn) and Yi Sung-in (Toŭn). He had them sent to the prison in Ch'ŏngju and dispatched officials to interrogate them. On the day of the interrogation there was a sudden heavy shower and water breached the city walls and rushed through the gardens of the house [where the interrogation was taking place]. The lives of the interrogation officials and the prisoners were barely spared, saved only by them holding onto trees in the garden. Upon hearing this, King T'aejo realized [the two prisoners'] innocence and ordered them to be freed. Yi Sung-in, whom Chŏng To-jŏn hated, however, was later put to death.

As the terrain [of Ch'ŏngju] is high to the east and unblocked to the north, it harbors murderous energy. There is a camp under the charge of a commander in chief in the town. In the year of *musin* (1728) a traitor, Yi In-jwa, led his army in an attack on the camp of a military commander. Yi

Pong-sang, the military commander, and Nam Yŏn-nyŏn, the commander of the camp, were killed in the night attack. Having finally occupied the castle, Yi In-jwa installed Sin Ch'ŏn-yŏng as military commander and led the rest of the army north up to Ansŏng, where he was defeated by O Myŏng-hang, the patrol command officer.

Over the Kŏdaeryŏng to the east sits Sangdangsansŏng and to the east again is Ch'ŏngch'ŏnch'ang, a storehouse. To the west of the storehouse is the village where the Sin clans live. To the south over a little hill are the pavilions Inp'ungjŏng and Ongnyudae. This is where the Pyŏn clans live. Valleys with streams and rocks among big mountains create a rather mellow atmosphere. To the east again over a big valley is Kwiman, whose valleys and mountains are very beautiful. Sangdang and Ch'ŏngch'ŏn together are called Sandong. They are windy and chilly because they sit atop the mountains. [The place] is therefore not as good as Ch'ŏngju, which is on flat land. [The place] is blocked to the south by Mount Songni and by Mount S'ŏnyu to the east. Extending to the north, a branch of Mount Songni circles around the area like a hook. The area is blocked to the north but open to the south. There are many famous villages in it. It produces iron and plenty of timber for building coffins and palaces. All of the people of flat land come here for trading. Several ten *ri* away from Ch'ŏngch'ŏn to the north is Songmyŏnch'ŏn. Along the borders of three counties known as Mun'gyŏng, Khoesan, and Ch'ŏngju, there are beautiful valleys and mountains. Yonghwadong, which is to the south of Ch'ŏngch'ŏn, is close to Mount Songni to the southwest, but it is not that rugged. It has a small area of open fields but the soil is barren. There is a village where people live together. To the south of the village is Yulch'i. The water from Ch'ŏngch'ŏn meets the water from Mount Songni and then flows to Songgye in Koesan to the north. There are many places with beautiful scenery north and south along the stream.

To the north [of Ch'ŏngju] is Chinch'ŏn. Compared with Ch'ŏngju, Chinch'ŏn has fewer fields and more mountains. Mountains are surrounded by many folds and there are big streams. It is not stifling, however, and the land is very fertile. Over the mountain range Taemullyŏng to the northwest are the lands of Ansŏng and Chiksan. As [the area] is only one hundred *ri* away from the sea, fish and salt can be easily purchased. Munŭi is connected with the Hyŏng River to the south. Although the mountains are less lush, there are many places with beautiful scenery along the river. Ch'ŏngan alone has a poor landscape and is not a suitable place to live.

From the west of the Maillyŏng [pass] in Mokch'ŏn to the east of Naep'o and to the north of Ch'arŏng there are seven towns called Ch'ŏnan,

Chiksan, P'yŏngt'aek, Asan, Sinch'ang, Onyang, and Yesan. Their customs are nearly the same. To the south of the Maillyŏng there are deep mountains. The land close to the remote mountains is fertile and suitable for growing grains and cotton. To the north, there is a shoreline. In the area close to the beach, the land is half barren and half fertile. Although fish are caught and salt produced here, and it is close to a sailing route, it is not suitable for growing cotton. Ch'ŏnan and Chiksan are on the major road connecting north and south. Twenty *ri* away from Chiksan across a plain, the Sosa River is where the plain ends. To the north of the Sosa River is the southern boundary of Kyŏnggi Province.

In the year of *chŏngyu* during the reign of King Sŏnjo, when the Japanese army defeated Yang Yuan at Namwŏn and moved north past Chŏnju to Kongju, the army had great spirit. At that time, Xing Jie was residing in Liaodong as the governor-general. Yang Hao, an intendant of the Ming army, led one hundred thousand soldiers to P'yŏngyang. He had recently arrived and was having dinner on Yŏn'gwangjŏng when an urgent message arrived by horse. Yang Hao stopped eating, fired cannons, and immediately got on a horse and rode south. The cavalry followed him straight away and soon after were followed by soldiers. The soldiers ran from P'yŏngyang and arrived at Hanyang, seven hundred *ri* away, in one day and two nights. Yang Hao and four Tartar generals—Xie Sheng, Bai Gui, Sai Gui, and Yang Dengshan—lead a four thousand-strong cavalry clad in iron armor; he hid several hundred monkeys among the troops under the bridge over the Sosa River, which was located where the plain ends. He saw that the [soldiers of the] Japanese army, who were coming north from Chiksan, were as thick as a forest. When the Japanese army got as close as one hundred steps away, he released the monkeys. The monkeys, on horseback, charged toward the Japanese army whipping their mounts. As monkeys do not originate in Japan, it was the first time the Japanese soldiers had seen monkeys. Every soldier was astonished at the sight. Although similar to human beings in their appearance, [monkeys] are not human beings. While still in their camps the soldiers just stared without moving. Monkeys that reached the edge of the camp got off the horses and entered the grounds. Soldiers ran around to catch them, but the monkeys ran away from the soldiers and moved deeper throughout the camps. As the camps [were thrown into] chaos, Xie Sheng and others let the cavalry attack. The Japanese army, without having fired any guns or used any bows and arrows, was soundly defeated and retreated to the south. The fields were covered with corpses. Having received the message of a victory, Yang Hao gathered his army and chased the Japanese army to the sea [abutting] Kyŏngsang Province.

Until this time there had been no such great victories during the Japanese invasion of Korea. The crafty plan and controlled execution by Yang Hao were greater than the victory that Li Rusong had achieved in P'yŏngyang. Ding Yingtai, the secretary for merit ratings, however, was furious that Yang Hao had performed such a meritorious action without informing him. He falsely reported that the story of Yang Hao's victory was not true, following which Yang Hao was impeached and recalled to his home country. This is a clear indication that the morals of the Ming court have become degraded. King Sŏnjo sent his envoy [to the Ming court] to defend Yang Hao's innocence, and Ding Yingtai soon took a new government position. Ding then joined the Donglin Dang (Eastern Forest Party)[163] and his son appealed his father's matter to the party. Qian [Qianyi] (Muji)[164] believed the appeal and recorded [the matter] in his literary collection. This [incident] reveals how lax the state of the party was and how easily deceived scholars could be. Once in awhile those plowing the field pick up spears and daggers and the like.

Asan County is where water flowing north of the port of Yugungp'o meets the Sosa River. A major mountain range stretches from Mount Ch'ilchang to Mount Sŏnggŏ in Chiksan. The range runs down the middle of a plain, which extends through Sŏnghwannyŏk and stops at Mount Yŏngin in Asan. It is the guardian mountain of the county. The mountain stands to the southeast and faces northwest. It is here that the Sosa River circles around and ends. Behind the mountain, the wide Kokkyo Stream flows from the southeast. These two streams meet at a point in the northwest and form a big lake. A mountain to the south of the lake extends from Sinchang and a mountain to the north of the lake extends from Suwŏn. These mountains embrace the outlet of watercourses and act like a gate. Once the water flows through the gate it immediately joins the downstream of Yugungp'o. This makes Mount Kong look like a big ship with a sail. As it is made up of rocks and stands tall mid-stream, it resembles Mount Jieshi towering over the Bohai Sea.

The court established a storehouse at the northern beach of Mount Yŏngin and loaded the in-kind taxes collected from nearby Ch'ungch'ŏng Province [in preparation to] sail them to Seoul on boats. This lake is, therefore, called Kongseho (Lake of Tribute and Taxes). This area was originally rich in fish and salt. Once the storehouse was erected, people and traders were drawn to settle in the area and the number of rich households increased. This situation is not limited to the settlement where the storehouse was erected. As the range of Mount Yŏngin is blocked by the two streams and its energy is not dispersed, every direction around the mountain is full of famous villages where there are many scholar-gentry homes.

Several villages to the east and west of Yugungp'o have access to water transportation. Among them, Yesan alone became a city where traders did their business. A mountain range to the west of the Ch'aryŏng range went far north and became Mount Kwangdŏk again before continuing on to become Mount Sŏlla to the east of Onyang. It reaches high up in the sky and looks like Mount Hugong in Putian of Fujian County, standing tall like a sceptre. The reason this mountain is thought to be auspicious is because many villages in Asan and Onyang produced high-ranking officials and scholars.

Ch'ungju is one hundred *ri* away to the northeast from Ch'ŏngju. The town of Ch'ungju can be reached from Ch'ŏngju by passing through the Yuryŏng [pass] in Ch'ŏngan and Koesan and crossing over the Talch'ŏn. It is three hundred *ri* away to the southeast from Hanyang. Water in the meandering valleys from P'ŏpchusa of Mount Songni flows to the north of Sandong in Ch'ŏngju and becomes Ch'ŏngch'ŏn before becoming the Koe River at Koesan and then the Talchŏn to the west of the town. It joins the Ch'ŏngp'ung River in front of Kŭmch'ŏn again to the north. In the year of *imjin*, a Ming general was passing by Talchŏn, sampled the water, and declared it as tasting the same as that of Lushan Falls. As the town is on the upper stream of the Han River, it is convenient for travel. From olden days, the scholar-gentry of Seoul have resided here. If one follows up the stream to the south from the Talchŏn, it becomes the Koet'an, and if one follows up the stream to the east, one reaches Chŏngp'ung. Many pavilions of the scholar-gentry were built here. People dressed in proper garments get together and boats and carts flock in. Situated to the southeast of the capital, it produced more students who passed the government examinations than any other town in the entire country. For this reason it is called a renowned town.

From the left side of Kyŏngsang Province, however, Chŏngp'ung is connected through Chungnyŏng and from the right side of Kyŏngsang Province it is connected through Choryŏng Pass. That is, the two roads from the two mountain passes join in the town and are connected to Hanyang via either water or land. This town, being a strategic point for traffic, inevitably becomes a battlefield in times of emergency. As it is really the middle of the country, as are Jingzhou[165] and Yuzhou,[166] the Japanese army defeated General Sin Rip here. Even during times of peace, murderous energy rends the sky and no sunlight penetrates it. As its topography leans northwest and vital energy does not accumulate here, few are rich. With a large population, people engage in a lot of gossip. It is frivolous and not a desirable place to live. This description, however, applies only to the town of Ch'ungju.

Across the Talch'ŏn to the west of Ch'ungju lies Mount Songni. A branch, which extends north of the mountain, rises high to the west of Ŭmsŏng County and becomes Mount Kasŏp and Mount Puyong. One branch from here ends at Kŭmch'ŏn, another at Kahŭng, and the rest circles to the west of Talch'ŏn. The land is good for growing grains and cotton and the soil is extremely fertile. The mountains and valleys are dotted with several villages where many rich people live. Among them, Kŭmch'ŏn and Kahŭng are the most prosperous. Two rivers join in front of the town of Kŭmch'ŏn and then flow around it to the north. For this reason it has the advantage of receiving goods from the Yŏngnam region to the southeast as well as access to fish and salt from Hanyang, that is, from the northwest. Houses of the residents line up one next to the other, as in all the towns along the river in the Hanyang region. Kahŭng is ten *ri* away from Kŭmch'ŏn to the west. The river flows southeast to northwest, and the town is on a hill to the south. A branch from Mount Puyong rises against the river flow and becomes Mount Changmi. This is the main mountain of Kahŭng. Having established a granary, the court collects grains for taxes from the seven towns of Kyŏngsang Province to the south of the mountain pass and the seven towns of Ch'ungch'ŏng Province to the north of the mountain pass. Assistant prefects then transport the grains by water to Seoul. The residents, as commission agents, vie to make profits by receiving and dispatching the rice, sometimes with enviable results. Many households in the two settlements are also successful in the civil service examinations, becoming high government officials.

Away from the Mount Kasŏp area, the mountain range that stretches to the west of Mount Songni is called Mount Sosongni (Small Songni). From here a branch range extends north again and becomes Mount Okchang and Mount P'alsŏng and stops at Malmari, which is the very place where Kim Se-p'il (Sipch'ŏng), a victim of the literati purge in the year of *kimyo* (1519), retired and lived. His descendants have been living here for generations. Several hundred households living here are well-off. In front of the village there is a big stream suitable for irrigation. A lot of rice paddies produce one *chong* for every *myo*. From olden times there have been few years of poor harvest. It is about two hundred *ri* away from Hanyang, which can be reached via the Yŏ River. It is therefore really a habitable place. The four towns to the north of the river, Kŭmch'ŏn, Kahŭng, Malmari, and Naech'ang, are known by people of the area as the four big towns of Ch'ungju.

Seven *ri* northwest of the town of Ch'ungju, and between two rivers before they merge, stands a small mountain. This is where Urŭk, a Taoist hermit, was playing the *kayagŭm*[167] [at a place] called T'angŭmdae

(Kayagŭm Playing Platform). To the north of T'angŭmdae is Pukch'ang (North Granary), where the scenery of rocks along the river is beautiful. West of the granary is where Yi Yŏn-gyŏng (T'ansu), another victim of the *kimyo* literati purge, used to live. As his descendants for ten generations continuously passed the civil servant examination, people called the place "an auspicious site on the riverside."

Following the river to the west one reaches Wŏlt'an, where the Hong families reside. Further to the west is Hadam, where Kim Si-yang, a late minister, used to live. Even further to the west is Mokkye, where boats loaded with fish and salt sail down the river to moor and pay tax. Fish from the East Sea and the produce from the mountains and valleys of the Yŏngnam region are gathered here, and all of the residents are rich as a result of being engaged in commerce. To the west of Mokkye is the valley of Ch'ŏngnyongsa. It is connected to Wŏnju to the west. The various villages from Pukch'ang to the east and Ch'ŏngnyongsa to the west are called "villages of the north of the river." Although the scenery along the river is beautiful, the land is barren. It is less favorable than the fertile land from south of the big river, to the west of the Talch'ŏn. Naech'angch'on, which is ten *ri* north from Mokkye, is a famous thousand-year-old town. As the field is spread out in the midst of the mountains, the wind is calm and its land is very broad. Many generations of scholar-gentry have lived here. To the east it connects to Wŏrŭnryŏng, and to the east of that is the very boundary with Chech'ŏn.

To the east of Ch'ungju is the city of Ch'ŏngp'ung. The Hanbyŏngnu is on the riverside. As it is rather pleasant and has a mellow atmosphere, [Hanbyŏngnu] is a famous pavilion on the upper stream. The Hwangch'ŏn River, to the east of Ch'ŏngp'ung, is where Kwŏn Sang-ha (Suam) used to live. To the east of Ch'ŏngp'ung is Tanyang and to the north of Tanyang is Yŏngch'un. These three towns have rugged streams and valleys and few fields.

Chech'ŏn County, which is to the northeast of Ch'ungju, is located on high ground surrounded by mountains and has a flat field within. It is open and cheerful, as the mountains are low. Many families of the scholar-gentry lived here for generations. It being at a high altitude, however, the wind is cold and the land is too barren to grow cotton. A few residents are rich but many are poor. To the north is the reservoir of Ŭirimji. During the Silla dynasty a big levee was created to store water. Rice paddies for the whole town were irrigated from this reservoir. To the west of the reservoir is Husŏnjŏng, which belongs to the Kim family. Although it is not as good as the lakes in the Yŏngdong (嶺東) region, it is good enough to relax on a boat. The north of Chech'ŏn is close to P'yŏngch'ang and is connected with Yŏngwŏl to the east. Because it is in a very remote mountainous area, it is truly a suitable place to escape from wars and the world.

Yŏnp'ung is to the south of Ch'ungju. No high officials came from here. However, the land is fertile and easily irrigated. It is suitable for growing cotton. To the west of Yŏnp'ung is Koesan. As Koesan is situated between the two mountain passes of Choryŏng and Yuryŏng, the terrain is narrow and rugged, but at the same time it is less affected by malevolent energy. As it faces a big river to the east, there are many scenic spots and famous towns with residents who held high official positions. The land is suitable for growing grains and cotton. The fact that it is close to Kŭmch'ŏn to the north also counts toward making this place livable. Over the Choryŏng to the east is Mun'gyŏng, and over the Yuryŏng to the west is Ŭmsŏng. To the west Ŭmsŏng is connected to Chuksan and Ŭmjuk in Kyŏnggi Province.

KYŎNGGI PROVINCE

The west of Ch'ungju borders on Chuksan and Yŏju of Kyŏnggi Province [see Plate 9]. Mount Ch'ilchang of Chuksan stands tall at the boundary between Kyŏnggi and Ch'ungch'ŏng Provinces. The mountain range extends northwest, ends abruptly at Suyu Pass to form plains, and rises again to become Mount Pua, Mount Sŏksŏng, and Mount Kwanggyo in Yongin. Having formed Mount Kwanak to the northwest of Mount Kwanggyo and Mount Suri directly to the west, the mountain range disappears into the West Sea [see Plate 9].

From Chuksan another branch range extends to the north and, having passed Ŭmjuk, it ends in Yŏju. Yŏngnŭng [in Yŏju] is where the Great King of Changhŏn is buried.[168] When the earth was dug up [for constructing the tomb] an old engraved stone was found on which was written the phrase "this is surely the place where a sage of the Eastern country will be buried." Geomancers call it *hoeryongjajwa* (the landform of a dragon turning its direction to the south) and *sinsuipchin* (water from the northwest flowing out to direct east). The tomb site is regarded as the best among those of Korean kings. To the south of Chuksan is Mount Kubong. As it is surrounded by mountain peaks, [Kubong] is a potential fortress site. It lies in the center of the road that connects Kyŏnggi and Ch'ungch'ŏng Provinces. Passing Yangji, to the west of Chuksan, the mountain range becomes diffused and several villages lie to the south of the Han River. As the villages are decaying and have bad geomantic conditions, there is no good place to live.

The waterway running west from Ch'ungju along the river passes

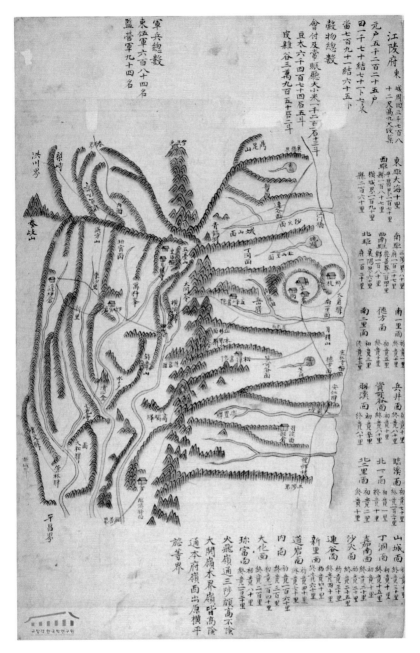

Plate 1: Kangnŭngbu (Kangnŭng City). Yi Chung-hwan's walk in 1703 can be traced along the red line from Un'gyoyŏk (indicated by three Chinese characters between two small mountain ranges at bottom, far left) to Taegwallyŏng (a mountain pass in the middle of the T'aebaek Range, the prominent range drawn down the center of the map). The route from Taegwallyŏng to Kangnŭngbu (shown as a walled city at center right) is also lined in red.

Source (all plates): *Haedong Chido* (Map of Korea), 1750–1751, Kyujanggak Institute of Korean Studies, Seoul National University.

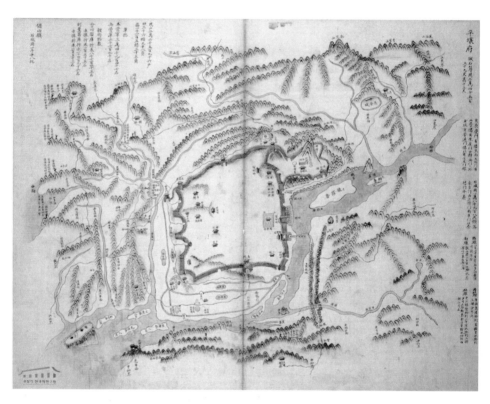

Plate 2: P'yŏngyangbu (P'yŏngyang City). To the south of the roughly square-shaped walled city at center is a wide plain located between the city and the Taedong River that is considered to be the area where the grid-pattern land division system, mentioned in the text, remained. Pubyŏngnu is at the upper far right corner of the city wall facing the Taedong River.

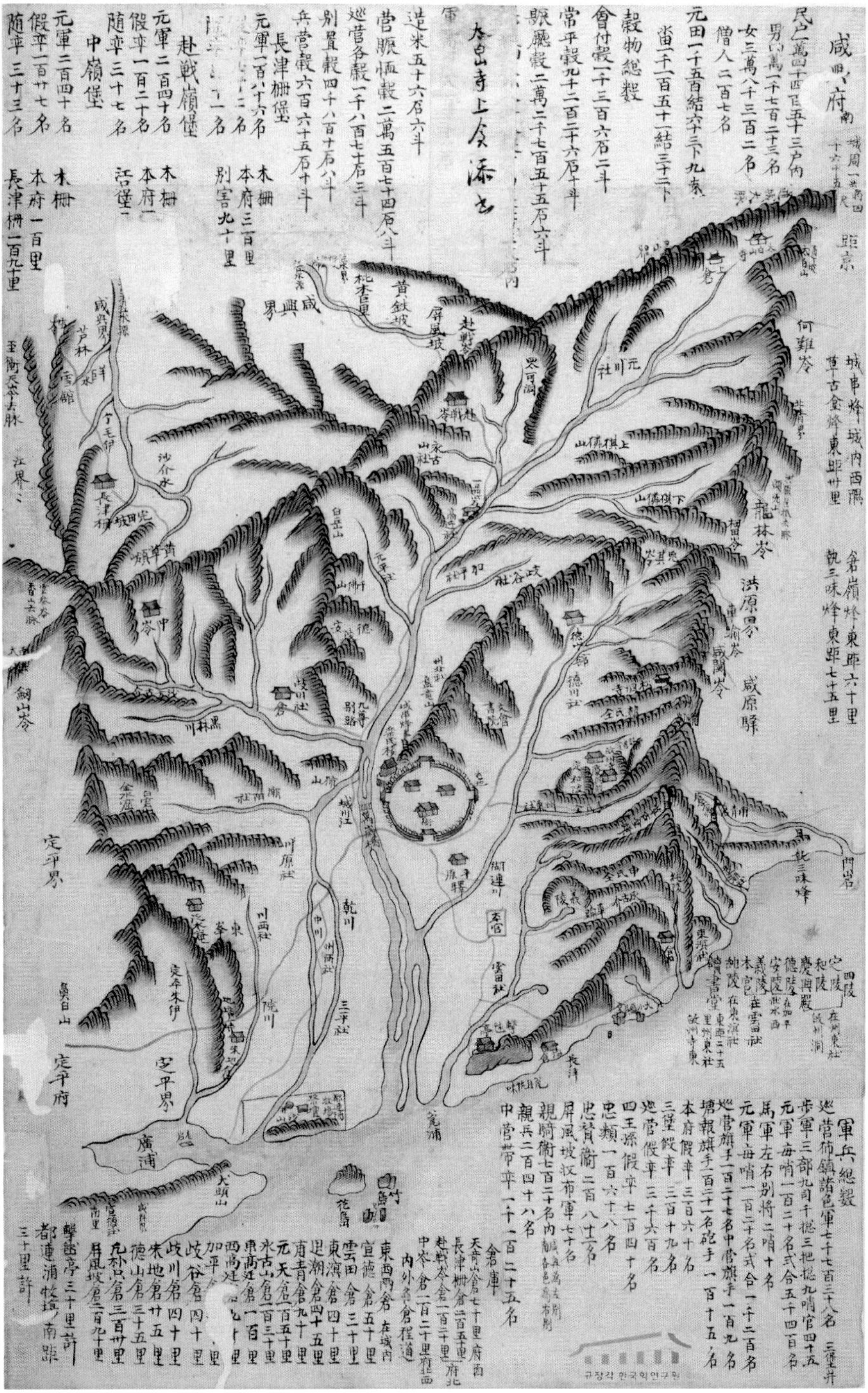

Plate 3: Hamhŭngbu (Hamhŭng City). The route over the Kunja River (map center), an alternate name of the Sŏngch'ŏn River, via the Mansegyo bridge to the walled city of Hamhŭng is lined in red. The Chinese characters for Chŏngp'yŏngbu (Chŏngp'yŏng City) appear below the road in red in the bottom-left corner.

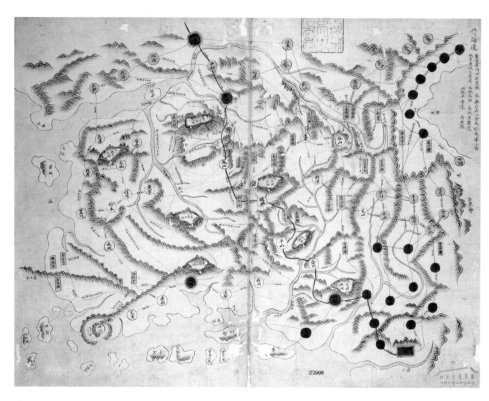

Plate 4: Hwanghae Province. The map shows cities, counties, mountains, and rivers of the province in relation to other provinces. It includes P'yŏngyang (top), Hamhŭng (top right), Mount Kŭmgang (center right), the Han River (bottom right), the Yellow Sea, and East Sea.

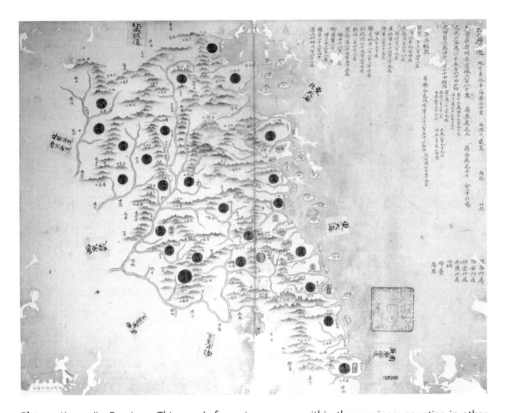

Plate 5: Kangwŏn Province. This map's focus is on areas within the province; counties in other provinces are represented by Chinese characters (for example, "Anbyŏn," Hamgyŏng Province, is at the top and "Yŏnghae," Kyŏngsang Province, is at bottom right). Nine counties to the east of the (T'aebaek) mountain range are indicated along the east coast by the green dots starting with Hŭpkok in the far north (top right) and continuing south, in order, to T'ongch'ŏn, Kosŏng, Kansŏng, Yangyang, Kangnŭng, Samch'ŏk, Ulchin, and P'yŏnghae to the far south (bottom-right corner). Mount Kŭmgang (upper middle) and Mount T'aebaek (lower right) are prominently drawn.

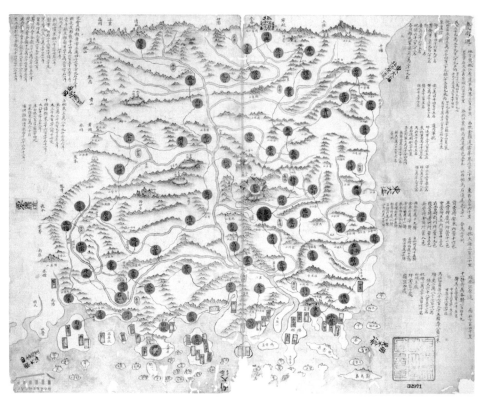

Plate 6: Kyŏngsang Province. This map shows Kyŏngsang Province with its provincial capital, Taegu, in the center (largest circle in red). The borders of the province are defined by Mount T'aebaek (top-right corner) and the range that extends across to the west, and on its western side by the range that runs south to Mount Chiri (bottom left). Several mountain fortresses are represented; most notable is the magnificent depiction of Ch'ilgok to the north of Taegu. Most of the province is connected to the Naktong River (center). On the peninsula to the southwest of Tongnae (bottom right), a special residential quarter for Japanese people is indicated by the Chinese characters for *waegwan* (倭館). Pusan, the largest port city in this area of present-day Korea, is not on this map.

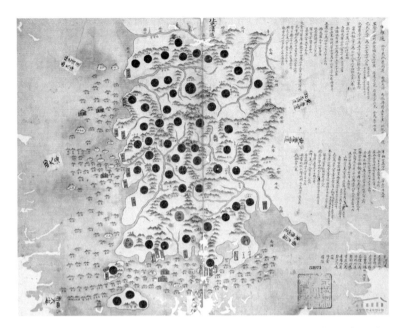

Plate 7: Chŏlla Province. Chŏnju, the provincial capital, is indicated in the north by the largest red circle. Numerous islands are identified by name; ports are indicated by blue rectangles. Chejudo is the largest island (bottom, middle to left) and Chindo, the site of Admiral Yi Sun-sin's great victory, is shown as the second largest island. Mount Tŏgyu (center right) is shown on the eastern boundary of the province.

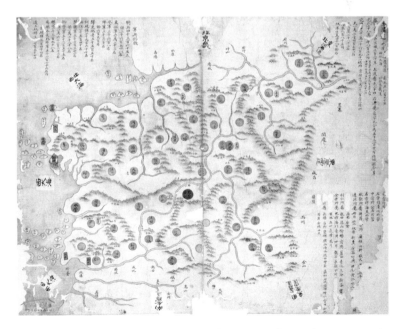

Plate 8: Ch'ungch'ŏng Province. Kongju, the provincial capital, appears in the center of the map. The river to the north of Kongju is labeled as Kŭmgang (Kŭm River); past Puyŏ it is labeled Paengmagang (Paengma River). Taedun (lower middle) is the most prominently depicted mountain in the province.

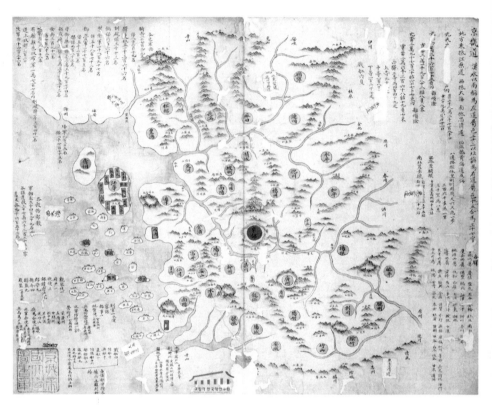

Plate 9: Kyŏnggi Province. The capital city, at center, is surrounded by a wall along low-lying mountains with Mount Samgak and Mount Pukhan to the north. Mount Kwanak is to the south across the Han River. Mount Mani appears on Kanghwado, the province's largest island, which is ringed by ports, indicated by blue rectangles. Kyodongdo is to its northwest; to the east is Munsusansŏng (Mount Munsu Fortress) in T'ongjin. Yŏngnŭng, the tomb of King Sejong, is shown to the northeast of Yŏju, which is in the southeastern corner of the province.

through Wŏnju, Yŏju, and Yanggŭn. After meeting the Yongjin River to the north of Kwangju, it becomes the frontal water flow for Hanyang. The township of Yŏju lies to the south of the river; it is less than two hundred *ri* away from Hanyang by both land and water. To the west of the township lies Paegaech'on. From the southeast a long, curving river moves northeast, passing in front of the village. This is the very best riverside settlement. The outlet of the water is concealed, and it is not visible where the river flows out. Both the township and the village join a plain. Opening to the southeast, it looks clear and cool. Many households of scholars have lived for generations in these two places. The residents in Paegaech'on, however, rely solely on boats for their living without tilling the land; their profit exceeds that of farmers. In the township is the Ch'ŏngsimnu; the scenery around the pavilion is beautiful. To the north of the river is the monastery Sinnŭksa and, nearby, the pavilion Kangwŏlhŏn. The rocks along the river are extremely peculiar. Below the southern bank of the river lies the rock of Maam. People say that a black dragon is living under the rock.

To the south of Yŏju lie Ich'ŏn (利川) and Ŭmjuk and they have similar customs. To the north of Yŏju are Chip'yŏng and Yanggŭn, which border Hongch'ŏn of Kangwŏn Province. As the mountains are dizzily high and the valleys deep, Chip'yŏng and Yanggŭn are not good places to live. To the north of Mount Yongmun in Yanggŭn is Miwŏnch'on. This is where Cho Kwang-jo (Chŏngam) wanted to settle because of the beautiful scenery. I have been there and found the place to be remote and blocked, although there is a fairly wide space in the mountains. The climate there, moreover, is cold, the surrounding mountains are not beautiful, and the stream running in front of the place flows in an unpleasant manner, the rapid current having the sound of a blocked throat. This is not a desirable place to live.

To the west of Yŏju lies Kwangju, which is formed by a northern branch from Mount Sŏksŏng that extends to the south of Han River. The administration center is on top of a mountain as high as ten thousand men. It was the old capital chosen by Onjo, founder of the Paekche kingdom. The inside of the place is flat and low, but when viewed from outside, it stands so steep and high that the [soldiers of the] Qing Chinese army, when [they] first invaded Korea, could not use their swords. Even during the Manchu invasion, which started in 1636, they could not in the end take the castle.[169] The reason King Injo descended from the castle was because the food stores were low and Kanghwado had fallen.[170]

Even after the peace negotiation was concluded, this place was considered important for the protection of the capital from foreign invasions.

Nine monasteries were thus built and monks asked to stay there. A chief executive was chosen from among the monks and made the monk-general. Every year sturdy monks were selected from various monasteries in every province and, as residents, were asked to look after the nine monasteries. An archery competition was held each month where winners were rewarded with a generous stipend. Monks therefore concentrated solely on archery and lived on the stipend. [This arrangement] was implemented because the court wanted to preserve the castle, relying on numerous monks from around the country. Inside, the castle is not rugged, but outside the castle, below the mountain, there is a murderous energy. In addition, the place is an important military camp, [which means that] it cannot avoid being a battlefield in case of emergency. The Kwangju area is therefore not a desirable place to live.

To the west of Kwangju lies Mount Suri, which is to the east of Ansan (安山). The branch range that extends to the northwest is the longest among the branches of Mount Suri. Having passed through Inch'ŏn, Pup'yŏng, Kimp'o, and T'ongjin, it becomes a lower-lying rocky range. Passing below the river, it rises to become Mount Mani.[171] This is Kanghwado, an island surrounded by the [Han] river to the northeast and by the sea to the southwest. It is a large island serving as the mountain beyond the homage mountain of Hanyang and protecting the merging of watercourses of the Han River.

The Han River changes course, turning to the southwest of T'ongjin; it then meets Kapkot Point and flows further south until it reaches a depression behind Mount Mani. From here the rocky range spreads horizontally across the water like a threshold. It is a little concave in the middle. This place is Sondolmok. To the south is the big West Sea. Ships from the three southern regions loaded with tax in grain sail to the edge of Sondolmok and wait for a high tide, which allows them to sail through. A small miscalculation [leading to] hitting a rock would result in shipwreck. The Han River flows straight to the western arc around the hill at Yanghwajin and joins with the Sŏ River. It then flows to the north of Mount Munsu and enters the sea.

The distance between the north and south of Kanghwado is more than one hundred *ri*, while that between the east and west is fifty *ri*. A resident commander is based in the city. To the north, Kanghwado faces Sŭngch'ŏnp'o of P'ungdŏk with a river in between. The river banks [here] are made entirely of rocks; ships cannot be moored lower down [where] the banks are muddy. Across Sŭngch'ŏnp'o there is only one area safe for mooring ships in high tide, which is why it is called a dangerous dock. No walls were built either to the right or the left. Instead, a *tondae* was built on the bank below the mountain.[172] Inside, weapons are stored and soldiers quartered to defend against foreign attack. From Kapkot in the east to Sondolmok in the south, the only place where boats can land is Kapkot. The rest of the coastline is completely muddy like that of the north shore of Sŭngch'ŏnp'o. A small wall was built along the riverbank on the hillside, the same as that on the north shore, with the result that all that needs to be done to protect the island is to defend Sŭngch'ŏnp'o and Kapkot; beyond the island is [the sea, which serves as] a natural moat. That is the reason the island had been the capital of Korea for ten years during the Mongol invasion; the Yuan soldiers had stampeded the Korean peninsula but could not invade the island. During the Chosŏn dynasty all of the ships loaded with taxes in kind from the provinces of Kyŏngsang, Chŏlla, and Ch'ungch'ŏng passed Sondolmok on their way to Seoul. Seeing the geographical importance of Sondolmok, the court placed a resident commander there to keep watch. The court also built a defense camp and kept an associate commander on Yŏngjongdo.

In the year of *chŏngmyo* (1627) during the reign of King Injo, Qing soldiers invaded P'yŏngsan in Hwanghae Province and, before returning home, made a peace agreement to form a brotherly relationship with Chosŏn. At that time, the Qing army was occupying Shenyang and fighting ceaselessly with soldiers of the Ming court,[173] while Kado[174] was under occupation by [the Ming general] Mao Wen Long. As our court was in contact with the Ming court[175] via sea through Dengzhou and Laizhou, the Qing court feared that our country might turn against them. The Qing court first sent a spy to pose as a servant in the Office of Diplomatic Correspondence so that he could detect the time when Chosŏn's power was weak. Fearing that the Qing soldiers might invade Korea, our court renovated Namhansansŏng. In the spring of *pyŏngja* the Qing court sent Long Guda as a spy. He pretended that he was going to see Sŏnyubong Peak on the Sŏ River. Kim Si-yang (Hadam), the then minister of home affairs, guessed that [Long Guda] would go out to look for Namhansansŏng and ordered low-ranking officials to line up in wait outside the East Gate. Having pretended he was heading for the West Gate on horseback, Long Guda suddenly changed direction to head toward the East Gate. He was puzzled when he noticed the low-ranking officials waiting under canopies on the roadside and asked the translator about them. The translator said, "The minister of home affairs knew that you were going to visit Namhansansŏng. That's why a small table of food is set up beside this road for you. Please come in and stay for awhile." Greatly surprised, Long Guda showed a forced smile and returned to the guesthouse without visiting the fortress. At that time there were many young and newly recruited officers in the Office of the Censor General. Having no clear grasp of the development of the situation and yet claiming the rightness of their cause, they petitioned that Long Guda be beheaded. Hearing of this, Long Guda returned home without saying goodbye, writing the character for "blue" on a wall in the guesthouse. "Blue" means December.

In December of that year Qing soldiers entered Chosŏn, not through Ŭiju but by crossing over the frozen Yalu River near Ch'angsŏng. Even though they encountered walled cities, they did not attack them. In three days the soldiers on the front line arrived at Hongjewŏn but stayed outside without entering it. They unsaddled the horses and made them rest as if they were not going to attack. In this way they awaited reinforcements. All the people in Hongjewŏn Castle were surprised and terrified. Ch'oe Myŏnggil, the minister of defense, brought beef and wine [to their camp] and asked why they had come. In the meantime, the crown prince and two princes born of the queen were first sent to take possession of the ancestral tablets of the royal shrine.[176] The queen and the royal concubines escaped to Kanghwado.

The king repeatedly went up to the upper story of the South Gate. Fearing that he might be captured by Qing soldiers, he took another route and entered Namhansansŏng. A battalion of Qing soldiers then arrived and seized the fortress. After four or five days, the Qing emperor finally arrived. Realizing that the highs would not be easy to conquer, he became angry and determined to kill Long Guda, Long Guda having suggested invading our country. Long Guda pleaded that he be granted ten days to conquer the island to atone for his mistake, which was granted. Long Guda climbed Mount Munsu in T'ongjin with a group of soldiers. When he looked down on Kanghwado, which seemed as small as his palm from that distance, he found that there were no guards on watch in Kapkot. Having demolished civilian houses and made rafts from their timber, he crossed over the water and conquered the island. On hearing this, King Injo decided to descend from the mountain fortress and surrender.

Earlier, because Prime Minister Kim Ryu thought that Kanghwado would never be conquered, he appointed his son Kyŏngjing as the defense general of Kanghwa and made him and his family retreat to the island. He also appointed Yi Min-gu to be deputy. Kyŏngjing was proud and foolish while Min-gu was insincere. Without thinking about matters in the longer term, they indulged every day in gambling and drinking. The princes and chief officials stated that soldiers needed to be sent to Kapkot for defense. Kyŏngjing laughed at this and said, "How can barbarian soldiers fly over and cross [the sea]?" After Kanghwa Castle was conquered, Kim Sangyong, a chief official, killed himself, and many of the wives and daughters of the noble class also died to preserve their honor. Because some of them drowned themselves in the sea, the scarves that had covered the women's faces were drifting on the water like clouds. It was impossible to tell which household these women belonged to. After peace was restored there were a few among the dead whose merit was acknowledged with the erecting of monuments, although they had actually been kidnapped [by Qing soldiers].

After the Manchu invasion, the court took disciplinary action for the past, repaired military equipment, and stored horse feed and various grains for emergencies. As nothing serious occurred for the next one hundred years, the amount of grain accumulated in Kanghwa reached nearly one million *sŏm*.[177] When lean years persisted toward the end of [the reign of] King Sukchong, much [of this] grain was shifted to other provinces to relieve the effects of the famine. After the harvest, grains were collected and stored in each city. When the ministries' budgets were low, transportation of the grains to Seoul was mandated. Therefore, the store of rice decreased each year and is now less than one hundred thousand *sŏm*.

In the year of *kyeyu* (1693), after hearing of the Manchu invasion from his close assistants among the court officers, King Sukchong ordered a fortress built on Mount Munsu. This was because defending Mount Munsu was crucial to the defense of Kanghwado. Later, the Border Defense Command and several generals requested that the seat of the T'ongjin County magistrate be shifted to the fortress and a camp built so that all of the soldiers could be mobilized in town and defend the place in case of a war or uprising. They could not agree on a single plan, however, and so the idea was not implemented.

In the year of *pyŏngin* (1746), during the reign of the present king, Kim Si-hyŏk, the resident commander of Kanghwa petitioned that a wall be built along the river.[178] The court granted this and Kim had the wall built starting from the east. The wall was erected from Yŏnmijŏng to the north and to Sondolmok to the south. When the work was finished, the king selected Kim Si-hyŏk as a chief official. The wall fell soon after due to a heavy rainfall. When the wall was built, the foundation work was carried out by filling up the marshy areas with earth and stone. Therefore, the river banks became solid enough for men and horses to walk on. It also became possible to moor boats at many places along the river stretching for forty *ri*. From then on, it was difficult to defend Kanghwado.

A [mountain] range beginning in Kanghwado extends along the west coast and then [the terrain] subsides into a low-lying rock outcropping. Passing over a small estuary, it becomes [the island of] Kyodongdo. This is the outer table mountain of Kaesŏng. To the north of the island is the Han

River, which serves as the facing watercourse of Kaesŏng. To the south is a large sea and to the south of the sea are places such as Haemi and Sŏsan. As both shores on opposite sides of the sea are not far away, mountains can be seen on both sides. To the northwest, Yŏnan and Kaechŏn of Hwanghae Province are seen at a tangent over the port. Kyodongdo is made of rock. It is smaller than Kanghwado and further out into the sea. The court set up a control camp and kept a naval commander in chief there so that it could direct the navies of the Kyŏnggi, Hwanghae, and P'yŏngan Provinces. Due to the salinity of the soil and frequent droughts, the two islands reap a poor harvest so that islanders are also engaged in fishing and salt making.

The branch range that extends from Mount Suri to the west is the shortest and stops at Ansan (安山). Along this range are many graves containing the ancestors of high-ranking officials who reside in the capital. Being abundant with fish and salt as well as being close to the capital, many households of the scholar-gentry have lived there for generations. The branch range that extends to the south from Mount Suri turns to the southwest and stops at Sŏnggonni in Kwangju. Sŏnggonni is a port village producing fish and salt. Merchant boats [coming] from the sea nearby gather here and villagers have grown affluent from selling fish.

The branch range that extends to the southeast forms several mountains in the vicinity of Suwŏn City and stops beyond an estuary at the sea facing Asan County in Ch'ungch'ŏng Province. In the middle [of the range] is Mount Kŭmsu, which has a pond on its summit. The water of the pond looks as if it has been dyed yellow. People say that there is a gold mine in the pond. A Tang person who was good at telling the energy of the land said that this mountain has the energy of gold treasure. Another branch from Mount Kŭmsu extends westward to join Namyang City. It passes through Munp'anhyŏn to the west of the city and stops at the sea. The area is close to Tangjin in Ch'ungch'ŏng Province and is separated from Tangjin only by a small sea. Its level of high and low tidal water corresponds to that of Tangjin. The land stretches to the sea, with seashores and ports on both the left and right. Several hundred houses that produce salt are scattered along the beach to the north and south reminiscent of the stars in the sky.

Where the land ends is the Hwaryangjin camp, at which an associate commander is stationed; it is about ten *ri* over the sea from Taebudo. As all residents are engaged in fishing, the villages to the west of Namyang City from the south of the Han River receive all the profits from fish and salt. The island was formed when a rocky outcropping was submerged by the sea. The winding rocky range stretches up to the island. The water above the range is very shallow. In olden days islanders found a path by following the cranes that walked along the rocky range, giving it the name "Cranes' indication." The path was known only to the islanders and not to outsiders. Chased by Qing soldiers, in the year of *pyŏngja*, islanders fled along the path, which because the rocky range zigzagged, it was difficult for the soldiers to find. The Qing cavalry, with no clear knowledge of the path, chased the islanders and drowned, thereby saving the island. The island has rich soil and many residents. Being the first crossroad of the sea route from the south, it serves as the outside gate for both Kanghwado and Yŏngjong Islands. Earlier, a navy camp was positioned here, but after the camp shifted to Kyodongdo, it became a horse-rearing ranch. Nowadays, there are no soldiers on guard. This is not right. It would be better if the Hwaryangjin camp moved to this island so that it and Yŏngjong Island could support each other.

Thirty *ri* to the west over the sea lies Yŏnhŭng Island. At the end of the Koryŏ dynasty, Prince Ingnyŏng Ki foresaw that Koryŏ would soon collapse. Having changed his name, he brought his family over to this island and hid. After the fall of the Koryŏ dynasty, he escaped from drowning and his descendants remained there. Their status has now declined and they are shepherds on the ranch. The three-room house where Prince Ingnyŏng once lived is closed up tightly and entry is prohibited. Rooms are filled with piles of books and kitchenware, the meaning and purpose of which are unclear. In the past when an official visited the island and tried to open the lock, several male and female shepherds pleaded, saying, "If the door is opened someone will be killed, so we made sure that the door is not open. It has been three hundred years since [anyone] dared open it." The official took pity on them in this and stopped trying.

Yangsŏng and Ansŏng lie to the east of Suwŏn. Ansŏng is on the strait between Kyŏnggi and Ch'ungch'ŏng Provinces. As abundant goods were gathered there and craftsmen and merchants flocked to the place, it became a city to the south of Hanyang. Outside the city, however, is an unlivable area, which, although flat, has murderous energy. To the north of Suwŏn is Kwach'ŏn, and fifteen *ri* to the north of Kwach'ŏn is Tongjakchin. Cross over the river and a further fifteen *ri* north of Kwach'ŏn is the South Gate in Kyongsŏng.

A mountain range from Ch'ŏllyŏng in Anbyŏn in Hamgyŏng Province extends five hundred to six hundred *ri* to the south and reaches Yangju, where it breaks up into [a group of] small mountains. Turning to the east at an angle [these small mountains consolidate and] suddenly rise to become Manjangbong Peak of Mount Tobong. As [the range] extends again to the southeast it becomes disbursed for a while and then [reconstitutes itself] to rise again to form Paegundae of Mount Samgak. From here it extends again to the south and becomes Man'gyŏngdae. One mountain branch extends to the southwest and another to the south to form Mount Paegak. Geomancers said that "as it is a landform of a wood-type mountain projected high into the sky, it is worthy to be the main mountain of a royal palace."[179] [This area] is surrounded by a big river to the north, south, and east, and is connected to the sea in the west. As it intertwines with waters from many places, the area is known as the place where the energy of the whole country is concentrated. *Yugi* (Extant records), by [the monk] Tosŏn (827–898), states that "the Yi family will succeed to the throne that is currently held by the Wang family and will choose Hanyang (Seoul) as the capital."

During the mid-Koryŏ period, Yun Kwan was assigned to nominate a place to the south of Mount Paegak and plant plum trees there.[180] Once they grew tall they were cut down. In this way vigorous energy was suppressed. When our dynasty took over from the former dynasty, Monk Muhak was sent to find a site for the capital. When Muhak went from Paegundae to Man'gyŏngdae along the range and then reached Pibong Peak to the southwest, he found a stele. Inscribed on it were six characters, "*Muhak osimdoch'a*," which mean "Muhak will make a wrong search and arrive here." The stele was erected by Monk Tosŏn. Muhak changed his course by following the range directly south and arrived at the foot of Mount Paegak. Observing that the three mountain ranges met and formed flat land, he finally decided on that place as the site for a palace. This is the very place where plums were planted during the Koryŏ dynasty.

The exact place for the outer mountain fortress wall that would surround the site remained undecided, however. One night during a heavy snowfall, it was noticed that the snow that had fallen on an outer area piled up while that on the inside melted. King T'aejo thought it a mystery and ordered the wall be built along the line marked by the snow. The line matches that of the present wall. The wall was erected in accord with the landform of the mountain. The parts of the wall to the direct east and the southwest, however, are low and weak. [Moreover,] because small fences were not built on the wall nor moats made, [the wall] could not defend [Seoul] at the time of the Hideyoshi and Manchu invasions. In the year of *ŭryu* (1705), during the reign of King Sukchong, the court discussed whether the city wall should be restructured. Some said, "The area to the east of the city is very low. If we block the river and irrigate water to the city, all the people in it will become fish." At this remark, the discussion finally stopped. For three hundred years, however, this place has been renowned as the center of culture and civilization, harboring a strong Confucian spirit and producing many scholars. In fact, it is a small China.

Yangju, P'ochŏn, Kap'yŏng, and Yŏngp'ŏng form the outskirts to the east, within one hundred *ri* of Seoul, and Koyang, Chŏksŏng, P'aju, and Kyoha make up those to the west. These areas are not desirable places to live, as the soil is barren and the residents poor. Those among the scholar-gentry who lost power and went down to the three southern provinces were able to preserve the fortune of their household. Those who went to the outskirts, however, became impoverished. After one or two generations many lost status [and became, for example,] low-ranking officials or commoners.

Hanyang is blocked by a big river in front and is connected in the west to Hwanghae and P'yŏngan Provinces by a road. Five *ri* away from the city is a hill, Sahyŏn, and over the hill is Nokpŏnhyŏn. It is said that passing through here a Tang general said, "If one man blocks the gate of the pass, not even ten thousand people would be able to open it." Forty *ri* further away is the mountain pass Pyŏkcheryŏng, where Li Rusong was defeated during the Hideyoshi invasion. Having returned to Hanyang after a defeat in P'yŏngyang, the Japanese army permitted only the weak soldiers go in and out of Koyanghhyŏn. Having heard of this in Kaesŏng, Li Rusong, out of his eagerness to perform a meritorious deed, left many soldiers there and let lightly armed soldiers attack the Japanese army. The Ming soldiers had barely climbed up the Pyŏkcheryŏng when the Japanese soldiers appeared from all directions; many stout men of Li's [force] were shot dead. Luo Shangzhi, who was also called Luo Qian Jin[181] because he was strong, alternated advancing and retreating [while] wearing two layers of armor and supporting Li Rusong under his arm. He managed to save Li's life. Having lost his fighting spirit, Li Rusong repeatedly withdrew his army from the battlefield. Only after hearing that the Japanese army had left Hanyang did he finally mobilize his army and chase the enemy south to the shore of Kyŏngsang Province before returning. It is worth building a gateway at the two hills and the Pyŏkcheryŏng. There is no place in the country, however, where a gateway has been built by blocking a road. It is a real pity, as there are places that can serve as natural fortresses.

Forty *ri* to the west of the Pyŏkcheryŏng is the Imjin ferry dock. It is downstream of the river and situated to the north of Hanyang. The southern bank of the river looks like a naturally formed fortress. The steep southern bank faces the river and is situated at a junction that leads to the west, and so the place is really worth guarding. It is rather unfortunate that a wall has not yet been built there.

Ferrying across the river and traveling a further forty *ri* past Chang-dan [one finds] the city of Kaesŏng, which was the capital during the

Koryŏ dynasty. Mount Songak is its guardian mountain and Manwŏtdae is at the base of the mountain. This is the very spot mentioned in the histories of the Song as a place where a palace was built against a big mountain. In Kim Kwan-ŭi's *T'ongp'yŏn* it is written, "this place is where a golden pig lay himself down."[182] Tosŏn said, "this is a field where non-glutinous millet is to be planted."[183]

[I have the honor of reflecting on the time] when Emperor Xuanzong[184] was young and, having left Shiliu Yuan,[185] had a hard time in a foreign land. He crossed the sea on a merchant boat and arrived at the northern side of the Husŏ River. Noticing that the riverbanks were all marshland, he paved the bog with coins, with which the boat was laden, and [therefore] landed. This is why the place is called Ton'gae (Coin Port). He then arrived at the house of Poyuk. Seeing that he was a noble born of the Tang dynasty, Poyuk had his younger daughter Chinŭi sleep with him. When Xuanzong left the house, he knew that she was pregnant. He gave her a red archer's bow and said, "If you gave birth to a baby boy let him come to China carrying the bow. Please name him Chakchegŏn." Chakchegŏn grew up practicing archery with the red bow left him by his father and became very good at it.

When he was on board a merchant vessel on its way to Tang China, the boat ceased sailing [forward] and circled around in the middle of the sea. People on the boat were greatly surprised and agreed to see whether their fortune was good or bad by throwing their hats into the sea. It happened that only Chakchegŏn's hat sank. In the end, they left him on a small island, with provisions, until the boat returned from China. When he was alone on the island a boy appeared out of the water and said, "The Sea God [Dragon King] wants to see you. You will get there if you keep your eyes shut." Chakchegŏn decided to follow the boy's instructions. Having arrived at the water palace, Chakchegŏn saw an old man, who said, "This old man has been residing here for a long time. Recently, however, a white dragon has been trying to rob me of my cave. Therefore, I promised that I would fight him tomorrow. I am guessing that you are a good archer. Please help me and shoot that white dragon." Chakchegŏn asked, "While you are fighting, how can I tell which one is which?" The old man answered, "It will be time to fight when it is windy and raining at midday tomorrow. When the battle is at its peak, both our backs will be above the water. My back is blue while the white dragon's is white." Chakchegŏn agreed to his request and returned to the island. The following day, he waited and saw what the man had said would happen. On the island, Chakchegŏn aimed at the white thing and shot it. A little while later as the sky cleared up and the sea calmed down, a boy appeared and again led Chakchegŏn to the palace. When they reached the water palace the old man brought a girl out and let Chakchegŏn take her as his wife. The man said, "As you are of noble birth you will be blessed once you return to your hometown." After staying there for a long while, Chakchegŏn and his wife bid farewell to him.

At the same time as they surfaced on the island, the merchant boat arrived. Chakchegŏn together with his wife returned to the shore of Ch'angnŭng [in Korea]. Having heard that Chakchegŏn had returned after marrying a princess of the Sea God, the prefect of Yŏmbaek collected goods and labor and had a house built for them. After they moved from Ch'angnŭng to the foothills of Mount Songak a son was born and was named Yung. Later, the princess of the Sea God reprimanded Chakchegŏn for his lack of fidelity. Having transformed into dragons, the princess and her young daughter entered a well and went to the West Sea.[186] Yung had a son and gave him the surname Wang and the first name Kŏn. In fact, his surname was Yi.

After Wang Kŏn ascended the throne, he made the place where his father had once lived into the royal audience chamber. He bestowed the title Queen Onsŏng on the princess of the Sea God and King Ŭijo on the late Chakchegŏn. When he founded the Koryŏ dynasty, it was the beginning of the Five Dynasties (907–959) in China.[187] While Emperor Zhaoxuan (r. 904–907)[188] of China met his doom abroad, the first king with the surname Wang rose and unified the three Han kingdoms. This is the legacy of Emperor Taizong of the Tang dynasty and is similar to the situation that, when the Chen state fell [in 478 BCE], the Tian family became strong in the Qi state. It is thus not fair to say that heaven is hardly benevolent to good people.

Some do not believe the story of the princess of the Sea God. It is said, however, that some children of the founder [of the Koryŏ dynasty] have scales under their arms because the mother of the founder was a dragon. The reason the princess of the Sea God returned to the sea, taking her young daughter and becoming a dragon, is that she was afraid that her daughter might give birth to a son who might later become king. Girls with no scales were therefore allowed to marry courtiers, while the girls with scales were made to become concubines of the kings who succeeded to the throne. In this way, immoral acts ended up being committed. In the middle of the dynasty there was a king who married his own sister, a situation criticized in the histories of Song dynasty. But this sort of thing happened only within the royal family and not among common folk.

After the withdrawal of the army in Wihwado, the founder of our [Chosŏn] dynasty expelled King U,[189] labeling him a child of Sin Ton.[190]

He then enthroned Yo as King Kongyang[191] and had the new king behead King U in Kangnŭng. Before King U was killed he raised his arms and showing the scales under his armpits said, "Although people say that my surname is Sin, it is in fact Wang, who are descendants of a dragon. I have scales under my arms. Take a good look at them." The attendants got near him and saw what King U had said was true. This is most strange.

In the year of *imsin* (1392), during the reign of Emperor Hongwu, our founder received the throne from King Kongyang and changed the capital to Hanyang. Among the renowned families and households who were courtiers of the Wang family, those who would not surrender to him remained in Kaesŏng. People living outside Kaesŏng called the place Tumundong. King T'aejo hated those who remained in Kaesŏng and prohibited the scholars of Kaesŏng from sitting government exams for one hundred years. As a result, their sons and grandsons eventually became commoners living off their merchant activities and stopped studying altogether. After three hundred years the name "scholar-gentry" itself finally disappeared in Kaesŏng and no scholar-gentry from Seoul went there to live.

Earlier on I saw a portrait of Queen Onsŏng in an old shrine in Tae-jŏngni (Big Well Village) and the wall of Ch'angnŭng T'osŏng. What I always found strange is that the remains/relics are too vivid for us to say that the [Princess of the Sea Palace] story is false. [At the same time,] if we accept that the story is true, it is untrustworthy. I do not know which to choose.

The most lamentable part is that Chŏng To-jŏn, who was a pupil of Yi Saek (Mogŭn) and at a level equal to the prime minister at the end of Koryŏ dynasty, sought to profit from the fallen dynasty, harmed his former teacher, and killed his own friends. This is similar to what Wang Jian and Chu Yuan did.[192] In addition, he even put forward a plan to get rid of royal members of the Wang family [of the Koryŏ dynasty]. He let all of the Wang family board a big boat on the pretext of sending them to Chayŏndo. He secretly made a diver drill a hole in the boat and the boat finally sank. At that time a monk who was close to the Wang family saw, from a hill, a family member of Wang and recited a poem:

The sound of slow paddling is heard over the blue wave.
The monk on the hill! What can you do?[193]

The place where the boat sank is now piled high with sand and mud and has become a large island in the sea. Chŏngjuhae, which is downstream of the Poryŏn River, is the very place.

When King T'aejo ascended the throne he made King Kongyang move to Kwangdong District. He demolished the royal shrine and loaded the ancestral tablets onto a big boat on the Imjin River. The boat sailed alone upstream and landed in front of a temple on the riverbank in Majŏn County. When the villagers informed the local magistrate of this, King T'aejo allowed the statues of the Buddha from the temple to be moved to another temple and the ancestral tablets [of the Wang family] to be kept in the temple [instead]. The temple came to be called Sungŭijŏn and a man with the surname of Wang was made the official in charge.

By this time, those among the Wang families who were known to the world or served in the court had already died or been killed and others ran away and hid under new family names. They changed their surname to Ma (馬), Chŏn (全), or Ok (玉) to hide the character of their original family and did not acknowledge themselves as Wang (王).[194] Only during the reign of the Great King of Changhŏn was a man, Wang Sun-rye, with the family name of Wang found. Following the precedent where the Sŏnu family was given charge of the Kijajŏn shrine, Wang Sun-rye was given rice paddies and slaves and was led to the hereditary position of caretaker so that memorial services could be offered at the shrine. This was implemented due to the benevolence of the Great King. The king had once said that the act of wiping out the Wang family was not what King T'aejo intended, that it was devised by the courtiers of King T'aejo who had helped him to become king.

The bridge of Sŏnjukkyo in the castle is where Chŏng Mong-ju was killed. When he was prime minister during the reign of King Kongyang, he alone did not play up to King T'aejo. Thus, several generals of King T'aejo had Cho Yŏng-gyu hit Chŏng Mong-ju with an iron hammer on the bridge. With this the lineage of Koryŏ's kinghood was finally passed on to the Yi family. The present court later granted Chŏng Mong-ju a posthumous epithet of prime minister of the State Council, a title of the present dynasty, and erected a stele in front of his grave. The stele was soon struck by lightening and destroyed. His descendants requested that the court rewrite the stele to state "chancellor[195] of Koryŏ dynasty." The [new] stele has stood safely so far. This demonstrates that the loyal and persistent spirit does not disappear even after death. This is also awe-inspiring.

More than ten *ri* to the southeast of [Kae]sŏng stands Mount Tŏkchŏk. On the mountain there is a shrine dedicated to Ch'oe Yŏng where his portrait is hung. Residents said that prayers offered to the portrait were answered. Having built a dwelling next to the shrine, the residents arranged for a maiden (shamaness) to reside there to look after the shrine. They have kept maidens there for the last three hundred years, replacing those who are aging with young ones. The maiden there herself said, "When night falls, Ch'oe Yŏng's spirit comes down to have intercourse with me." I would say that Ch'oe Yŏng was brave but reckless. He had his daughter become the queen of Wang U and did not serve the country well, letting the governance of the dynasty fall into the hands of others. As [his spirit] could neither rise to heaven nor enter earth it became a ghost to which no ancestral rites were offered from the court. The fact that he did not forget the pleasure between man and woman alone reveals that he did not submit to being dead. This is foolish and lascivious. They say that the efficacy of this shrine ceased several decades ago. This is also strange.

Manwŏtdae is a long hill that must be looked up at to view it. It is written in Tosŏn's *Yugi* that a place must be built not by disturbing the natural state of the earth, but by adding more earth and rocks on the ground. This is why King T'aejo of the Koryŏ dynasty built a palace on a reinforced slope terraced with rocks. When the Koryŏ dynasty collapsed, the palace was demolished but the terrace of rock remained. Having been neglected by offices of authorities over time, rich merchants in Kaesŏng secretly carried the rocks away and made them into gravestones. Nowadays, few rocks remain there.

Behind Manwŏtdae is the valley Chahadong, which is beneath Mount Songak. The stream and rocks are deep and strange. Within the castle grounds is Mount Nam (男山) to the southeast. This is where the traitor Ch'oe Ch'ung-hŏn lived. When the Wang family lost power, King Kongmin built a flower garden and a hall P'algakchŏn within it. This is the place where Wang U was beseiged. Mount Yongsu and Mount Chinbong to the south are also branches of Mount Songak and serve as table mountains in the castle. Geomancers said that Mount Chinbong has the landform of "the cosmetic table of a beautiful woman." This is why kings of the Koryŏ dynasty married Chinese princesses. As there is a writing brush- [pointed peak-] shaped mountain, many from our country achieved first place in civil service examinations in China. But the mountain range on the right is high and that on the left is low. Therefore, there were no excellent prime ministers and several military uprisings ensued.

Sandaeam, to the northeast of the castle, is where King Ŭijong encountered an uprising. The Yŏngt'ongdong to the northwest is where Poyuk lived. In the olden days Kwibŏpsa, which no longer exists, was there. To the north of the valley is the pond of Hwadam. This is where Chingsa Sŏ Kyŏng-dŏk lived in hiding during the reign of King Chungjong.[196] One mountain pass away is the old site of Hyŏnhwasa. Presently, monuments and a pagoda alone remain there. To the west of the monastery is Taehŭngdong, a wide valley situated between Mount Ogwan and Mount Sŏnggŏ. A mountain wall was erected here during the reign of

King Sukchong. The outside of this place is rugged and inside it is flat, making it a natural fortress. The government office stockpiled grains and military equipment there and built a large monastery so that monks could guard [these store] in case of sudden mishaps. Inside the valley the rocky wall is grand and high, and the stream is also deep and wide. At the base of the valley is a big waterfall. This is Pagyŏn Fall.

On Mount Mansu, which is outside the west gate of the castle, are the tombs of seven Koryŏ kings. One mountain pass away from here is Ch'ŏngsŏktong. A long valley of ten *ri* stretches out in a winding manner. Both sides of the valley are surrounded by walls, like hills, one thousand men high, and in the middle a big steam gushes forth. The place is ringed several times around by mountains, which are like gates. When a Qing emperor invaded our country and arrived here he was greatly terrified and intended to kill Long Guda [who led him here]. Long Guda conjectured that certainly no [Chosŏn] soldiers were guarding the area. Before passing by here, however, he made a secret investigation and found that [indeed] there was no one. On their return to China they avoided this route and went through Paekch'i, which is to the northeast of Kaesŏng.

To the south of Kaesŏng is P'ungdŏk City and to the east is Changdan. The Yŏngpyŏng River, which flows in from the east, and the Chingp'a River, which flows in from the north, meet at Majŏn. They then flow around the south of Changdan to become the Imjin River, which to the west joins the Han River at Sŭngch'ŏnp'o in P'ungdŏk.

Changdan County is to the north of the Imjin River and below Mount Paekhak. To the north of the county is Mount Hwajang. In the monastery are the *Pattra Sūtra*[197] and sandalwood. These were left by Chigong, a monk from India. The south of Mount Hwajang is made up of beautiful foothills and meandering streams. The place is compared to Mount Beimang in Luoyang in China, as many graves of high-ranking officials of Koryŏ and Chosŏn can be found there. To the east of the Imjin River are Yŏnch'ŏn and Majŏn, and to the north is Sangnyŏng. They are over one hundred *ri* from Hanyang and connected with the two capitals [of Hanyang and Kaesŏng] by water. These three places, however, are barren and the people are poor. They are thus not good places to live. Among them Sangnyŏng has better soil and good views facing the river. In Yŏnch'ŏn is a place where Hŏ Mok (Misu) used to live.

Discourse on the Selection of Habitable Places

The first consideration in the selection of a place to live should be its geomantic conditions. The other factors to be considered are its economic potential, social characteristics, and natural scenery. If any one of these four factors is found to be lacking the place will not be a happy choice. A place with the best of geomantic qualities but poor economic conditions is not fit for long-term inhabitation, nor is a place with good economic conditions but poor geomantic qualities. Even if a place is good in geomantic and economic terms but situated in an undesirable neighborhood, the social climate will certainly be a regrettable. Finally, without easily accessible natural scenic beauty, one is denied the opportunity for temperament-molding.

GEOMANCY

How should geomantic conditions be approached? First of all, the outlet of the watercourse is to be examined, then the terrain and the shape of mountains. Then one needs to look at the color of the soil, the nature of watercourses, and the homage mountain and homage water flow.[198] Generally, if the outlet of the water is gaping and wide open, even if the area is endowed with extensive good-quality farmland and big mansions, the people there cannot endure for many generations; they are bound to be ruined and scattered. That is the reason why, when one looks for and evaluates a place to live, one must look for a broad but enclosed plain with a tight water outlet. It is easy to discover such a compact place in mountainous areas but difficult to find such a place on the plains. On the plains one must look for a geomantic landform where water flows against the current. Despite a place being mountainous or shady, if water flows in vigorously and the place is sheltered, it is auspicious. It is good for the place to be surrounded by one fold [of a semicircle range of hills] and even more auspicious if it is surrounded by three to five folds; such a place is suitable for a family to inhabit for generation after generation.

In general, people live by benefiting from *yang* energy and the sky supplies *yang* light (sunshine). An area with a very limited view of the sky is certainly not a good place to live. Thus, the wider a plain is, the better accommodation it provides. In such places the sun, the moon, and the stars shine brightly and the climatic conditions of rain, wind, cold, and warmth are moderate and comfortable; thus, many great men of ability are born and there is less incidence of disease. The places to avoid at all costs are where the surrounding mountains are oppressively high, where the sun rises late and sets early, or where the Big Dipper is not seen at night. This is because such a place is low in spiritual brightness and susceptible to the inroads of *yin* energy. Various evil spirits gather there to form foggy and poisonous vapors in the morning and evening that easily cause illness.

That is why living in a narrow valley is not as good as living on a plain. A vast plain surrounded by low hills cannot be called mountainous; it is still a wide plain. The reason is that the sun is not blocked and the water energy (水氣)[199] has far-reaching influence. Even in the high mountains, if a place has extensive areas of flat land it can also be an auspicious place.

Generally, the best mountains are shaped like high towers and pavilions, as explained by geomancers. If the main mountain is in general beautiful, neat, clear, and with gentle contours, it is the best choice. The second best is a mountain range that stretches flat into the distance and then rises suddenly to form one peak after another. The branches of these mountains encircle a small, flat basin and the setting looks like a palace [surrounded by walls]. The main mountain looks imposing and magnificent, like a huge mansion. A place in a spacious plain with surrounding mountains, and where the mountain ranges descend to the plain by a watercourse to become fields, is the next best choice. The place to avoid by all means is where the incoming mountain range has a weak, dull, and lifeless look, or where there is little auspicious due to a landslide or steep slopes. Generally, if the ground is lifeless and lacks auspicious energy, no men of great talent will be born to the place. For this reason, one must choose [auspicious] mountain shapes.

On the whole, in rural settlements, whether in the water (水中)[200] or beside water, if the soil and sand are firm and dense, the water from a well or spring will be clean and cool. Such a place is a livable locality. If the soil consists of red clay, black gravel, or is fine and yellow, it is dead soil. Water from a well or spring in such soils always contains harmful elements. Such a place is not suitable. In general, a place that has no water is naturally not suitable for habitation. Mountains can accomplish nature's wonders only when they are accompanied by watercourses. However, the incoming and outgoing directions of the water flow must accord with [geomantic] principles; only then can the place harbor the auspiciousness of engenderment and nurture.[201] This is not discussed here in detail because there are geomancer's books [on the subject]. House sites are different from grave sites, however. As water controls wealth, there are many affluent households by the edge of the water. Famous and prosperous villages, even if they are in mountainous areas, are also situated at the confluence of streams, which are [good] places to live for many generations.

Generally, if the mountains in front of the abode have rough rocky peaks, skewed solitary peaks, peaks that threaten to collapse, have strange rocks seen from either a peak or the bottom of the mountain, or have, in a long valley, a high landform that can be seen from all sides of the house, such a site is definitely not suitable. The auspicious mountains are those that have beautiful and delicate contours when seen from afar and that look bright and clear when seen from nearby. Such mountains make people feel joyful at first sight and not threatened or upset.

Incoming water is called water outside the [inner] watercourse. If a small stream or a small brook flows toward [a house site] it is auspicious. A big stream or a river should not flow toward a site. Generally, whether a site is for a house or a grave, if a big river flows toward it, the site may enjoy initial prosperity but later be doomed to misfortune. One must watch incoming watercourses. The incoming water must accord with the direction of an incoming mountain and meander slowly in order to mix the *yin* and *yang* energies. It is not auspicious if the incoming water flows straight in like an arrow.

If one intends to build a house or mansion to be handed down to descendants for many generations, one must choose [a site] with reference to its geomantic qualities, of which the six points discussed above are the very essence.

Economic Potential

Why and how should economic potential be discussed? Humans cannot survive just by breathing air, drinking dew, and covering themselves with feathers and fur. They must produce food and clothing. In order to support their elders and parents and look after their wives, children, and servants, they need to extend their means of living beyond mere food and clothing. Even Confucius taught that teaching comes after material well-being. How can one allow people to sit and discuss the moral principles of benevolence and righteousness if they are virtually unclad beggars unable to offer sacrifices to their ancestors, look after their parents, or fulfil their duties to wives and children?

For a long time those who sought empty reputations have avoided doing practical work. In their compulsion to achieve fame by attempting the impossible, they cannot help hiding their darker side so as to flaunt their virtue. To concern oneself with proper moral conduct without first addressing one's material well-being actually means to expect manifest virtue without hidden vice. To have green pines for friends and white clouds for company, to pillow one's head on a rock and rinse one's mouth in a clear stream, to till misty fields and fetch water under the moon... surely these are virtuous things to do to earn a fine reputation. But these were only practiced in ancient times, when rituals were not yet perfected and all members of the community were commoners. If these practices were accepted as [proper] rules, there would be no need to have a master of ceremony[202] at a coming-of-age ceremony, no need to follow protocols at a wedding,[203] no need to prepare a coffin for a funeral, and no need to prepare proper ceremonial vessels for a sacrificial ritual to ancestors. How could these be practiced nowadays?

For all of their lives human beings require wealth for their own survival and for properly sending off their dead. Since wealth does not drop out of the sky nor spring up from the ground, fertile land is the best source of wealth. The next best is a metropolis where ships, vehicles, people, and goods gather for trade between sellers and buyers. Fertile land means land that is good for growing five grains and cotton. Top-grade rice paddies are those where one *mal* of rice [seed] is sown and sixty *mal* harvested. The next grade yields forty to fifty *mal*. Land that produces only thirty *mal* or less is unsuitable for human habitation. The most fertile areas in the nation are counties such as Namwŏn and Kurye, in Chŏlla Province, and Sŏngju (星州) and Chinju, in Kyŏngsang Province. From the most fertile land in those counties one hundred forty *mal* are harvested and even the least fertile yields eighty *mal*. The other counties [of the country] are not able to produce this amount.

On the left side of Kyŏngsang Province the soil is barren everywhere and the people are poverty-stricken. Only on the right side of Kyŏngsang Province is the soil fertile. The left side of Chŏlla Province is the land around Mount Chiri, which is fertile, but the counties along the sea are dry and experience frequent droughts. In Ch'ungch'ŏng Province, south of the Naep'o and Ch'aryŏng ranges, there are equal proportions of fertile and barren land. Even the most fertile land there often yields no more than sixty *mal*. The land from the north of the Ch'aryŏng range to the south of the Han River also consists of equal proportions of fertile and barren areas but is not as fertile as south of the Ch'aryŏng range. Much of the so-called fertile land there does not yield even forty *mal*. The land to the north of the Han River is generally barren, and from Kangwŏn Province in the east to Kaesŏng City in the west, no more than thirty *mal* is harvested. From the nine counties to the east of the [T'aebaek] mountain range from Kangwŏn Province to Hamgyŏng Province, the land is very infertile. Hwanghae Province has an equal measure of fertile and infertile land. In P'yŏngan Province the mountainous areas have barren soil, but along the sea coast the soil of many counties is as fertile as that of Ch'ungch'ŏng Province. As for dry fields, in narrow valley settlements millet is the main crop, and in seaside settlements only soybeans and barley are cultivated. Settlements on the plains, being far away from both mountains and sea, find it easy to grow any type of crop.

For cotton crops the provinces of Kyŏngsang and Chŏlla are the best and, whether narrow valleys or coastal areas, the land is good for cotton cultivation. From the area to the east of the T'aebaek Mountain Range (嶺東 Yŏngdong) in Kangwŏn Province to Hamgyŏng Province to the north, cotton is never sown. Even if cotton were sown it would not grow. As for the area to the west of the T'aebaek Mountain Range (嶺西 Yŏngsŏ) of Kangwŏn Province, the mountain air is so cold that it is even less suitable [than Yŏngdong 嶺東] for growing cotton. Cotton, however, is cultivated in small quantities in fields near Wŏnju and Ch'unch'ŏn. The mountainous districts to the north of the Han River in Kyŏnggi Province are not suited for cultivating cotton because the mountains are high and the water is cold. In the plains, cotton is cultivated in some places. Only in Kaesŏng City is it widely grown. Various counties along the [western] coast to the south of the Han River and those of Ch'ungch'ŏng Province such as Naep'o, Imch'ŏn, and Hansan are not suitable for cultivating [cotton]. Because of the poor quality of the soil, even if it is sown the plants may grow lush but will not bear cotton bolls.

Away from the sea to the south of the Han River cotton is cultivated intensively, but such places are rare. Only in the vicinity of Ch'ungju, Koesan, Yŏnp'ung, Ch'ŏngp'ung, and in the Tanyang area is it cultivated widely. Still, such places cannot match the district to the south of the Ch'aryŏng range, where cotton is grown everywhere. Hwanggan, Yŏngdong (永同), Okch'ŏn, Hoedŏk, and Kongju are the best places for cultivating cotton; the next best are [areas such as] Ch'ŏngju, Munŭi, Yŏn'gi, and Chinch'ŏn. In Hwanghae Province only the districts near the sea are unsuitable for growing cotton, while, thanks to good soil, both the mountains and the plains are suitable. In P'yŏngan Province only in the mountainous areas is cotton cultivated here and there. But anywhere on the plains is suitable for cotton cultivation.

Apart from these areas, the tobacco fields in Chinan, ginger fields in Chŏnju, ramie fields in Imch'ŏn and Hansan, and sedge fields in Andong and Yean rank first in Korea and have become the source of profit for wealthy people. This is a brief overview of agricultural practices in Korea.

Transport and trading were invented by the sage Shennong.[204] Without these no wealth can be created. In terms of capacity, the horse is not as good as the cart and the cart is not as good as the ship. Because in Korea there are many mountains but few plains, wheeled transportation is inconvenient. If merchants carry goods on horseback on a long journey, the profit suffers due to the high cost of transportation. Therefore, when profits are considered, moving goods by horse is not as good as transporting goods by ship.

Korea is surrounded by sea to the east, west, and south; there is no place in the country that cannot be reached by boat. Due to strong winds and waves in the East Sea, however, ships coming from the southwest, which are not accustomed to rough seas, seldom make trips to the East Sea, although many seaside villages in Kyŏngsang Province, the Yŏngdong (嶺東) region of Kangwŏn province, and the whole area of Hamgyŏng Province are in contact by boat. Because the currents of the sea are gentle in the southwest, commerce continues unceasingly and reaches even further, to Hwanghae and P'yŏngan Provinces in the far north.

Normally, at the junction of rivers and seas, merchant ships make profits and practice trading in credit. Ch'ilsŏngp'o in Kimhae County and Kyŏngsang Province is situated on the estuary of Naktong River and developed in this way. From here ships can sail up to Sangju to the north and Chinju to the west; Kimhae controls the sole entrance to those places. In fact, being located at the mouth of the river, which flows through the whole of Kyŏngsang Province, it controls the commercial advantages of land and sea to the north and south. Both government agencies and private merchants make enormous profits from traffic in salt.

In Chŏlla Province there is the Yŏngsan River of Naju and other waterways such as Pŏpsŏngp'o of Yŏnggwang, Sajinp'o of Hŭngdŏk, and Sat'an of Chŏnju. Although these waterways are short, they are accessible by means of tidal currents from the sea and thus attract many merchant ships. The Kŭm River in Ch'ungch'ŏng Province is a long river with distant headwaters, but it is shallow to the east of Kongju and has too many rapids in this part [of its course] for ships to sail. Up to Puyŏ and Ŭnjin the river is influenced by tidal waters from the sea, and ships can sail in all the waterways in the Chin River area below the Paengma River. Being situated on the Kŭm River between the sea and the inland of Ch'ungch'ŏng and Chŏlla Provinces, the settlements of Kanggyŏng and Ŭnjin form big towns in the middle of the plains to the south of the Kŭm River. Seaside dwellers and valley households all bring out their goods for exchange. During the fishing season, from spring to summer, the smell of fish and seaweed permeates whole villages, and big and small ships form a wall, queuing up day and night along the waterways. Big markets are held six times each month making available goods from near and far.

In the district of Naep'o, both Kongseho in Asan and Yugungp'o in Tŏksan are connected by deep and long waterways. Kwangch'ŏn in Hongju District and Sŏngyŏn in Sŏsan District, although [located] on streams, have access to tidal waters and are therefore ports where merchant ships can anchor and transport goods. Even though seaside towns in Kyŏnggi have the advantage of tidal waterways, merchant ships do not gather there much because it is too close to the capital city. Yongsanho is seven *ri* southwest of Hanyang. In olden days the main course of the Han River flowed below the southern bank and one tributary flowed below the northern bank and formed a lake ten *ri* long. To the west the Yŏmch'ang sandbar blocked water from seeping out and thus water lilies grew in the middle of the lake. During the Koryŏ dynasty royal tours often went there to enjoy the view of the water lilies. After the present [Chosŏn] dynasty moved the capital to Seoul, the Yŏmch'ang sandbar was breached due to the sudden inflow of tidal waves. Since then tidal water has reached Yongsan and ships from all over the country anchor there.

To the west of Yongsan is a string of riverside villages such as Map'o, T'ojŏng, and Nong'am. These villages are joined to the West Sea by waterways, and thus ships from the whole country gather there. Noblemen and royal in-laws living in the city have built pavilions there so that they may hold banquets and enjoy a leisurely life. About three hundred years ago the Han River became increasingly shallow, and today tidal water cannot reach its upper part. At the Yŏmch'ang sandbar, mud sediment builds up year after year and it is difficult to know whether or not the river will be blocked off.

In Kaesŏng City, ten *ri* out from Sugumun Gate, is the East River, a tidal waterway where merchant ships anchor. After the end of the Koryŏ dynasty the tidal water receded, the river became shallower, and ships could no longer enter. Sŭngch'ŏnp'o was some forty *ri* from Kaesŏng City but since the Husŏ River is within thirty *ri* of the city, at present ships from other provinces sail through there. Big ships sail far out to sea to trade in foodstuffs, and small boats transport goods along rivers, sailing north to Kangŭm, west to Yŏnan, and east until they reach the Han River.

The two big islands of Kanghwa and Kyodong are situated to the south of the Husŏ River. Being surrounded by the river and the sea, they are producers of fish and salt. Merchants from Hanyang and Kaesŏng make much profit from the towns on the islands.

In P'yŏngan Province, both the Taedong River in P'yŏngyang and the Ch'ŏngch'ŏn River in Anju enjoy the advantage of being navigable. But to the south is Changsan Cape, which is dangerous for navigation, meaning that ships sailing from the south are rare. Changsan Cape is in Changyŏn County in Hwanghae Province. It stretches out into the sea and is shaped like a sharp horn. Because of the rapid currents and dangerous reefs, sailors are afraid of the place. To the west of T'aean [Peninsula] in Naep'o County in Ch'ungch'ŏng Province is Anhŭng Cape, which protrudes into the sea like Changsan Cape. There are two rocks standing up out of the sea that ships have to navigate between. Sailors are also afraid of Anhŭng

Cape. Because these two capes in the north and south stand firm in the sea facing each other, many ships passing by them are wrecked.

The taxes-in-kind collected from the southern provinces of Chŏlla, Kyŏngsang, and Ch'ungch'ŏng are transported north to the capital by ship. Naval units are therefore dispatched to every shipping route and item after item of taxed goods are transported during the year. There is not one household among the royal family or scholar-gentry who does not own farm estates in the three southern provinces. These families also require transport of their farm revenues by ship. Sailors are very familiar with the sea route, and there are many merchants who sail through the Anhŭng Cape as if strolling about their own courtyards. The taxes-in-kind from the counties in P'yŏngan and Hamgyŏng Provinces are not transported by ship to the capital but are kept in each region as provisions for the royal envoy's visits or as government supplies. Since the scholar-gentry do not reside here, there is no private shipping. For this reason, merchant ships from these provinces sail to and from the capital only very rarely. Sometimes merchant ships from other provinces sail there, but not as often as they go to the three southern provinces. The sailors from there are therefore not experienced at crossing the rapid currents, and their fear of Changsan Cape is much greater than that of sailors from provinces south of the Anhŭng Cape.

Apart from shipping on the tidal waterways, there are smaller river-boats that, due to their size, are unable to venture out to sea to make profits. The Han River is the biggest and longest waterway [in the whole country] and enjoys the advantages of abundant tidal water. The following places are connected by shipping routes where trading on credit is carried out: the Hwang River (黄江) in Ch'ŏngp'ung County, Kŭmch'ŏn and Mokkye in Ch'ungju, Hŭngwŏnch'ang in Wŏnju, and Paegae in Yŏju County to the southeast; Uduch'on in Ch'unch'ŏn and Wŏnam in Nangch'ŏn to the northeast; and Chingp'ado in Yŏnch'ŏn directly to the north. Only Hanyang has the advantage of being connected to the sea on the left and right, and on the rivers to the east and west ships gather carrying merchandise from all over the country. Many people have sought profits and become rich here, and the capital is the best place for that. This is a brief survey of the waterways and shipping in the nation.

Rich merchants with large sums of capital have established central bases and carried out business extending to Japan in the south and Beijing in the north. Over the years these merchants have exported and imported goods from all over the world and have sometimes accumulated enormous personal wealth. Most of these merchants live in Hanyang or Kaesŏng and often in P'yŏngyang and Anju. All are located along the road to Beijing and have become rich [through trade]. These merchants are much wealthier than those who have made their fortunes from shipping, and there are no such merchants in the three southern provinces. The scholar-gentry, however, traditionally cannot engage in such work and thus look for places to keep ships where fish and salt are traded. What can be wrong with this, since the profits enable them to meet expenses for the four rituals of coming of age, weddings, funerals, and memorial services?

Social Characteristics

Why should social practices come into consideration? Confucius said, "Villages with benevolent people are good places to live. Those who do not choose to live among benevolent neighbors may be regarded as unwise." In ancient times Mencius' mother moved her dwelling three times in hopes of providing a better education for her son. Failure to adopt correct customs is harmful not only to oneself but also to one's descendants through the bad influence incorrect customs exert; that is why one must consider local customs when choosing a place to live.

Among the eight provinces, P'yŏngan is the best for the hospitality of its people. The next best is Kyŏngsang because of the integrity of its people. Because Hamgyŏng is bordered by barbarians, the local inhabitants are strong and fierce. The natural environment is harsh in Hwanghae, and therefore many of the people are cruel and brutal. The people of Kangwŏn are from remote mountain valleys and are boorish. People from Chŏlla indulge in craftiness and are prone to evil. As for the villages situated on plains around the capital in Kyŏnggi, the inhabitants' fortunes have dwindled and become depleted. The inhabitants of Ch'ungch'ŏng pursue only power and profit. This is a brief comment on the characteristics of the people of the eight provinces.

The above characterization is true of common folk; the customs of the scholar-gentry are different. Present-day government organization in Korea is different from earlier times. Even though three chancellors[205] and six ministers[206] are appointed to supervise and control various government offices, great importance is attached to the Office of the Inspector General and the Office of the Censor General. These offices were given the exclusive right, after discussion, to execute the investigation of officials' alleged wrongdoings based on hearsay, [to oversee] the resignation of officials to avoid conflict of interest, and to implement appropriate measures for [restitution on behalf of] wronged officials.

Generally, the power to appoint central and local government officials does not belong to the three chancellors but to the Ministry of Personnel.

Fearing that this ministry would rival the three chancellors, the right to recommend officials to the Three Remonstrative Offices[207] was not given to the minister of personnel but was instead assigned to the selection secretaries, the senior fifth- and senior sixth-rank officials of the ministry.[208] Therefore, these officials were given the right to recommend candidates to the Office of the Inspector General and the Office of the Censor General. Although the positions of the three chancellors and six ministers are most prestigious, if their conduct is even slightly disagreeable, selection secretaries can have the officials of the Three Remonstrative Offices debate the matter and bring about immediate impeachment. Since the court esteems a sense of honor and takes personal reputation and integrity seriously, once an official is faced with impeachment he has no option but to resign from his post.

The power of the selection secretaries is therefore similar to that of the three chancellors. It is arranged so that superior and inferior posts are interrelated and hold each other in check, [with the result that] throughout the past three hundred years there have been no wicked government officials who abused their power or who have become uncontrollable. This [system] was wisely instituted by the forefathers of the present dynasty, who, benefiting from the lessons of the Koryŏ dynasty, saw to the prevention of a situation where a weak king is pitted against a powerful bureaucracy. For this reason, only men of good reputation and high moral standards will be selected from the staff of the Three Remonstrative Offices and appointed to be selection secretaries, who have the right to recommend their own successors. The reason this right does not belong to the minister of personnel is that such a serious matter warrants a fair and just evaluation by all concerned.

When it comes to recommending personnel for promotion, the selection secretary's position is considered first and then afterward people for other positions are recommended. So long as he does not commit a wrong, a selection secretary can easily become a chancellor or minister. For these reasons no young or newly appointed officer would fail to aspire to the position of selection secretary, which carries both prestige and power. Since this system has been practiced for a long time, there are bound to be grounds for argument in the selection process, either in the order in which candidates are listed or in the approving or rejecting of the recommendations.

During the reign of King Sŏnjo, Kim Hyo-wŏn enjoyed a high reputation and was recommended to the post of selection secretary. At that time Sim Ŭi-gyŏm, who was in the third highest rank in the Ministry of Personnel and a relative of the queen,[209] did not endorse the recommendation and thus Kim Hyo-wŏn could not become a selection secretary. Coming from a reputable family, Kim Hyo-wŏn was well known not only for his high scholarship and meritorious conduct, but also for his penchant for recommending the wise and conceding to the capable. He appealed, therefore, to the hearts of young scholars. The scholars rallied and challenged Sim Ŭi-gyŏm for abusing his power in obstructing the appointment of the wise. Although he was related to the queen, Sim Ŭi-gyŏm had earlier played a part in the purging of powerful yet deceitful officials and for protecting the scholar-gentry. The elders and high-ranking government officials came to support him. In this way the difference between senior and junior officials developed from trivial issues into a serious division.

During the years of *kyemi* (1583) and *kapsin* (1584), the names Easterners (Tongin) and Westerners (Sŏin) emerged. Because the house of Kim Hyo-wŏn was situated in the eastern part of Seoul, he and his followers were called Easterners; and because the residence of Sim Ŭi-gyŏm was situated in the western part, he and his followers were called Westerners. The Easterners were headed by Kim Hyo-wŏn, Yu Sŏng-nyong, Kim U-ong, Yi San-hae, Chŏng Chi-yon, Chŏng Yu-gil, Hŏ Pong, Yi Pal, and others, while the Westerners were headed by Sim Ŭi-gyŏm, Pak Sun, Chŏng Ch'ŏl, Yun Tu-su, Yun Kŭn-su, Ku Sa-maeng, and others. This was the beginning of factionalism in Korea.

Earlier, on his deathbed, Chancellor Yi Chun-gyŏng left a message, saying, "In the future, factionalism will spread among the court officials." In a memorial to the king, Special Adviser Yi I rejected this, saying, "He said it to sow discord between the king and officials." He rebuked Yi Chun-gyŏng, saying, "The dying man said wicked things." Later, when Yi I realized that his statements had been proven wrong, he tried hard to harmonize the two factions.

The purges of scholars were often caused by the queens' families [who came to exercise power and pursue their own agendas through the queen], who were unpopular among the scholars. As Sim Ŭi-gyŏm was the queen's relative, he became the main target for the hatred of a huge scholar faction. Even though Queen Insun had passed away and a distant kinsman of the royal family had succeeded to the throne and Sim Ŭi-gyŏm was no longer related to the palace, the Easterners nevertheless vehemently attacked him and denounced anyone who helped him. The junior scholars, in their keen pursuit of a good reputation, also swelled the ranks of the Easterners.

Yi I had originally tried hard to mediate between the factions. Aware of the heated debate among the scholars when he became inspector general, he impeached Sim Ŭi-gyŏm, thus showing that Yi I had never been a Westerner. When he was minister of military affairs, [Yi I] once went to the residence of Hong Chŏk of the Office of Special Advisers. On reading a poem by Hong Chŏk containing the lines "Flower petals cascade high and low / Not dropping all at once." He praised the poem as comparable to a good Tang poem. Hong Chŏk said to Yi I and the many prominent people gathered there, "The reason we are gathered here is to discuss how to impeach you." Yi I replied, "Since this is a public discussion, I won't stay." He then got up and left.

When Hŏ Pong presented the king with the memorial impeaching Yi I, the king grew angry and banished him. When Censor General Song Ŭng-gae impeached Yi I, the king also banished [Song Ŭng-gae]. The general royal transmitter, Pak Kŭn-wŏn, led his fellow officials to protest on their knees to the king and the king banished [Pak] as well. This was called the "three banishments." But what Hŏ Pong argued in his impeachment was full of nonsense and of no substance. Many people among those who supported Sim Sim Ŭi-gyŏm now supported Yi I and the number of Westerners increased. Yi I had a good reputation as a Confucian scholar and did not identify himself as a Westerner. It was unfortunate that he was involved in the "three banishments" because it changed the whole political situation at the court beyond recovery and he could not escape being responsible for this event. Before long Yi I passed away.

In the year of *kich'uk* (1589) Chŏng Yŏ-rip was purged and imprisoned. The king ordered Commissioner Chŏng Ch'ŏl to administer the purge. During Chŏng Ch'ol's administration Easterners who were acutely critical were either put to death or banished. The court became virtually empty. From the year of *kich'uk* (1589) to *sinyu* (1591) trials and imprisonments continued and spread far and wide. Yi San-hae was at that time chancellor and Chŏng Ch'ŏl was first deputy chancellor. Fearing that Chŏng Ch'ŏl might topple him under the pretext of the imprisonment mentioned above, Yi San-hae spread rumors [about Chŏng Ch'ŏl]. One day when Chŏng Ch'ŏl was presiding over a trial at court, the king sent a message ordering that Chŏng Ch'ol be divested of his office and expelled. At that time the offices of the inspector general and the censor general jointly issued a statement denouncing Chŏng Ch'ŏl and he was banished to faraway Kanggye. Both offices wanted him to be given further punishment but Yi San-hae prevented them. After Chŏng Ch'ŏl was banished, Yi San-hae recalled the Easterners banished by Chŏng Ch'ŏl and appointed them to the court; he expelled the Westerners who had been following Chŏng Ch'ŏl. This was the changeover in the political balance during the year of *sinmyo* (1591). From then on the Easterners dominated.

During the year of *imjin* (1592) King Sŏnjo evacuated the capital because of the Hideyoshi invasion and temporarily stayed at the city of Kaesŏng. At that time a member of the royal family petitioned the king to punish Kim Kong-nyang for disrupting the normal procedures of government in collusion with certain members of the court. The petitioner also accused Yi San-hae of misgoverning the country and asked that he be banished. In response, the king banished Yi San-hae to P'yŏnghae. When the king went up to Nammunnu he received a petition to bring Chŏng Ch'ŏl back. The king pardoned Chŏng Ch'ŏl and let him return to the king's temporary headquarters. When the king came to Ŭiju, he composed a poem and passed it to the royal secretariat. It read,

> I weep seeing the moon o'er the mountain pass.
> My heart aches as the wind from Amnok River blows across.
> Will the court officials from now on
> Still be bickering over Westerners or Easterners?

After the king returned to the palace, the Japanese army refused to pull out of the South Sea. The court was busy defending the country from the Japanese army and accommodating the Ming generals. The Easterners and the Westerners worked together in the court and did not have time for infighting.

In the year of *musul* (1598), when Toyotomi Hideyoshi died, the Japanese army retreated. By that time Yi San-hae had been pardoned, had returned to the capital, and was reappointed to the chancellery. Yi Kyŏng-jŏn, the son of Yi San-hae, had already passed the civil service examinations. Recognized for his literary talent as well as for being the son of a high government official, Yi Kyŏng-jŏn was eligible for nomination by the selection secretaries as a candidate for the position of special adviser. The old tradition at the court was that when a special adviser was to be selected, the selection secretaries would nominate suitable candidates and then [before choosing the special advisers] select the best candidates as their own successors; this [custom] is called the Record of Special Adviser in the Personnel Office.

Chŏng Kyŏng-se, a man from the Yŏngnam region, was a selection secretary at that time. He wanted to block Yi Kyŏng-jŏn from selection. He declared that from the time that Yi Kyŏng-jŏn was a young Confucian student he had been in the habit of slandering people, so it was not appropriate to appoint him as a selection secretary. Yi San-hae and his followers were infuriated. Yi Tŏk-hyŏng, who was a minister, invited Yi Chun to his house and told him, "Please tell Kyŏng'im [Chŏng Kyŏng-se's pseudonym] that if he blocks Yi Kyŏng-jŏn from nomination for selection secretary, there will inevitably be big trouble. This is certainly not the way to pacify the court. I am not saying this for personal reasons." Yi Tŏk-hyŏng did this because Yi Chun was from the same hometown as Chŏng Kyong-se and Yi Kyŏng-jŏn was his own brother-in-law. Chŏng Kyŏng-se, however, did not listen.

Later on, when Nam I-gong became a censorial official, he brought [an act of] severe impeachment against Chancellor Yu Sŏng-nyong. Chŏng Kyŏng-se had been a pupil of Yu Sŏng-nyong. Yi San-hae had Nam I-gong impeach Yu Sŏng-nyong, suspecting that he might have instigated Chŏng Kyŏng-se's actions, but Yu Sŏng-nyong was not in fact involved. Those who supported Yu Sŏng-nyong were Yi Wŏn-ik, Yi Tŏk-hyŏng, Yi Su-gwang, Yun Sŭng-hun, and Han Chun-gyŏm; they were called Southerners (Namin) because Yu Sŏng-nyong was from the southern region. Those who supported Yi San-hae were Yu Yŏng-gyŏng, Ki Cha-hŏn, Pak Sŭng-jong, Yu Mong-in, Pak Hong-gu, Hong Yŏn, Im Kung-no, and Yi I-ch'ŏm; they were called the Northerners because the residence of Yi San-hae was in the capital. Although the Easterners were [further] divided into Southerners and Northerners, there were few Southerners among them.

The Northerners held power for ten years, from the last year of King Sŏnjo (1608). When Prince Kwanghae ascended to the throne both the Westerners and the Southerners lost their power. Before long the Northerners split into the Major North and the Minor North factions. Those who advocated the abdication of the queen[210] became the Major North and those who opposed the abdication became the Minor North. The Major North was led by Yi I-ch'ŏm and included Hŏ Kyun, Han Ch'an-nam, Yi Song, and Pak Tae-hyŏng. The Minor North was headed by Nam I-gong and included high-ranking officials such as Ki Cha-hŏn, Pak Sŭng-jong, Yu Hŭi-bun, and Kim Sin-guk. Even though these members of the Minor North were higher in rank than Nam I-gong, they assisted him by opposing the abdication of the queen.

Yi Kyŏng-jŏn was on good terms with Yi I-ch'ŏm in the beginning. Noticing later that many people hated Yi I-ch'ŏm, he realized he was flirting with disaster by his association with Yi I-ch'ŏm. In the year of *kyech'uk* (1613) he had his son Pu, a literary licentiate,[211] petition the king to sentence Yi I-ch'ŏm to death. One day while Yi I-ch'ŏm and Yi Kyŏng-jŏn were playing a game of *go,* a daily report from the royal secretariat arrived with the news of Yi Pu's petition for the punishment of Yi I-ch'ŏm. Astonished, Yi I-ch'ŏm exclaimed, "Your son wants to kill me." Yi Kyŏng-jŏn asked, "How can it be? This must be another person with the same name." Believing Yi Kyŏng-jŏn, Yi I-ch'ŏm finished the game and got up and left. Later, on discovering that he had been deceived, Yi I-ch'ŏm severed his friendship with Yi Kyŏng-jŏn. Yi Kyŏng-jŏn finally joined the Minor North faction.

In the year of *kyehae* (1623), King Injo took over the throne with the help of Westerners, including Kim Ryu, Yi Kwi, Hong Sŏ-bong, Chang Yu, Ch'oe Myŏng-gil, Yi Sŏ, and Ku In-hu, and killed many of the Major Northerners. The Westerners took power and appointed both the Southerners and the Minor North faction to important positions. The Minor North did not become very strong—some became Southerners and others became Westerners—until the number of those who still called themselves the Minor North became so small that they have been insignificant ever since.

Among the officials who helped the king take over the throne many were impudent and proud. Because of this, King Injo wanted to suppress the strong and support the weak. Whenever the offices of the inspector general and the censor general, which were of southern origin, attacked the Westerners, without fail the king sided with the Southerners. Thinking it impossible to change the will of the king and afraid of losing his power, Kim Ryu secretly told his people, "You may appoint Southerners as deputy minister of personnel or below. But do not appoint them to the Ministry of Personnel or the State Council." Southerners therefore held offices together with Westerners among the lower level of officials,[212] from special advisers and officials of royal decrees, and selection secretary to vice deputy and deputy minister of personnel. When a Southerner reached vice ministerial rank, promotion to the first-grade ranking was not granted. Even if it had been granted, a Southerner could not have become minister of personnel. During the chaos of the Manchu invasion Yi Sŏng-gu acquired the position of deputy chancellor, the highest position [among the Southerners].

In the early years of King Hyojong, Song Si-yŏl and Song Chun-gil were favored with special appointments in order to eliminate Kim Cha-jŏm. After Kim Cha-jŏm was killed, both were promoted to the position of minister. In the last year of King Hyŏnjong, the Southerners Hŏ Mok, Yun Hyu, and Yun Sŏn-do accused the two Songs of making mistakes in a national ceremony in the year of *kihae* (1659). King Hyŏnjong agreed with the accuser and had the practice corrected. At that time the Southerner Hŏ Chŏk was chancellor and was asked by the king to look after the country after his death.

In the first year of [the reign of] King Sukchong [who succeeded King Hyŏnjong], Hŏ Chŏk was administering the country. Earlier Kim U-myŏng, the father of the queen, had adopted the *sudo* (隧道) system[213] for the burial of his father, which Song Si-yŏl severely criticized. Kim

U-myŏng, in turn, attacked the two Songs for allowing Min Sin to be chief mourner in place of his father at his grandfather's funeral rite. Therefore, Kim U-myŏng and the two Songs became estranged. At that time Kim U-myŏng's nephew Kim Sŏk-chu, together with Hŏ Chŏk, appointed some Southerners to government office and accused Song Si-yŏl of malpractice at a national ceremony, sending him into exile. This is how the feud between the Westerners and Southerners started. Kim Sŏk-chu was promoted from special adviser to minister of military affairs within a year.

In the year of *kyŏngsin* (1680), Hŏ Kyŏn, Hŏ Chŏk's illegitimate son, who had always been impudent and proud, passed the civil service examinations. Resentful at not being promoted to a higher rank[214] and overly ambitious, he started associating with the brothers of Chŏng and Nam of the royal family and gradually drifted away from Kim Sŏk-chu. Suspicious of Hŏ Kyŏn's behavior, Kim Sŏk-chu had his man Chŏng Wŏn-no spy on him. Chŏng Wŏn-no discovered that Hŏ Kyŏn was plotting treason with Chŏng and Nam.

At that time, the king had bestowed on Hŏ Chŏk a special cushion and walking stick and was to be a feast with wine and music. He ordered all the officials to attend the banquet as a sign of respect. Instead of attending the banquet, Kim Sŏk-chu visited the king at his palace and told him what Chŏng Wŏn-no had discovered. The king immediately ordered the establishment of a special court and the arrest of Ho Kyŏn, who was made to confront Chŏng Wŏn-no at the special court. Hŏ Kyŏn pleaded guilty and was executed by dismemberment. The purge escalated and Chŏng, Nam, Hŏ Chŏk, Yun Hyu, and O Chŏng-ch'ang were all killed. It also adversely affected Yun Hyŏg-yŏn, Yi Wŏn-jŏng, Cho Sŏng, and Yi Tŏk-chu, who were all ministers. Thus, the [power of the] Southerners receded and the Westerners gained power.

In the year of *imsul* (1682), Hŏ Sae was put to death. This event stirred public sentiment. Conflicting public opinion led to the division of Westerners into the Old Doctrine and the Young Doctrine factions. The Old Doctrine Faction was headed by Kim Sŏk-chu and Kim Man-gi and aided by Song Si-yŏl, Kim Su-hang, Min Yu-jung, and Min Chŏng-jung. The Young Doctrine Faction was headed by Cho Chi-gyŏm and supported by Han T'ae-dong, O To-il, Nam Ku-man, Yun Chi-wan, Pak T'ae-bo, and Ch'oe Sŏk-chŏng. They were divided because the Old Doctrine Faction wanted to kill the Southerners and the Young Doctrine Faction opposed the Old Doctrine.

A decade after the year of *kyŏngsin*, the Southerners Min Am and Min Chong-do gained power and, except for Chŏng and Nam, exonerated all those who had died at the time of the *kyŏngsin* literati purge (1680). They also killed Song Si-yŏl, Kim Su-hang, Yi Sa-myŏng, and Kim Ik-hun. Six years later the Southerners regained power and killed Min Am and Yi Ŭi-jing. From then on and for decades both factions ruled the country and carried on their disputes. In the last years of King Sukchong, members of the Old Doctrine Faction were appointed and members of the Young Doctrine Faction were rejected.

In the year of *sinch'uk* (1721) during the reign of King Kyŏngjong, Cho T'ae-gu and Ch'oe Sŏk-hang came to power and banished the Old Doctrinarians. In the year of *imin* (1722), they imprisoned and killed chancellors of the Old Doctrine Faction, Yi I-myŏng, Kim Ch'ang-jip, Yi Kŏn-myŏng, and Cho T'ae-ch'ae.[215]

At the beginning of the reign of the present king [Yŏngjo], Old Doctrinarians were reappointed and all Young Doctrinarians were rejected. In the year of *chŏngmi* (1727), Young Doctrinarians were favored for government posts. In the year of *musin* (1728), there was an upheaval and Kim Il-gyŏng and then Pak P'il-mong were killed for treason. Yi Sa-sang, Yi Chin-yu, Yun Sŏng-si, So Chong-ha, and Yi Myŏng-ŭi were killed for their association with them.

At the time, Cho Mun-myŏng, a Young Doctrines chancellor, and Hong Ch'i-jung, an Old Doctrines chancellor, advocated the Policy of Impartiality. People from the Old and Young Doctrines, Southerners and Northerners factions were appointed together. In the year of *kyŏngsin* (1740), during the present king's reign, the officials who gave lectures to the king told him that factional divisions began with the position of the selection secretaries and advised the abolition of its power so as to eliminate factional strife. Acknowledging the point, the king granted the request and ordered that the selection secretaries' right to recommend their own successors and the rules about the recommendation of officials to the Three Remonstrative Offices be abolished. In this way the status of selection secretaries was reduced to the same level as that of officials of the senior fifth and senior sixth ranks of other ministries. The system that had lasted three hundred years thus came to an end.

During the reign of King Sŏnjo, which was the mid-era[216] of the present dynasty, there were many talented men. All ambitious young officials tried very hard to cultivate their reputation so as to gain nomination as a selection secretary. One official, in the presence of peers, asked a child servant to give more beans to his horse, and another official, again among a gathering of colleagues, raised his hands to chase away the birds sitting on the rice sheaves spread out in the courtyard. All the celebrities present despised them, and they were not recommended to the Ministry of Personnel. Any responsible or open-minded person could have acted the way these two people did, and [the rejection of their nomination] had nothing to do with their character or integrity. That they were nevertheless rejected by their fellow officials is laughable, but even so, [one can appreciate] the strictness applied in selecting people and the way scholars tried to exercise self-control to behave properly at the time. These are the means and devices whereby the present dynasty encouraged people to esteem untainted reputations and good government officials.

During the reign of King Injo there was another political purge related to the Ministry of Personnel, the result of which was a petition in favor of a reduction of the ministry's power. When the king inquired of the ministers whether or not to grant the petition, they replied that the long-established practice of the present dynasty should not be changed too quickly. The ministers on the whole knew it was the present dynasty that gave the Ministry of Personnel the important role of preventing ministers' misconduct, and therefore, in order to avoid suspicion, they did not want to take upon themselves the responsibility of abolishing this role. As the old rule was abolished, the newly appointed officials found that they were not responsible to anyone. Everybody behaved in an arbitrary fashion and sought promotion without following procedure. They no longer esteemed a sense of honor and sought only personal advantage. They preferred provincial posts to posts at court, desiring to become governors or country magistrates. They did not value dignity or loyalty, and so they did not reflect on or feel ashamed of their conduct. As the Policy of Impartiality had been in force for some time, members of all four factions received appointments. Because few government posts were vacant and applicants numerous, competition became severe. Furthermore, with the removal of the rights of the selection secretaries, people aspired to rise quickly to high posts with the result that the usual conduct of the court officials declined irremediably and the ministers came to hold all the power that used to belong to the court.

Because members of all four factions resided in Seoul, different customs developed in the city. Apart from the three northern provinces, members of the four factions lived scattered in the five southeastern provinces. Only the people of Kyŏngsang Province respected the teachings of Yi Hwang (T'oegye) of Yean County. Yu Sŏng-nyong was a student of Yi Hwang, and the term Southerner actually started with Yu Sŏng-nyong. All the scholars of the province were Southerners and shared the same [political and social] views. In other provinces, however, members of the four factions lived side by side. After his retirement, Kim Chang-saeng, a former student of Yi I (Yulgok), resided in Yŏnsan County and taught students. Song Si-yŏl and Song Chun-gil from Hoedŏk County and Yun

Sŏn-gŏ and his brother from the town of Isan all came to Yŏnsan County and studied under Kim Chang-saeng. Yun Chung, son of Yun Sŏn-gŏ, became Song Si-yŏl's student, although they later became estranged. After the year of *kyŏngsin* (1680), Song Si-yŏl joined the Old Doctrine Faction and Yun Chung became a member of the Young Doctrine Faction. As they drifted apart, students from Hoedŏk County and the town of Isan came to be at odds with each other as if they were water and fire.[217] The area of Yŏnsan and Hoedŏk is inhabited by the descendants of students from the Kim and Song families. Only the town of Isan follows the Young Doctrine because of the three Yuns [who were from Isan].

Many houses and pavilions facing the rivers in Kangwŏn and Kyŏnggi Provinces used to belong to the Southerners. Few people in Chŏlla Province have held high-ranking government offices since the mid-era of the present dynasty. Few prominent people have been raised there and the scholar-gentry are grouped according to their relatives and friends who lived in Seoul. There were in old times many Southerners and Northerners, but nowadays there are more Old and Young Doctrinarians. There are only ten or so renowned clans in this province, although there are many wealthy families. That is because, apart from Ki Tae-sŭng and Yi Hang, there are no teachers or elders capable of guiding and disciplining young scholars. The sentiment of this province is rather volatile and cannot compare with better provinces.

Wherever the scholar-gentry live public morality declines. To foster their own factions they draw in vagrants, and to increase their power they exploit the powerless peasants. While they cannot keep their own behavior under control, they resent those who criticize them. They like to dominate an entire area. If they fail to do so, they argue and scheme against one another even if they are neighbors on the same street or in the same village or locale. From the years of *sinch'uk* (1721) and *imin* (1722), the feud between the three factions of the Old and Young Doctrines and the Southerners deepened with each passing day. They accused one another of treason and this [acrimony] reached into the countryside, transforming it into a factional battlefield. People from different factions do not intermarry and do not tolerate one another in various respects. If someone from one faction gets on well with someone from another, he is branded as disloyal or capitulating to the other faction. Once a vagrant or a slave is known to have associated with a certain family, he is not allowed to serve other families. One's wisdom and integrity as a scholar are acknowledged only within one's own faction and not by other factions. Once a person is criticized by another faction, his own faction comes to value him all the more. He may have committed the world's gravest crime, but once he is attacked by another faction all the members of his faction get together to support him without regard to the right and wrong of the case. If a man of good deeds and virtue does not belong to one's own faction, one's first concern is to scrutinize him for faults.

The factions, which started off small, have grown after two hundred years to be indestructible parties, as the descendants of each faction adhere to their ancestors' views. Because the Old and Young Doctrinarians have been separated from the Westerners for only forty years or so, brothers, uncles, or nephews can belong to either of the two factions. Once such relatives join opposing factions, their relationship is like that of the ancient Chinese states of Chu (?–233 BCE) and Yue (?–306 BCE). Although they share their ideas and discuss things within the same faction, they will not speak to members of the same family who belonged to other factions. Hence, genuine human relationships do not seem to exist anymore.

In recent years, as members of all four factions are eligible for promotion, they are interested only in a position at court. They discard as mere pedantry the sense of justice and propriety that has been observed over the years. Right and wrong, patriotism and treason, king and country, all are dismissed as things of the past. Although the incidence of fierce, bloody infighting has decreased, the new vices of inertia, degeneracy, spinelessness, and glibness have been added to the old habits. Even if members of all factions are divided in their hearts, they speak with a pretense of consensus. When many people gather to discuss government affairs, they try to avoid issues by concealing their differences of opinion. If they find it difficult to answer questions, they dodge the situation with facetious jokes and smiles. It seems that when officials gather together, only loud laughter is heard. When it comes to the implementation of policies, many seek to benefit only themselves and few endeavor to serve the public and the nation. They do not take official life seriously and regard official buildings as taverns. Ministers are called capable and benevolent when they show mediocrity disguised as moderation. The Three Remonstrative Offices are highly respected when they keep silent and provincial officials regard integrity and frugality as sheer idiocy. If this continues, will not the present mad stampede soon end in a total disaster? Ever since the cosmos was created, in the myriad of countries there have been few cases of distortion and deprivation of human nature that can compare with the plague of factionalism of our present age. If it is not cured, what kind of world will this become? Small and far removed from China,[218] Korea has a million residents. What if all of these souls were to lose their humanity and have no hope of redemption? This worries and saddens me.

One can see from the preceding discussion that when one wants to settle in the countryside, the hospitality and friendliness of the neighborhood and natural conditions such as humidity and airiness are primary considerations. What one must find is a place where people of the same faction live. Only then can one get on well with the neighbors, enjoy conversation with them, and emulate them in one's studies. A better choice, though, is to find a place where scholar-gentry do not reside at all and one can keep to oneself without associating with others. Whatever one chooses to be—farmer, artisan, or merchant—one should find happiness in the occupation of one's choice. In this way there is no need to be concerned about what the neighbors may think or feel.

SCENERY

The following is a description of the natural scenery of our country.

Mount Paektu lies on the border of Jurchen and Chosŏn and acts as a royal parasol for the nation. At the peak of the mountain there is a large lake with a circumference of eighty *ri*. The western stream from the lake becomes the Amnok River, the stream to the east becomes the Tuman River, and the northern stream is the source of the Huntong River. To the south of the Tuman and Amnok Rivers lies Korea.

From Mount Paektu to Hamhŭng, the main mountain range runs down the middle of the northern part of the country. An eastern branch stretches toward the south of the Tuman River, while western branches stretch toward the south of the Amnok River. Because the ridge of the range tilts sharply toward the East Sea at Hamhŭng, the eastern branch is not quite one hundred *ri* in length while the western branches run seven to eight hundred *ri*. The main mountain range runs continuously south for several thousand *ri* to join Mount T'aebaek in Kyŏngsang Province.

Ch'ŏllyŏng, the main passage leading northward, is where Hamgyŏng Province borders on Kangwŏn Province. To the south, there are many mountains and passes: Ch'ujiryŏng, Mount Kŭmgang, Yŏnsuryŏng, Osaengnyŏng, Mount Sŏrak, Mount Han'gye, Mount Odae, Taegwallyŏng, and Paekpongnyŏng. After these there is Mount T'aebaek. All are rugged mountains with steep valleys, dangerous ridges, and peaks towering over steep valleys. Parts of the mountain ranges that are low and flat enough allow roads to connect with the eastern side of the T'aebaek Mountain Range are called passes; the rest are all called mountains.

The mountains throughout the whole of P'yŏngan Province, whether north or south of the Ch'ŏngch'ŏn River, are formed by the branch ranges that stretch northwest from Hamhŭng.[219] Those of Hwanghae Province and Kaesŏng City [of Kyŏnggi Province] are formed by a branch that runs west between the Kowŏn and Munch'ŏn Districts. Those of Ch'ŏrwŏn and Seoul are formed by the range that begins at Ch'ŏllyŏng in the Anbyŏn area. All the mountains in Kangwŏn Province extend from the west of the T'aebaek Mountain Range. They are confined to the west of Yongjin District, and they make up the shortest mountain range in the country. Beyond this area, there are no big mountains.

From Mount T'aebaek the mountain range divides in two, forming the left and right ridges. The left one follows the coastline of the East Sea, while the right one continues south from Mount Sobaek but is not at all comparable to the grandeur of the T'aebaek Mountain Range. Even though there are many mountains, as described above, some ranges continue and others discontinue. There are four big and seven small mountain passes where the ranges disconnect. Chungnyŏng below Mount Sobaek is the main pass and below that are the [two] small passes named Ch'ŏnju and Hwawŏn. Choryŏng, which lies below Mount Chuhol, is the mountain's main pass and below that are the smaller passes of Yangsan and Yulch'i. Hwaryŏng and Ch'up'ungnyŏng below Mount Songni and Mup'ungnyŏng to the south of Hwangak are all small mountain passes. Yuksipch'i and P'allyangch'i to the south of Mount Tŏgyu are wide passes; beyond this point lies Mount Chiri.

The small mountain passes, which join the northern region to the south, are on mountain ranges that run through flat land. In this area Mount Songni and Mount Tŏgyu divide into many branches of ranges. The mountain range that runs out from the south of Mount Songni undulates down to the southern and northern plain of the Kiho region.[220] The vital energy of Mount Tŏgyu flowing to the west created Mount Mai and Mount Ch'ut'ak and to the south created Mount Chiri. Two mountain ranges of Mount Mai to the northwest terminate Chinjam and Man'gyŏng Counties. The longer branch divides into three sub-branches at the mountain pass of Noryŏng. The northern two extend toward the districts of Puan and Muan and then disburse to form many islands in the West Sea. The longest [of the three branches] stretches from west to east and forms Mount Ch'uwŏl in Tanyang and Mount Mudŭng in Kwangju.

The mountain ranges of Mount Mudŭng and Mount Ch'uwŏl zigzag and extend again to the west and make up Mount Wŏlch'ul in Yŏngam County. From Mount Wŏlch'ul the range again runs to the east but terminates at Mount Paegun in Kwangyang County. The curvilinear shape of the mountain ranges is like the Chinese character chi (之). One branch of Mount Wŏlch'ul runs separately to the south past Kwanduri in Haenam County to form islands in the South Sea. One thousand ri across the sea this branch extends to form Mount Halla of Chejudo. Some say that

Mount Halla extends toward the Ryukyu Islands [now known as Okinawa] over the sea. This cannot be confirmed, but it is certain that the Ryukyus are very close to us.

During King Injo's reign, Japan invaded the Ryukyu Islands and kidnapped the king of Ryukyu. The crown prince loaded a ship with treasures from his country and left to pay the ransom for his father. But the ship drifted and reached Chejudo. When the county magistrate there asked him what the treasures in the ship were, the crown prince replied that they were *chuch'ŏnsŏk* and *mansanjang*. *Chuch'ŏnsŏk* was a many-sided hollowed-out piece of rock. When water was poured into it, the water would change into fine wine. *Mansanjang* was a tent woven from spider webs and dyed with herbs. If it was opened out a little it would cover one room, but if opened out fully it could cover a mountain. Not a single drop of rain could leak through it. Rare indeed are these two treasures. When the county magistrate demanded them, the prince refused to hand them over, whereupon the magistrate sent soldiers to arrest him. Seeing them approaching, the prince threw the rock into the sea. The county magistrate confiscated all the goods on the ship and planned to put [the prince] to death. Before his execution, the crown prince asked for some paper and a brush and wrote a poem.

> The words of Emperor Yao fall on the deaf ears of this King Jie.[221]
> Faced with immediate punishment, how can I have time to appeal to
>   heaven?
> The three good officers[222] are about to be interred, who will pay the
>   ransom?
> To the two royal princes[223] on the boat the brigand shows no
>   benevolence.
> When the bones are thrown on the sandy beach, weeds will grow
>   over them.
> Even if the soul returns home there will be no relatives to mourn.
> Running ceaselessly under the Ch'uksŏru, the water will carry this
>   grief for ten thousand years.

After putting [the prince] to death the county magistrate reported him to the court as a foreign invader who was trespassing. The incident was later exposed and [the magistrate] barely escaped a death sentence himself.

As for the water channels of the country, all of those on the [eastern] side of the backbone range [i.e., T'aebaek] from as far north as Hamhŭng to Tongnae in the south flow east and empty into the sea. All the rivers of Kyŏngsang Province and the Sŏmjin River flow southward and enter the sea. On the western side of the mountain range from as far north as Ŭiju to Naju in the south, all the water channels flow westward to pour into the sea. The long channels form rivers and the short ones become ports or inland waterways. This is a sketchy outline of the mountains and rivers of our country.

Since ancient times, there has been a saying that Korea is shaped like an old person sitting with his head to the north-northeast and his feet toward the south-southeast and that the western side is open toward China, forming the shape of a person bowing to China. Therefore, from olden days Korea has been on friendly terms with China.[224] It has also been said that because there is neither a river stretching one thousand *ri* nor a plain wider than one hundred *ri,* Korea cannot produce great men. Barbarians from the west, north, and east as well as the Jurchen entered China and in turn became emperors, but Korea alone maintained its boundaries and never dreamed of doing this.[225] Korea is situated far away from China with a sea in between. When Kija did not want to serve the Zhou regime he came to Korea and became king. It is therefore recognized as a country of loyal people. This [loyal] spirit has continued to the present dynasty. Although we have surrendered to Qing invaders, we kept our friendship with [Ming] China by not forgetting its assistance when we Koreans were under attack during the Hideyoshi invasion.

Upon the sixtieth anniversary of the fall of the Ming dynasty in the third month of the *kapsin* year (1704), during King Sukchong's reign, the Altar of Great Gratitude was erected in the west of the rear garden of the [Ch'angdŏk] palace. A special sacrificial ritual was performed with extensive offerings for the Wanli Emperor of the Ming dynasty. It was ordered that the ceremony be performed once a year. It is good that in the year of *kyŏng'o* (1750) the present king (Yŏngjo, r. 1724–1776) ordered his people to offer a sacrificial ceremony to the Chongzhen Emperor[226] along with the other emperors. The memorial ceremony is always performed at night. Even though it begins with a clear sky and fine weather, suddenly cold harsh winds arise and thick clouds cover the sky during the ceremony. When the ceremony is completed, however, it becomes clear again. This phenomenon is extremely mysterious. I suggest that we keep the tablets of Shi Xing, Xing Jie, Yang Hao, and Li Rusong together with those of the two emperors because of their contribution during the Hideyoshi invasion.

A story goes that Hong Sun-ŏn, a young translator, went to Beijing and found a beautiful girl who would spend the night with him for several thousand *kŭm.* An old female go-between led the way to a big house, where he saw a young lady surrounded by many maidservants with lamps. When she saw Sun-ŏn, [the young lady] burst into tears. Asked the reason she was crying, she replied, "My father was from Sichuan and was appointed a local magistrate. Since both of my parents have died I have to sell myself to raise the money for a proper burial in Sichuan. I have twice vowed not to marry. After we have spent tonight together we will part forever, which is why I'm crying." Realizing that she was from a noble family, he was surprised and asked her to become his adopted sister. Weeping, she thankfully accepted the suggestion and gave him his money back. Sun-ŏn refused to take it and insisted that she keep it for the burial of her parents. Years later in the *imjin* year, Sun-ŏn accompanied a government envoy to the house of the minister of military affairs [of China], Shi Xing. There, in the inner quarters of the house, the minister introduced him to his wife. Sun-ŏn realized that she was none other than his adopted sister. Moved by the integrity of Sun-ŏn, Shi Xing did his utmost to help Korea during the Hideyoshi invasion. Because Shi Xing fell victim to court intrigue that arose from our country's war with Japan, we have all the more reason to make offerings at a sacrificial ceremony. Shi Xing's wife spent a great deal of her time weaving brocade, and on every roll she embroidered the two characters *po* and *ŭn*, which mean "repaying the benefactor." She gave the embroidered brocade rolls to Sun-ŏn and they were valued at several thousand *kŭm*.

In the year of *chŏngyu* (1579), King Sŏnjo ordered his subjects to erect a shrine for Xing Jie and Yang Hao within the capital to honor their achievements in defeating the Japanese troops at Sosa. Failure to include Li Rusong in the project was a grave mistake, however.

Mountains

I have not been to Chŏlla and P'yŏngan Provinces, but I have been many times to the provinces of Hamgyŏng, Kangwŏn, Hwanghae, Kyŏnggi, Ch'ungch'ŏng, and Kyŏngsang. The following is based on what I have seen and heard.

The twelve thousand peaks of Mount Kŭmgang (Diamond Mountain) are all just bare rock. There are caves in the rocks and streams and waterfalls passing over the rocks. Since peaks, valleys, springs, ponds, and waterfalls are made exclusively of white rocks, Mount Kŭmgang has from olden days had the nickname Mount Kyegol (All Bones). It is so named because there is not a single handful of soil. The peaks, as high as ten thousand men, are formed completely of rock. Even a lake one hundred fathoms deep can nestle in one of the huge rocks, making this mountain truly unique.

In the middle of the mountain range is Chŏngyangsa, and in its temple grounds, occupying the most important spot, is Hŏlsŏngnu. Sitting in this pavilion one can enjoy the grand view and spirit of the mountain. As if sheltered inside a jade cave, the atmosphere is so clear and refreshing that one cannot help feeling that one's stomach and intestines are cleansed of all dust and dirt. To the west of Chŏngyangsa are two other monasteries, Chang'ansa and P'yohunsa. Inside are many relics of the Yuan and Koryŏ dynasties as well as precious treasures donated by the royal palace. To the north of Chŏngyangsa in Manp'oktong are nine scenic waterfalls, and on the side of the valley are eight big Chinese characters by Yang Saŏn (1517–1584):[227] *pongnae p'ungak wŏnhwadongch'ŏn.*[228] The strokes of the characters seem to be flying and moving like live dragons or tigers; they look as if they are flying into the sky with their wings. In the Manp'oktong are the Mahayŏn temple and a cave, Podŏkkul, that look as if they are hanging high on the cliff. The magnificent, mysterious scenery seems to be divinely created, so that no one can comprehend how it came into being.

Chunghyangsŏng sits on the peak of the ten-thousand-men-high mountain. The ground is entirely covered with white rocks arranged on different tiers like beds and shelves. On top of these stands an upright rock, which looks like a statue of the Buddha without eyebrows or eyes. Small stone statues form two rows, left and right, on the rock bed; they too have neither eyebrows nor eyes. It is said that Tanwujie stayed here.[229] To one side of Chunghyangsŏng is a deep and precipitous valley; to gain access to it one must follow a narrow footpath from the northwest. All around are numerous white peaks, a blend of water, rocks, ponds, and valleys. It is exquisite beyond description.

Famous pavilions and small hermitages that dot the entire area look like the Buddha's palaces [located on] the seven golden mountain ranges[230] and the mountain of the man-bird.[231] [The place] does not seem to be part of the human world. Strong winds blow straight up the highest peak, called Pirobong, making it so cold that when one climbs up to the summit one needs to wear warm garments even in summer. To the northwest of the mountain is Yŏngwŏndong, which forms a separate realm. To the east is Naesuch'am Mountain Ridge. Over the ridge is Yujŏmsa. To the northeast of the monastery is the big waterfall of Kuryongdong (Nine Dragon Cave). As the water tumbles down from the highest peak it hollows out rocks, making nine big stone ponds at nine levels, each of which is said to be guarded by a dragon. Water falling from the cliff glistens brightly, and white rock cliffs incline too steeply and dangerously to stand on. It is fascinating and frightening at the same time.

Yujŏmsa has a great many relics. A monk once said that fifty-three Buddhist statues arrived there by sea from Ch'ŏnch'uk [India], and

Noch'un, the landowner, erected the temple to house them. Much of the monk's story, however, is absurd and unreliable. What we can accept is that in previous generations those who revered and esteemed the pagodas and shrines certainly arranged them most splendidly. To the west of Yujŏmsa is an area called the Inner Mountain and to the east lies the Outer Mountain; it is from here that water flows into the East Sea. Mysteriously, from ancient times there have been no snakes or tigers in these areas, allowing people to travel freely at night. It is not surprising that Mount Kŭmgang Range is the most famous in the country and so great that many [foreigners] have said, "I wish I had been born in Koryŏ [Korea]."

The Buddhist *Flower Garland Sūtra* (*Hwaŏmgyŏng*)[232] was composed during the latter part of the reign of King Zhao of the Zhou dynasty. At that time, India and the western region did not communicate with China, so [one wonders] how they could have known of a country east of China. When one considers that Mount Kŭmgang in the northeastern sea[233] is mentioned in a Buddhist scripture, however, one wonders whether the recording [there] is the result of the far-sightedness of the Buddha.

From here to the south are Mount Sŏrak and Mount Han'gye, which are also formed of rocks. They consist of high, steep cliffs and deep valleys. Densely wooded forests block out the sky and sunlight. On Mount Han'gye is a waterfall the height of ten thousand men. During the Hideyoshi invasion a Tang general saw this fall and said it was better than those of Lushan.[234] Further south is Mount Odae, which is covered with earth. It is surrounded by many rocks and deep valleys. On the highest level are five terraces with good views and a hermitage on each. In one of the hermitages are kept the *sarira* of the Buddha.[235] Here also, Han Mu-oe achieved Taoist enlightenment and became a supernatural being. That is why the mountain is regarded as one of the best places for the cultivation of Taoism. From ancient times this area has escaped destruction in war. Having established national archives at Wŏljŏngsa further down the mountain, the court has kept annals of the Korean kings, which are guarded by government officials. From here the range gradually flattens, becoming the pass of Taegwallyŏng, which connects Kangnŭng to the east. Below the pass is Kusandong, famous for its scenic beauty of springs and rocks.

Mount T'aebaek and Mount Sobaek are also earth mountains and the soil color is excellent. On Mount T'aebaek is the excellent scenic spot of Hwangji, and on top of the mountain is a plateau where settlers reside. They practice rotation cultivation by burning the fields that lie fallow. Since the location is high, it is cold and has an early frost, [which is why] only millet and barley are cultivated as staples. Over the lake of Hwangji and under the peak of Chagyakpong is a burial site into which public entry is forbidden. The royal family is said to have chosen the burial site but have not yet used it. On the plain below the mountain stand Kakhwasa and the hermitage of Hongjeam. Buddhist monks who have acquired a higher degree of buddhahood as well as eccentrics sometimes dwell there. Because the three disasters of war, famine, and plague have not visited since ancient times, the court has set up another archive here. On Mount Sobaek is Ukkŭmdong, from where springs, rocks, and beautiful scenery can be seen for several tens of *ri*. Further up on the mountain is Pirojŏn, an old temple dating from the time of Silla, and a lecture hall of Yi Hwang (T'oegye). The springs and boulders on Mount T'aebaek and Mount Sobaek are generally in low, flat areas of the valley. There are no rocks on the upper slopes of the mountains. Therefore, even though the view is majestic, it does not have an oppressive atmosphere. In the distance the peaks do not rise particularly high, and the undulating hills are rather like moving clouds or flowing water. The northern horizon is blocked from view and sometimes there are red and white clouds on it.

When the Taoist sage Nam Sa-go saw Mount Sobaek he got off his horse, bowed to the mountain and said, "This mountain will save the lives of many people." It is written that Mount T'aebaek and Mount Sobaek were ideal places for seeking refuge during war. From Mount Paektu to Mount T'aebaek, the mountain range is not divided but remains a single range. Below Mount Sobaek the mountain range subsides. Mount Songni is the first mountain to rise after the discontinuation of the range. Mount Songni is called by geomancers a stone-fire mountain. There are large boulders and the summits are sharp-edged peaks that look from a distance like lotus flowers starting to bloom, or an array of torch lights. Below the mountain a deep and wide valley is formed purely of rocks, and there is also a place known as Eight Foldings and Nine Turnings. The rocks of the mountain are splendid, and the water of the springs is pure, clear, and blue in color because it comes from the rocks. This forms the upper part of the Talch'ŏn of Ch'ungju (City). Around the whole mountain are so many wide and spectacular valleys, deep springs, and peculiar rocks that the exquisiteness and elegance of the scenery is second only to that of Mount Kŭmgang.

Hwanjŏktae to the south of Mount Songni is rocky and consists of thousands of peaks and valleys that are so steep and dangerous that people have the greatest difficulty finding a pathway [through them]. The waters from these valleys converge to make a small stream. This stream, called Pyŏngch'ŏn, flows across small fields to the south of Mount Ch'ŏnghwa and enters into a deep pit to the east. To the south of Pyŏngch'ŏn lies Mount Tojang. A branch of Mount Songni stretches out and joins Mount Ch'ŏnghwa. The area between the two mountains and the upper part of

Yongch'u is called Yongyudong. The flat area of the valley is made up of rock beds over which a big stream flows from west to north. Upon reaching steep base rocks, the stream breaks up into many small waterfalls. When the stream passes through a narrow notch in the rocks it becomes a brook. It forms a pond on broad rock bases and becomes a small well in a round pit. Upon encountering a flat rock, it looks like curtains made of strings of pearls, and circling the rock it looks like incense smoke curling up into the air. Some rocks have unusual shapes such as a manger, a tripod, a cauldron, a mortar, a garden rockery, a group of little islands, a goat, a tiger, a chicken, a dog. The water can flow round in a circle, stay still, crash down, or froth and churn. The rustling of the vegetation on both banks of the stream sounds like the autumn wind and the cool valley wind adds to this extraordinary scenery. In the middle of all this stands the pavilion of the Song family.

To the northeast of Mount Ch'ŏnghwa lies Mount Sŏnyu. A flat summit is formed on top of the mountain with very long and deep valleys below it. On the mountain is the pavilion of Ch'ilsŏngdae and a cave, Hosogul. In olden days Ch'oe To, [known as] the Enlightened, and Namgung Tu, the Taoist priest, practiced self-cultivation here. A text reads that those who want to practice self-cultivation can reside peacefully on this mountain. The water from this valley flows past the scenic spot of Nangp'ungwŏn and joins the water running in front of the Yangsansa. It then flows down to the east of Kaunch'ang and enters into the big stream, Mun'gyŏng. Over the ridge, to the west of Ch'ilsŏngdae, is Oesŏnyudong (Outer Sŏnyu Valley), and further down is P'agot. The valley is cosy and deep and a big brook runs through the rocks and off the steep hills, tumbling and winding many times. The exquisite scenery is beyond description. Although not as majestic as the Manp'oktong of Mount Kŭmgang, some say it is more delicate and intriguing. On the whole, no other scenery except Mount Kŭmgang can match this place, and naturally this is the best place in the three southern regions.[236]

Behind Mount Ch'ŏnghwa lie the valleys, Inner and Outer Sŏnyudong, and to the front is Yongyudong. The extraordinary scenery of both the front and back of the mountain excels that of Mount Songni. The mountain is not as towering as Mount Songni nor does it have the same dangerous features. The earthen peak surrounded by rocks is bright and does not appear harsh. The place can be regarded as auspicious because of its sedate and gentle appearance and its benevolent and magnificent atmosphere.

Hwayangdong lies below P'agot. Upon reaching this place, the stream from P'agot widens and the rocks have a more distinctive look. Imitating Zhuzi's building of a study at Mount Yungu, Song Si-yŏl (Ujae) built a house here.[237] Again imitating Zhuzi's restoration of the good cause [i.e., Confucianism], he offered the sacrificial ceremony to Emperor Shenzong of the Ming dynasty in the middle of the valley. Later he had a shrine built there and named it Mandong Shrine. Earlier on he had composed a poem.

> Loud is the blue water, as if angry.
> Quiet is the verdant mountain, as if frowning.

The mountain range extends to the south from Mount Songni and forms the passes of Hwaryŏng and Ch'up'ungnyŏng. Both areas provide quiet, peaceful seclusion. The land is mostly low and flat, which is good for rural settlement. One can hardly describe the whole area as mountainous.

Mount Tŏgyu is an earth mountain. On the upper part is Kuch'ŏndong, with deep springs and far-reaching rocks. Below the mountain lies Chŏksangsansŏng, which is surrounded by rock walls and has a flat top. The fortress was built by the court and historical records and chronicles were kept there. To the east of the mountain is Anŭm and Jirye. To the north is Sŏlch'ŏn and Mup'ung. Nam Sa-go referred to Mup'ung as being an auspicious place. Beyond the valley, the fields on the mountain slope are so fertile that there are many rich villages. Mount Songni and other mountains in the north do not have this advantage.

Mount Chiri is located close to the South Sea. Because it is the end of the mountain range that began at Mount Paektu, it is also known as Mount Turyu. Mount Kŭmgang is also known as Mount Pongnae, Mount Chiri as Mount Pangjang, and Mount Halla as Mount Yŏngju. These make up the so-called Mountains of the Three Gods. In a regional gazetteer, Mount Chiri is referred to as the place where the Taoist god T'aeŭl lives and where many supernatural beings gather. Its valley is deep and vast. The rich and deep-layered soil facilitates human habitation over the entire mountain. Within the mountain is a valley one hundred ri long that seems narrow [when viewed] from the outside but is actually broad. There are places in the valley that are not known to outsiders, so taxes are not collected there. Since it is close to the South Sea, the climate is mild and bamboos, persimmons, and chestnut trees are abundant. Fruit that is ripe drops by itself. Even the broomcorn millet and millet sown on the high mountain summit thrive. Because most of the fields on the flat area are arable, there are villages and Buddhist temples on the mountain. Monks and commoners cut bamboo and gather persimmons and chestnuts without much effort. They can support themselves comfortably. Farmers and artisans are also well-off without much toil. Since people on the mountain do not suffer from poor harvests it is called a rich mountain.

The valleys of Hwagaedong and Agyangdong are also inhabited, and the scenery is beautiful. During the middle of the Koryŏ dynasty Han Yu-han noticed the arrogant and violent behavior of Yi Cha-gyŏm and sensed an impending disaster. He gave up his office and hid himself along with his family in Agyangdong. Later the court searched for him and tried to recall him to a government post, yet Yu-han remained hidden. To this day nobody knows where he died, and some say that he became an immortal. To the west are the monasteries of Hwaamsa and Yŏn'goksa, and to the south are the monasteries of Sinŭisa and Ssang'gyesa. In Ssang'gyesa there is a portrait of Ch'oe Chi-wŏn (Koun) of the Silla dynasty. On the stone wall along the stream are large inscriptions in Koun's calligraphy. It is said that he attained enlightenment and even now roams Mount Kaya and Mount Chiri. In the year of *sinmyo* (1591), in the reign of King Sŏnjo, a Buddhist monk picked up a piece of paper from between two rocks. It read,

> The Flowering Vale in an Eastern land,
> Is an Immortal's abode in a vase.
> A push to my jade pillow
> And I awake to find that one thousand years have passed.[238]

The strokes of the Chinese characters looked newly written and the calligraphy seems to be that of Koun as known to the world.

Since olden days people have talked about the valleys of Mansudong and Ch'ŏnghaktong. Mansudong is now called Kup'umdae and Ch'ŏnghaktong is called Maegye; only recently have people been able to pass through these valleys. The land to the north of Mount Chiri belongs to Hamyang County and in it is situated Yŏngwŏndong, Kunjasa, and the village of Yujŏmch'on. The famous Nam Sa-go assessed this place as auspicious. The valleys of Pyŏksoundong and Ch'usŏngdong are scenic spots. The brooks in the narrow valleys to the north of Mount Chiri converge to form [the streams] Imch'ŏn and Yongyudam, and then reach Ŏmch'ŏn, which runs to the south of the country. The scenery of both the upper and lower streams is magnificent and extraordinary. This area is, however, remote and secluded. In the village many fugitives have settled and sometimes there are robberies. Shrines for various deities are scattered all over the mountain. Every spring and autumn, shamans from around the area gather here to chant. Sometimes men and women get together in the open air. Furthermore, the prevailing smell of wine and meat makes the place most unclean.

Large and small mountain ranges from Mount Chiri stretch to the southwest and gather at the upper stream of the Sŏmjin River. Most of the springs there are miasmic. A great disadvantage in this place is the absence of a clear and clean atmosphere on the mountain. Along the ridges of the whole of T'aebaek and Sobaek Mountain Ranges, these eight mountains are the best. As for mountains not situated in these ranges, there are none in the whole of Hamgyŏng Province worthy of fame because the mountains are too high and the valleys too barren. Only in the valley of Mount Ch'ilbo in Myŏngch'ŏn County close to the East Sea do the rocks appear to be sculpted by supernatural beings. Mount Myohyang of Yŏngbyŏn County in P'yŏngan Province is covered in earth, and the peaks have an earth-mountain shape. However, the lower part of the mountain is formed of rocks, which look beautiful and magnificent and are not ominous. There are many flat areas with big and broad streams running through them. On the inner side of the mountain these areas look rather like villages on a plain. The mountain branches embrace the valley row upon row and form the shape of a fortress-city. There is no access to the valley except through the southwestern outlet of the watercourse and people must enter there one at a time. There is a legend that says that on top of Mount T'aebaek is a rock cave where Tan'gun was transformed and born. Inside the mountain are three big temples and numerous small huts, and monks who practice deep meditation give lectures there.

There are no fire-type mountains to be found in the whole of Kyŏngsang Province. Only on Mount Kaya in Hapch'ŏn County do the tapering rock peaks line up like flames shooting up in the air, thus presenting a splendid sight. At the entrance to the village are Hongnyudong and the bridge of Murŭng'gyo. The splashing waterfall and the bed of rocks stretch several dozen *ri*. People say that Ch'oe Ko-un left his shoes here, but nobody knows where he went. His calligraphy in large characters is engraved on the wall; it is still as clear as it was when it was first written. His poem reads,

> The water races o'er the rocks, folds of mountain peaks echo
> the roar.
> It is even difficult to distinguish people's voices nearby.
> Lest the bickering noise of the world reach my ear,
> Let the water's echoes cover the whole mountain.

This is the very place to which the poem refers. During the Imjin War, Mount Kŭmgang, Mount Chiri, Mount Songni, and Mount Tŏgyu did not escape the intrusion of Japanese troops, but the invasion did not reach Mount Odae, Mount Sobaek, or this mountain. It is said that the three disasters of war, famine, and plague did not affect this place. On the mountain is Haeinsa. With regard to this monastery, there is a story about King Aejang of Silla, who came back to life after he had died and was prepared for burial. The king promised a guardian of the netherworld he would send an envoy to Tang China to bring home a copy of the Tripitaka. After he had [the wooden blocks] engraved, lacquered, and decorated with bronze and nickel, he had a pavilion of 120 *kan* built to store the Tripitaka on the shelves. The building is over one thousand years old now yet the blocks in it still look newly engraved. Birds are said to keep clear of the building and never rest on the roof tiles. This is extraordinary, especially when one considers that the same thing would not happen if Confucian scriptures instead of Buddhist ones were kept inside.

To the northwest of the temple is the summit of Mount Kaya, which appears to be too steep for people to climb. There may be a flat area up on the summit, but no one knows for certain. It is always cloudy on the top and firewood collectors and herdsmen often hear music coming from the peak. The monks of the temple say that on a foggy day they can hear the sound of horses trotting on the summit.

Along the Kaya River, outside the valley, the rice paddies are so fertile that usually 120 to 130 *mal* can be harvested from one *mal* [of seed]. At its worst, at least eighty *mal* can be produced. Since water is abundant, this area has not experienced drought. It is the best area for cultivating cotton and is known as "the hometown of ample food and clothing." To the northeast of the mountain lies the deep, long Mansudong. It is an auspicious place worth living in, away from all worldly troubles.

Mount Chŏngnyang of Andong County is on the side facing the Yean River. The mountain range from Mount T'aebaek becomes a plain and then rises up again to form this mountain. From the outside, the mountain looks like a couple of mounds of earth. When one crosses the river and enters the valley, however, one notices high rock cliffs all around that form an extraordinary scene beyond description. Inside lies Nangadae, where Ch'oe Ko-un played games of *go*. There is a rock shaped like a square *go* board and a statue of an old woman inside a rock cave. People say that she was the maid who prepared meals for him while he was living on the mountain. On the mountain is Yŏndaesa, where many Buddhist scriptures copied by Kim Saeng of the Silla dynasty are stored. In recent times a Confucian scholar who was reading in the monastery stole a volume of the scriptures. Upon arriving home, he became ill and died. Terrified, his family immediately returned it to the monastery.

These four mountains, together with the other eight great mountains, are the famous mountains of the country and make ideal places for retreat and meditation. There is an old saying that the famous mountains of the world are occupied mostly by monks. Since Buddhism and not Taoism is popular in Korea, all of these twelve famous mountains are occupied by Buddhist monasteries.

Apart from the monasteries mentioned above, Pusŏksa is famous for the miracles and extraordinary events that took place there. It was built during the Silla dynasty and is situated between Mount T'aebaek and Mount Sobaek. Behind the monastery is a big rock lying on its side. On top of the rock is a bigger rock covering it like a roof. At a glance, both rocks seem to be touching each other, but after careful examination, one will find that there is a space between them. One can easily pull a rope through the small crevice to find that the top one is a floating rock. Thus, from this intriguing phenomenon the monastery acquired the name Pusŏksa (Monastery of the Floating Rock). Outside the temple gate there is a pile of "live" sand. It has not eroded since ancient times but [instead] always seems to replenish itself. During the Silla period, a monk called Ŭisang attained enlightenment and intended to travel to India. He put a walking stick into the soil under the eaves of the door to the room where he used to live and said, "After I leave, this stick will grow branches and leaves. If this tree does not dry and die, you will know that I am not dead." After he left, monks at the temple moulded a statue of Ŭisang and kept it in his dwelling. The stick put forth branches and leaves at once. Standing outdoors, it reflects the light of the sun and moon but does not get wet with either rain or dew. It neither pierces through the roof nor outgrows a man's height; it has been alive for a thousand years. In the era of King Kwanghae, Governor Chŏng Cho of Kyŏngsang Province came to the monastery and saw the tree. He said he wanted to make a walking stick out of the tree that was originally used as a walking stick by the supernatural man. He had the plant sawn off and took it away. But the tree soon grew back as it was before. During the reign of King Injo, Chŏng Cho was executed for treachery. The tree is green through all the seasons and neither blossoms nor sheds its leaves. Monks at the monastery called it "the Tree of the Flying Immortal." T'oegye once composed a poem about the tree.

> As if carved out of jade, it stands beside the temple gate.
> From a walking stick, the monk says, was this tree transformed.
> With Chogye (曹溪) must this walking stick be connected,
> For it does not need heaven's blessing of dew and rain.

Behind the mountain lies Ch'wiwŏllu, a magnificent structure towering in the sky. Its majestic appearance seems to dominate the whole of Kyŏngsang Province. On the wall is a board inscribed with T'oegye's poem. When I went to Mount T'aebaek with the court official Yi In-bok in the autumn of the year of *kyemyo* (1723), I came up to this monastery and wrote a poem to rhyme with T'oegye's.

> From this towering pavilion's twelve handrails the grand view to
>   the southeast,
> A thousand *ri* away lies before one's eyes.
> On earth there exists this remote Silla
> Under heaven, one finds the deep Mount T'aebaek.
> Homing birds disappear into the twilight mist of the autumn valley.
> Scattered clouds over the sea reflect the sunset.
> On and on you may walk, still you cannot reach the temple above.
> And begin to understand the hardship of pilgrimage.

I also wrote another poem.

> Far and wide, Mount T'aebaek touches the sky,
> To the east of the sea towers the ancient temple.
> To these, rivers and mountains thousands of *ri* away pay tribute.
> The Buddhist shrine and pavilion soar high between heaven and
>   earth.
> The famous monk is gone, yet his tree is still in blossom.
> The ancient kingdom prospers and falls into decay; always the birds
>   fly by.
> Who would understand the wanderer from the land of the *Book of
>   Songs?*
> Endless are my thoughts on the floating clouds and the sunset.

Deep in the corner of the pavilion there is a room in which more than ten portraits of the most famous monks of this monastery, since the Silla dynasty, are hung. The portraits look ancient and dignified; their expressions are so serene and solemn that they seem to be facing the visitor in person. Above the pavilion the mountain range extends with many curves; somewhere below is a small hermitage where monks lecture on scriptures and practice meditation.

The Pusŏksa belongs to the district of Sunhŭng City in Kyŏngsang Province. Also in Kyŏngsang Province is T'ongdosa in Yangsan County and Tonghwasa in Taegu City. In Chŏlla Province is Togapsa in Yŏnggwang County, Ch'ŏnjusa in Haenam County, Taedunsa in Kosan County, Kŭmsansa in Kŭmgu County, Songgwangsa in Sunch'ŏn County, and

Nŭnggasa in Hamyang County. These are the greatest monasteries since the Silla dynasty.

In the early Tang dynasty the dharma master Chajang visited India and acquired the skull and *sarira* of the Buddha. He buried them behind T'ongdosa and erected a pagoda. Years later the pagoda started to lean. When Monk Sŏngnŭng dismantled it for renovation in the *ŭryu* year (1705) of King Sukchong, he found a note saying that this pagoda would be rebuilt by a person from another province by the name of Sŏngnŭng. In the silver chest was the skull, as big as a clay pot, wrapped in a silk cloth. The silk cloth was already over a thousand years old but had not decayed. In a small golden chest, the *sarira* was kept. It is dazzling to human eyes. The pagoda was rebuilt and a monument was erected. The words on the monument were composed by Ch'ae P'aeng-nyun (Haksa) and inscribed by my own father.

Monk Chinhong of the Silla dynasty threw his tin walking stick into the air and on the spot where it landed he built the Tonghwasa and lived in it. The huge monastery is surrounded by mountains and it has housed many famous monks and novices over the years. Monk Tosŏn of the Silla dynasty won fame at the Togapsa. Outside the valley he erected two boulders and wrote the three characters *hwangjangsaeng* on one and another three *kukchangsaeng* on the other. The meaning of the writing, however, is not clear.

Ch'ŏnjusa is located near the South Sea. It stands out like a mountain in the deep valley where it is situated. Pine, bamboo, tangerine, and pomelo trees grow in abundance. The magnitude of the monastery and the surrounding vegetation make it one of the great monasteries in the province. The mountain range to the back of Taedunsa extends from Mount Kyeryong, which is the lesser ancestral mountain. Behind the monastery is Paegunam. Having lost his mother in his youth during the Imjin War, Son Sun-mok, from Hamyŏl County, later arranged for a Buddhist prayer service in the hermitage. On the seventh day of prostrations he had a dream in which a disciple of the Buddha told him that his mother was on the facing mountain. Surprised, he got up and looked around to find an old lady sitting on a rock on the mountain. He hurried over and found out that she really was his mother. She said, "I was held in Japan as a war captive. One morning I was on my way to fetch water when a monk carried me on his back and brought me here. But I do not really know why it has happened." People were astonished and renamed the hermitage Tŭngmoam (Hermitage where a Missing Mother Returned).

The site of Kŭmsansa to the south of Mount Moak was originally a pit where a dragon once lived. It was too deep to be measured. During the Silla dynasty the founder monk filled the pit with ten thousand sacks of salt and drove the dragon away. He prepared the ground and built the main hall of the temple. Below the terrace, under the four corners of the temple building, brine seeps out and circles around. Due to its shining tall pavilion and the deep valley around it, Kŭmsan is a famous monastery in the Honam region. It is near the administrative center of Chŏnju City. This is where Kyŏn Sin-gŏm kept his father, Kyŏn Hwŏn, in custody, as mentioned in *The History of Koryŏ*.

Songgwangsa consists of numerous temple buildings, halls, pavilions, and hostels for monks. All were erected in a refined manner. The water and rocks in this secluded place are clear and clean. The mountain peaks gleam high above, and the scenery all around is harmonious and charming. In front of the bell tower is a water chamber, before which stands a tree. Long ago, on his deathbed, National Master Pojo said, "This tree will at first wither. If the branches and leaves come out again, however, you will know that I am reincarnated." One thousand years have passed since then, but the tree does not yet have any leaves. When one cuts the tree with a knife, however, it is still moist and alive inside. Had it really dried up it would have decayed and fallen. But since it has been standing straight until now, it certainly poses a mystery.

Nŭnggasa lies below Mount P'aryŏng. Long ago, a prince from Ryukyu drifted here. He prostrated himself in front of the monastery and prayed to the bodhisattva for a safe return home. After seven days and seven nights of prayer, a giant warrior appeared and, carrying the prince under his arm, strode over the sea. A monk drew a picture portraying this event and it remains on a wall of the temple.

Mountain Forms

Only if a mountain's peaks are formed of splendid-looking rocks does it look magnificent and have clear-water springs. If a mountain lies where rivers and the sea meet it has powerful energies. There are four such mountains in the country. One is Mount Ogwan in Kaesŏng City, another is Mount Samgak in Hanyang (Seoul), still another is Mount Kyeryong in Chinjam County, and the last one is Mount Kuwŏl in Munhwa County.

Monk Tosŏn said that Mount Ogwan consisted of a summit of the water-mountain type with a main body of the wood-mountain type (*sumo mokkan*). Its energy reaches far and lasts long. It then ends abruptly and forms Mount Songak, which geomancers call an earth-mountain reaching up to the sky. Mount Ogwan is grand and majestic and its spirit seems willing to embrace the whole area. The Majŏn River is to the east, the Husŏ River to the west, and Sŭngch'ŏnp'o Harbor in front. The two big islands of Kyodong and Kanghwa form a line that blocks the sea to the south and holds back the lower stream of the Han River to the north. They look like guards standing quietly outside the mountain. The whole area is so deep and wide that Tongwŏl said the landscape here is better formed than P'yŏngyang City. There are many valleys around Mount Ogwan. To the west are the Pagyŏn Falls and to the east, the pond of Hwadam. All the other springs and waterfalls are very beautiful too.

Mount Samgak of Hanyang City stands out splendidly in the blue sky; it can be seen one hundred *ri* away from the southeast. The area in front is flat and blocked by high mountains to the northwest. To the southeast it opens far out to make a naturally prosperous marketplace. Its only drawback is the lack of a wide and fertile plain. Together with Mount Tobong, Mount Samgak forms a beautiful landscape. The rocky summit is shaped like numerous flames rising in the sky. It has a special aura that is difficult to describe. This mountain, however, has no supporting mountains nor many valleys. In olden days there used to be Chunghŭngsa Valley, but it was flattened when Pukhansansŏng was built. Since Mount Paegak and Mount Inwang on the inside of the fortress look rather ominous, they are no match for Mount Songak, which is free of any malevolent energy. The only good point about them is that a branch called Mount Nam (南 山) stretches up the Han River to form a geomantically favorable area. Its outlet of water is low and gaping, and it faces Mount Kwanak. Though separated by the Han River, Mount Kwanak lies too close to the area. Although a fire-mountain type lies in front, geomancers regard it as inauspicious because it is situated directly to the south. Inside the surrounding hills, however, it is bright and serene. Since the soil color is clear and white it is all right to pick up and eat even food dropped on the road. The men of Hanyang City are bright and intelligent, but unfortunately they lack a manly spirit.

Mount Kyeryong is not as grand as Mount Ogwan nor as splendid as Mount Samgak. Nor is there an abundant watercourse in front of it. The Kŭm River alone flows around the mountain. When the oncoming mountain circles around and looks back upon the main mountain range, the landform generally has little energy in it. For example, Jinling [present-day Nanjing] is a place fit only for a marginal power. Although the founder of the Ming dynasty unified China and made Jinling the capital of the Ming empire, as time passed it was inevitable that the capital would have to be moved. Compared with Hanyang and Kaesŏng, the southern foot of Mount Kyeryong has much less energy, and the flat area inside the surrounding hills is small and not open to the southeast. The incoming mountain range stretches far and the valley area is deep and contains a tremendous amount of energy, however. To the northwest of this geomantic land formation is a deep and extensive dragon pond that overflows to form a big stream. The cities of Kaesŏng and Hanyang do not have a dragon pond. There are many scenic spots to the north and south of the mountain. To the east is Pongnimsa, and to the north are the extraordinary views around the monasteries of Kapsa and Tonghaksa.

Mount Kuwŏl also has the shape of an oncoming mountain turning around to look at the original mountain range. To the northwest it faces the sea and to the southeast it receives watercourses from P'yŏngyang City and Chaeryŏng Town that are influenced by the tide. Because of the profit from fishing and salt making, [the area] around the mountain enjoys advantages over the rest of Hwanghae Province. Five *ri* to the south are rich fields covering an area one hundred *ri* square. The natural protection provided by the landform and the richness of the fields make this area superior to Mount Kyeryong. The outline of this mountain is as rugged as Mount Ogwan or Mount Samgak. Throughout the mountain there are more than ten monasteries and on top of the mountain a fortress has been erected. A folktale says that the descendants of Tan'gun escaped from Kija and moved the capital from P'yŏngyang to this place, which is called Changjangp'yŏng. There is still a shrine to the three lords of the Tan family, and every spring and autumn the government sends incense for the sacrificial ceremony. The Tans lived on one part of the mountain rather than occupying all of this magnificent area, which will become a first-rate city one day.

Mount Ch'ŏngp'yŏng in Ch'unch'ŏn is another famous mountain. It was once the site of the capital of Yemaek. But it does not have powerful energy, since it is situated between two rivers and far away from the West Sea. A flattish valley area below Mount Moak in Kŭmgu County would be a good site for a capital, but this mountain does not have powerful energy either. Mount Hakka of Andong County lies between two rivers, and the shape and aura of the mountain is similar to those of Mount Ogwan and Mount Samgak. Regrettably, however, the rocky peaks are too small. Some say that the P'ungsan Plain below the mountain is a site good enough for a capital. All these three mountains, however, are no match for the four mountains mentioned before.

Although the mountains in the plains are generally small, their scenery is worth describing. Mount Chŏgak of Wŏnju is an earth mountain, but there are many valleys to the east and west. Furthermore, the mountain has much supernatural energy and hunters do not dare hunt there. Mount Saja lies to the northeast of Mount Chŏgak. A valley with springs and rocks stretches for thirty *ri* and the Ch'unch'ŏn River starts here. To the south are the valleys of Tohwadong and Murŭngdong whose streams and springs are outstanding. They are also said to be auspicious places and very suitable spots for retreat.

Mount Musŏng of Kongju joins Mount Kwangdŏk of Ch'ŏnan; both are earth mountains. There are, however, quite a few long valleys to the north and south. Not only do Buddhist monasteries and hermitages occupy good spots in every valley, houses and fields also are mingled together, skirted by long forests and meandering streams, forming a veritable picture of paradise on earth. As for Mount Kaya in Haemi County, the mountain to the southeast is covered with soil, but that to the northwest is covered with boulders. The valley of Kayasa to the east was in ancient times the site of the palace of All the Enlightened Ones (*sangwang*).[239] To the west lies Suryŏmdong with extraordinary boulders and waterfalls. The valleys of Kangdangdong and Murŭngdong to the north have beautiful scenery. Since they are close to villages, they are habitable places. Even though they are not as good as Mount Kaya of Hapchŏn County, the coastal scenery is still quite good. As for Mount Sŏngju (聖住) of Namp'o County, a big valley lies between the mountains to the north and the south. The ground is fairly flat, the valleys and peaks bright and clear, and the water and rocks clean and cool. Black jade, which is produced near the mountain, makes excellent ink stones. In olden days, Kim Si-sŭp (Maewŏltang) was said to have become an immortal in Muryangsa in Hongsan County; this is in fact the very mountain where it took place. In between the streams and valleys are many habitable areas.

A branch of the Noryŏng Mountain Range stretches to the north and enters the middle of the West Sea at Puan County. It faces the sea to the west, south, and north. In the center of the mountainous area are numerous peaks and valleys, which make up Mount Pyŏnsan. Tall pine trees grow on high peaks, steep ridges, flat areas, and tilted cliffs. They seem to pierce the sky and cover the sun. Salt and fish are produced near the valley. On the mountain there are fertile fields. Villagers go up the mountain to collect vegetables and go down [to the sea] to get fish and salt. Firewood, charcoal, and mussels are so abundant that people do not have to buy them. The only shortcoming is that the water and springs are miasmic. Among the various mountains mentioned above, big ones are suitable for a city site and the small ones are good for eminent persons and hermit retreats.

Some mountains are not suitable for people to live on, yet they have beautiful scenery. Mount Paegun of Yŏngp'yŏng County has the grand waterfall of Sambuyŏn. Mount Kodal of Koksan County is extremely remote and has caves and extraordinary holes in the rocks. In Mount

Mudŭng of Kwangju one finds dozens of rows of tall boulders jutting out in the air like huge tablets [held up by court officials receiving the king's audience]. This mountain has a very stern aura and dominates the whole province with its solemn dignity. Mount Wŏlch'ul of Yŏngam County has sharp-edged boulders that look as if they are ready to fly, like those of Mount Tobong and Mount Samgak, but it is too close to the sea and has few valleys. Mount Ch'ŏn'gwan of Changhŭng County has an extraordinary aura, and red and white clouds always float above it. Mount P'aryŏng of Hŭngyang County enters the sea like an island. Nam Sa-go called it an auspicious place because during the Imjin War, although Japanese warships sailed around the area, the soldiers did not enter the mountain. Mount Paegun of Kwangju is the place where Monk Tosŏn practiced his Buddhist faith and the scenery is beautiful. To the south of Mount Chogye (曹溪) of Sunch'ŏn are the scenic spots of Songgwangsa Valley. Mount P'algong of Taegu City has a rocky summit that extends a long way, and the streams and mountains to the east and west are quite beautiful. To the west of the mountain, however, an ugly mountain wall was erected for defense. In Mount Pip'a of Taegu City there is a rock from which water springs. Mount Unmun of Ch'ŏngdo County and Mount Wŏnjŏk of Ulsan County have connected peaks and many folds. The valleys are deep, and monks say that these places will produce one thousand sages; they are auspicious sites for escaping from wars. The boulders and waterfalls of Mount Naeyŏn in Ch'ŏngha County are exquisite and secluded; they surpass those of Mount Ch'ŏngnyang. Surprisingly, the valley area of Mount Chubang of Ch'ŏngsong County is entirely made up of rocks; it has splendid springs and waterfalls.

These mountains are good only as habitations for hermits or Buddhist monks. They are good for people to tour around for a short while but unsuitable for permanent residence. Apart from these there are many other mountains. I have not, however, discussed and recorded any mountains without valleys, springs, or rocks.

Mountains in the Sea

There are many extraordinary mountains in the sea. On Mount Halla of Chejudo, which is also called Mount Yŏngju, there is a huge pond, and every time a human noise is made, large clouds and mist gather around. On the summit is a square boulder that looks as if it has been sculpted. The grass below lines small paths and a fragrance fills the whole mountain. Occasionally the sounds of bamboo pipes and flutes are heard, but we do not know where the sounds come from. It is said that this is the place where supernatural beings enjoy themselves.

To the north of the mountain lies Cheju Town. The island used to be the ancient state of T'amna and later belonged to the Silla dynasty. The Yuan dynasty regarded it as a fourth-star area[240] and started many ranches where horses grazed on the mountain. Good horses are produced there to this day and are offered as a yearly tribute to the court. The towns of Chŏngŭi and Taejŏng (大靜) to the east and west of Cheju Town share its customs. From olden days, governors of Cheju and local magistrates of the two towns traveled by boat, without drifting or drowning. It was the same with the numerous officials of the court who came here in exile. From this we can see that the kings' grace has reached far, and hundreds of gods have responded compliantly.

Namhaedo lies in the sea near Kosŏng (固城) County in Kyŏngsang Province and is ten *ri* from the mainland. On the island there is a small basin, Kŭmsan, where Ch'oe Ko-un visited on his travels. The big characters Koun wrote remain inscribed on the rock walls. Wando lies in the sea near Kangjin County in Chŏlla Province and is ten *ri* from land. It was called Ch'ŏnghaejin during the Silla dynasty and Chang Po-go used it as his base. There are many good scenic places on the island and a military base has been established there.

Kunsando is in the sea near Man'gyŏng County in Chŏlla Province; it also has a military base. The whole island is made of rocks, and many peaks block the island at the back and embrace it from both left and right. In the middle lies a harbor where ships can berth. In front of the harbor lies a fishing ground and in the fishing season, every spring and summer, merchant ships from various places gather here like a cloud or fog to trade at sea. The residents compete with each other in spending their money on houses, clothes, and food, and they live much more extravagantly than people on the mainland.

Tŏkchŏkto lies in the sea to the north of Sŏsan County in Ch'ungch'ŏng Province. This is the place where Su Dingfang of the Tang dynasty stationed his troops when he invaded Paekche. Three rock peaks stand tall at the back and a branch from the foothills of the mountain circles around to make a port. Even though the water is shallow, it is possible to moor boats. A waterfall flows slowly to form a steady stream. Tiers of rocks and rock beds lie around looking splendid. Every spring and summer, when azaleas and rhododendrons blossom all over the mountain, the area between the valleys becomes as splendid as silk. The beach is of white sand and often wild roses blossom on it. Though just an island in the sea, it is certainly a fairyland. All the residents have become rich through fishing. While many islands have miasmic springs, the islands of Tŏkchŏk and Kunsan do not have any.

Ullŭngdo lies in the sea near Samch'ŏk County in Kangwŏn Province. If on a clear day one climbs up high and looks out to sea, the island looks like clouds. In the Sukchong era, Chang Han-sang, the famous general from Samch'ŏk, left Anbyŏn City in Hamgyŏng Province and went southeast by boat along the current to visit the island. Assisted by the wind, after two days he saw a rocky mountain standing up in the middle of the sea. Nobody was then living on the island, but there were traces left by people who had lived there long ago. He saw many rocky walls, rocky streams, and valleys. Cats and rats did not run away from people. Bamboo was as thick and tall as flag poles, and peach and plum and mulberry trees, wild mulberry trees, and wild vegetables also grew there. There were many exotic and unknown trees and plants. This might have been the ancient Usan state.

In the East Sea, which lies between Japan and Korea, there used to be a current that, like a mountain range on land, kept people of both countries from coming in contact with each other. Nowadays, however, the ocean current has changed, enabling Japanese boats to drift to the Yŏngdong (嶺 東) region, which is worrisome.

The above discussion focuses on mountains only. In what follows we turn to a description not of places located near famous mountains or in valleys with rivers or streams running through, but of places that are noted for their scenic springs and rocks or their verdant hills and beautiful lakes in the wilderness.

Scenic Spots in the Yŏngdong (嶺東) Region

The Yŏngdong region of Kangwŏn Province has the best scenery in Korea. [Lake] Samilp'o in Kosŏng is pure and clear and at the same time splendid and gorgeous. It is secluded and quiet yet open and bright. Like a lady in full dress, it is adorable and commands respect. The lake at the Kyŏngp'odae of Kangnŭng District has the spirit of the founder of the Han dynasty. Its loftiness, vigor, immensity, and serenity are all almost impossible to describe. The lake at Sijungdae in Hŭpkok County is bright yet austere and simple and inscrutable. It is like a great official sitting in his office, amicable, but brooking no familiarity. These three lakes rank first in their scenery. Next comes Hwadam of Kansŏng County, which may be compared to the moon's reflection in a clear fountain. Yŏngnangho looks like a pearl hidden in a big pond. Ch'ŏngch'oho of Yangyang County looks like a mirror reflecting pictures. These three lakes come next to the above three in terms of scenic beauty.

While not all the eight provinces of Korea have lakes, the six lakes of Yŏngdong are so marvelous that they do not seem to belong to the human world. In the middle of [Lake] Samilp'o is Sasŏnjŏng, where Yŏng-nang, Sullang, Namsŏngnang, and Ansangnang used to have a good time. These four friends agreed not to serve as government officials but instead to lead relaxed, natural lives. People say that they later attained enlightenment and became immortals. The names of the four immortals were written in red on the rocky wall to the south of the lake. It is amazing that the traces of the red ink on the wall have not been erased even after a thousand years.

Haesanjŏng lies to the east of a guest house. It has a view of the Kŭmgang Mountain Range to the west and the distant blue sea to the east. To the south it faces an immense, majestic river, which has along its course landscapes, both big and small, secluded and open. Paryŏnsa lies in the upper stream of the Nam River and next to Kamho. In olden days Yang Sa-ŏn (Pongnae) erected a pavilion on the lake, wrote the three Chinese characters *piraejŏng* on a board, and hung it on the wall. One day, the character *pi* suddenly flew away in the wind and disappeared into the sky without a trace. When the time and the date of that incident was checked, it turned out to be the precise time of Yang Saŏn's death. People said that *pi* was the very Chinese character that symbolized his spirit throughout his life. At the time of his death his energy dissolved and the Chinese character *pi* went also. This is truly an extraordinary story.

A small foothill stretches toward the east at Kyŏngp'odae; a lookout tower stands on the hill. In front of the hill there is a lake with a circumference of twenty *ri*. With the water level just waist-high, only small boats sail on the lake. To the east is the bridge of Kangmun'gyo and beyond it lie many rows of sandbars. The lake joins the sea, and beyond the sandbars the sea looks as if it meets the blue sky. The young poet Ch'oe Chŏn went up into the lookout tower and composed this poem.

> Since I entered the immortal's land, three thousand years have
>   gone by.
> Far away is the silvery sea under the sky; clear and shallow is the
>   water on the sand.
> Only the immortal phoenix has flown back, too.
> Under the peach blossoms, seen by nobody.

It has now become one of the most famous songs ever written. Some say that this poem is so perfect and free from error that it must be the words of immortals. Others believe its haunting quality suggests the words are from a ghostly hand. Ch'oe Chŏn is said to have died when he returned home immediately after he wrote the poem.

People also say that a rich man once lived where the lake is now. One day a monk begged him for some rice, but the rich man gave him human feces instead. Suddenly his house sank and formed a lake, while his piles of grain turned into small shellfish. Nowadays whenever there is a poor harvest, there is a good crop of shellfish, while in a good [harvest] year the crop of shellfish is much smaller. Since the shellfish are tasty and nutritious people call them starvation provisions. In spring and autumn, men and women come from distant places to carry away a harvest of shellfish on their backs or heads. They form long lines on both sides of the road. At the bottom of the lake there remain some tiles and tableware, which are often picked up by divers. Minister Sim Ŏn-gwang used to live somewhere on the southern bank of the lake. While serving at court he kept a picture of the lake on the right-hand side of his desk and said, "Since I have [a house] on the hill with a lake to the north my descendants will not prosper, surely they are doomed."

Several *ri* to the south of the lake is Hansongjŏng, where there are several objects such as stone pots and mortars. This is the place where the four immortals mentioned previously used to enjoy themselves. There is no pavilion on Sijungho but many rows of sandbars. The shore is sandy but the water is calm, clear, and serene. The scenery is excellent. Governor Han Myŏng-hoe first heard word of his promotion to minister while he was having a party here, so the villagers named it Sijungho (Lake of the Minister).

At Ch'ongsŏkchŏng in T'ongch'ŏn County a foothill from Mount Kŭmgang stretches right into the sea and stands out like an island. To the north of the foothill large natural stone pillars form a line into the sea. The pillars are as high as the foothill, measuring well over the height of one hundred men and with less than one hundred steps between them. They are called pillars rather than peaks because stone peaks have a broad base with a tapering top while these do not. The pillars are round and show traces of having been chipped all over, as if masons had shaped them with chisels. In places, a few old pines grow at the foot of the pillars. Below, in the waves, there are numerous small stone pillars. Some stand erect while others lie toppled. The pillars look as if they are being chewed and eaten by the waves. One could swear that these pillars were made by human hands, but they are the extraordinary and intricate work of the creator! They present exquisite scenery unique in the world.

Chuksŏru of Samch'ŏk County is a scenic spot next to Osipch'ŏn. When water reaches a hidden hole under a cliff, some of it shoots up and falls back down like rain. The rest of the water runs along the cliff in front of the pavilion and passes by the town. Once a man was rowing a boat and fell into the hole. He could not be found. People say that because the town was founded on an empty and doomed site it has never produced any talented people.

Naksansa of Yangyang County, Ch'ŏngganjŏng of Kansŏng County, Mangyangjŏng of Ulsan County, and Wŏlsongjŏng of P'yŏnghae County all stand by the sea. The blue sea is welded to the blue sky; nothing blocks the view. On the seashore, as on the banks of rivers and streams, small stones and magnificent rocks are vaguely reflected in the waves. The beaches are bright and made of white sand that looks like snow and crunches under one's feet as if one is walking on beads. On the sand wild roses blossom beautifully and scattered pine tree groves stand tall, seeming to pierce the sky. Upon entering the landscape one's mood changes suddenly and one comes to forget the distinction between oneself and the world. It is so enchanting that one feels as if one is flying through the air. One who has experienced this becomes a person of a different world. Even after ten years, the spirit of the misty scenery still lingers on one's face.

Anbyŏn City in Hamgyŏng Province is to the north of Hŭpkok County, outside the nine counties of the Yŏngdong region. A branch of Ch'ŏll-yŏng stretches eastward to the sea and spreads out in many terraces like high parasols or screens, thus forming a broad, picturesque view. Two other branches to the left and right encircle the channel like a man clasping his hands together. In between the branches, smaller cliffs are scattered around like bonfires in a field. Inland is a big lake called Hakp'o. Its circumference is over thirty *ri;* the water is deep, yet clear and transparent. There are sand dunes around the shores and wild roses poke out and blossom in the sand, exhibiting their beauty in full. Breezes blow grains of sand to form small mounds and big dunes. They move so frequently that one cannot figure out the number of such changes in a day. It is as amazing as the golden sands in the West Sea. At the back of the lake fine peaks and verdant hills look cosy and beautiful. At different times of the day they can look either close or further away. To the front, clear, gentle waves ripple out evenly, seeming to move and stay still at the same time.

The Chinese compare Xi Hu in Zhejiang to a beautiful lady with fine makeup. [In Korea] only the lake of Hakp'o is as good as Xi Hu. It is more beautiful than the six lakes of Yŏngdong. It used to belong to Hŭpkok [in Kangwŏn Province], but later it was incorporated into Anbyŏn City.[241] The people of Hŭpkok, submitted petitions against the people of Anbyŏn, to the court reclaiming it, yet they could not achieve their aim. Eventually it became part of a northern province. As the northern provinces are not desirable places for scholar-gentry to live, the lake's beautiful scenic spots by the edge of the sea have been deserted. Only passersby come and appreciate its beauty. It is a shame that chance should make such a tremendous difference to such a scenic spot being appreciated or neglected.

In the sea one thousand *ri* from the mainland is an island belonging to Korea. At the back of the island stand stone pillars, and peaks are formed from huge rocks with grass growing in between. In the middle of the island bamboo groves grow. The bamboo is very good for making arrows. Nobody lives there, and when tourists come for sightseeing and blow a bugle or a pipe, a storm with thunder and lightning will occur in the dragon pit down below.

Scenic Spots in the Four Counties

Even though the four counties of Yŏngch'un, Tanyang, Ch'ŏngp'ung, and Chech'ŏn lie within the boundary of Ch'ungch'ŏng Province, their actual location is in the valleys of the upper Han River. The banks of the river consist of many rocky walls and rock bases. Tanyang is the most rocky among these counties. Since the whole county lies among mountains, it does not contain a plain even ten *ri* wide. It nevertheless has many scenic spots with streams, rocks, and caves. Of these, Two Lakes and Three Cliffs are particularly noteworthy. Todam, one of the two lakes, is in Yŏngch'un County. The Han River flows into this deep and wide lake. In the middle of the lake stand three rocky outcrops forming a line like the string on a bow. They have an intricately sculpted look, as if they were miniature rock hills in a private garden. They are small and low, however, and have no towering precipices.

Kŭidam is in Ch'ŏngp'ung County. Rocky cliffs loom on both sides and block the sun. The river runs between the cliffs, which are parallel to each other like [open] gates. To the left and right are Kangsŏndae and the peaks of Ch'aeunbong and Oksunbong. Kangsŏndae faces the river, where a huge flat rock, which would accommodate one hundred people, rises high above the water. The two peaks are as high as ten thousand men and both come from the same crag. The Oksunbong peak is the straighter and stands like a giant with his arms folded.

In the summer of the year *muja* (1708), on my way to the capital from Andong County, I boarded a boat near the town of Tanyang. As it passed by Oksunbong I composed a couplet which reads,

> High above the water stands a gigantic peak, looking like an upright
>   scholar standing there,
> Deep in the lake stirs an ancient dragon.

Another couplet reads,

The superior spirit manifests itself in magnificent scenery,
The soaring energy upholds the form of the universe.

In the middle of the river are many mammoth rocks. When the water level falls, the rocks appear and when the water rises they disappear. There are three famous precipices in the valley to the southwest of the county. A big brook follows the rocky valley; the banks of the brook are all formed of rocks. There are strange rocks on the banks: some make small peaks, some look like beds, and some look like bricks piled up into a wall. On top of these rocks are old pine trees, some of which bow low, tangling with each other. When water flows over a long, grooved rock base it looks like a stone manger filled with water. When water flows over a round pit it looks like a stone pot full of water. The water crashing on the rocks makes such a loud noise day and night that people cannot hear each other when they stand near the stream. To the left and right are densely wooded mountain ranges, and birds in their hundreds chirp there. This is hardly a world of mortal beings. There are three places with similar scenic features in this area. The one on the very top is called the Upper Precipice, the one in the middle, the Middle Precipice, and the one below, the Lower Precipice.

Passing through Tanyang in the year *muja* (1708) I composed a couplet while I was visiting these precipices with Kim Chung-u, the county magistrate, and Yi Tŏg-un, the township's assistant magistrate.

Finding myself in the midst of ten thousand valleys,
I wondered whether my fond dream had come true.
For a thousand years I have longed to enjoy such an immortals'
    realm on earth.

I do not know whether I will have the chance in my future years to pay off this debt to the immortals.

To the southeast is the Unam Crag, which is formed by the foothill of a small mountain coming down toward the plain. [The crag] stands high like a rock wall. Brooks from the southeastern valley converge to make a stream that flows around the rocky wall. On top there is Sŏae's old pavilion, which has quite a good view of the valleys and mountains. Sŏae (Yu Sŏng-nyong), having bought the site with the leopard skin bestowed upon him by the king, built a pavilion with several rooms. In the year of *musul* (1598), when Nam I-gong impeached Sŏae as a favor to Yi Kyŏng-jŏn, even he compared this site with Meiwu.[242] In Sŏae's writings, the sentence "Red cliff and blue walls are also cited in the accusation" refers to this place. After Sŏae was dismissed and returned to his hometown, King Sŏnjo ordered the ex-minister Yi Hang-bok to select an irreproachable public servant from among the court officials. The minister immediately designated Sŏae out of regret at the false accusation made by Nam I-gong. As Sŏae reached Kwangnaru wharf outside the city gate, he wrote a poem.

> Three thousand *ri* long is the return journey home.
> For forty years in my work I have received His Majesty's great
>   favor.[243]

In this poem one can feel his sadness as he ended his service to the king. Immediately after Sŏae died, the pavilion was demolished. Yŏngdong (嶺東) is an outlying county close to the sea, and Tanyang is rugged and narrow. They are not desirable places to live.

Riverside Settlements

High mountains with rugged valleys and dashing streams are beautiful to appreciate for a while and they make suitable sites for Buddhist or Taoist monasteries. They definitely do not make good sites for the dwelling of ordinary residents over many generations. What these inhabitants must choose are either places on plains with a landscape of streams, rivers, and mountains, or places that are broad, bright, and beautiful yet sheltered and secluded, or locations near charming hills and clear streams with extraordinary rocks and strange stones that do not look ominous. If in a town, these locations will make the town famous, and if in a village will make the village popular.

As for riverside settlements, the outer city wall of P'yŏngyang is the best in the eight provinces. P'yŏngyang City has open fields of one hundred *ri* to the front and back; being wide and bright there is a feeling of openness and spaciousness. The mountain has splendid scenery and the river does not flow fast but gently forward. The mountains are broken up by plains and the plains are broken up by water. The water channels are flat, magnificent, and very wide; various merchant ships come and go on the waves. Splendid layers of rock zigzag along the riverbanks. To the northwest, fertile fields stretch endlessly and the whole scene has an otherwordly look.

Government houses and houses of public servants are within the inner wall; commoners live within the outer wall. The wall outside was built with clay during the Wiman and Chumong eras. Even though it has been destroyed and flattened, the site of the city wall remains and a settlement has developed on it. In the spring and summer women do their washing by the river to the south, and on the banks brightly colored washing is spread out to dry over ten *ri*. Seagulls and ducks fly away from the beating noise made by the laundry paddles. There are many houses next to each other and the shops along the streets are bustling. Since the Kija period the city has not gone through any abrupt changes, which can be attributed to the beauty of its landform. It has been said, however, that since P'yŏngyang has the landform of a sailing boat, the digging of wells is forbidden here. When wells were dug in the past, fires broke out in the town many times and eventually those wells were filled in. The entire population of the city fetches water from the river for daily use. Since they have to go a long way to fetch firewood, fuel is very scarce and expensive. These are the shortcomings of this city.

Next to P'yŏngyang comes Uduch'on of Ch'unch'ŏn, which is situated between the two branch streams of the upper Soyang River. Along the streams are rocks and beyond the streams are mountains. Though located in a narrow valley, the area opens wide further on. It is therefore full of vitality. Since boats sail up carrying fish and salt from the lower reaches of the river, many residents engage in commercial activities and become wealthy. The population has not decreased since the time of the Maek [Yemaek] state. Next comes the town of Yŏju, which is on the southern bank of the upper Han River. It is on the plain that stretches over forty *ri* south of the Han River. The air is clear, cool, and open. The river, which runs from east to northwest, is neither too grand nor too fast flowing. Cliffs like Maam and Pyŏksa on the upper reaches reduce the speed of the water flow. Yŏju is flat in the northwest; it has been a town for several thousand years.

In general, riverside settlements rarely benefit from agriculture. If, for example, a settlement is situated between two mountains and blocked by a river in front, there may be no farmland for cultivation because the soil will be sandy. Even if there is farmland, it may be too far away to cultivate and harvest. Or the land will be so low as to be prone to flooding. Riverside settlements are only benefited by attractive scenery, not by ample food and clothing. The three places mentioned above are the best because they have open fields around them.

As to Sŭngch'ŏnp'o in P'ungdŏk County and the Husŏ River that runs near Kaesŏng City, the water is muddy and miasmic. The riverside villages in the vicinity of Hanyang City all face mountains that are too close. Villages around Ch'ungju, with the exception of Kŭmch'ŏn and Mokkye, are lonely and isolated. Kongju is the only scenic spot on the cliff on the Kŭm River, yet it is too narrow and secluded. The Naktong River of Sangju has barren valleys on both banks, and Mokp'o City in Naju County, the Sŏmjin River in Kwangyang County, and the Yŏng River in Chinju County are situated in the remote countryside. Only from Puyŏ County to Ŭnjin County in the south and Imp'i County in the west are there many riverside villages; [they are] in the central area of the three southern provinces and not far from the capital. These [villages] have fields nearby whose soil is fertile enough for the cultivation of rice, ramie, and hemp and that benefit from catching fish and crabs. The transport of these goods to the south and the north is entrusted to these villages, and riverboats and seagoing ships gather there. These are the only desirable places to live apart from along the Han River. So far, I have left Amnok and Tuman out of the discussion.

Streamside Settlements

It is said that settlements along streams are not as good as those along rivers, and settlements along rivers are not as good as those beside the sea. This statement is based on two criteria, namely, easy access to goods and money and the profits from fishing and salt production. In reality, however, the strong winds from the sea darken the human skin and many diseases such as beriberi, dropsy, endemic diseases, and malaria are common near the sea. Freshwater springs are rare. The soil contains salt, and the turbid tides can affect the area, which seldom gives it a feeling of cleanliness. The landform of Korea is high in the east and low in the west. Water pouring from gorges forms rivers, and these rivers are not characteristically steady and tranquil; on the contrary, they twist and turn, rush and dash. In general, the fortunes of the inhabitants on riversides fluctuate because of the geomantic shortcomings of the sites. Only settlements along streams can enjoy the tranquility, the scenery, and the advantage of irrigation. Some people reverse the adage quoted above by saying that seaside settlements are not as good as riverside settlements and riverside settlements are not as good as streamside settlements.

Good settlements along streams should not be far from mountain passes, for then they may be permanent sites of habitation suitable in times of both peace and war. The best streamside settlements are the villages of Tosan in Yean County and Hahoe in Andong County in the Yŏngnam region. In Tosan two moderately high mountains join up to make a long valley. Upon reaching Tosan the volume of water from [Lake] Hwangji starts to increase and becomes a big stream outside the entrance to the valley. The feet of both mountains consist of rock cliffs that look beautiful against the stream. The stream is deep enough for boats to sail along. Numerous old trees in the middle of the valley provide a quiet, beautiful sense of seclusion. Behind the mountain and to the south of the stream are fertile and level fields. A hall called Amsŏhŏn, with its two houses where Yi T'oe-gye used to live, is still there and his ink stones, a wooden case, a walking stick, some shoes, and paper instruments for observing the sky are still kept there.

Hahoe is situated on a gentle, flattish hillside that stretches toward the northwest from south of the Hwang River where Sŏae's old house is located. The river flows around and is deep in front of the hill. The mountain to the north of the river is an extension of Mount Hakka and stretches along the river. It is magnificent and beautiful without having any threatening shapes. On top of the mountain, Ogyŏnjŏng and small hermitages can be seen among the rocks covered with pine and fir trees. This place is truly a splendid scenic spot.

On the lower part of Tosan Stream is Pun'gang, beside which Yi Hyŏn-bo (Nongam) used to live. U T'ak (Cheju) used to reside to the south of the river. These places are both noted for their wonderful secluded scenery. Settlements such as Samgwijŏng, Sudong, and Kail are located either upstream or downstream. These are all famous waterside settlements. Since there are many rapids downstream, merchant ships from the Naktong River cannot sail there. However, small boats can sail in front of the villages and arable land is not far away. One can till the land in peaceful times and hide on nearby Mount Sobaek in times of war. Among the streamside settlements these two places [Tosan and Hahoe] are the best in the whole country. But they are not valued merely because prominent people have lived there. Apart from these places, to the southeast of Andong is Chŏngsong Town facing a stream that runs down and meets the Hwang River.

In Imch'ŏn there is a county where Kim Sŏng-il (Hakpong) used to live. To this day his descendants prosper and the village is well known. In the nearby upper stream are scenic spots like Mongsŏn'gak and a retreat called Toyŏnsŏnch'al (Toyŏn Taoist Temple). To the north of the county is Naesŏngch'on, where Kwŏn Pal, a deputy minister, once lived. Ch'ŏngamjŏng is located on an enormous rock in the pond that looks like an island. The pavilion is surrounded by flowing water, so it has marvelous scenery. To the north on the sunny side of Mount T'aebaek is Ch'unyangch'on. Hansujŏng, an inheritance of Kwŏn Tu-gi, the policy monitor, faces the stream and has delicate, intricate scenery.

Ch'ŏngsong County lies on the upper stream [that eventually merges with] Imhach'ŏn. Two large streams join in front of the town where a vast stretch of field opens up. Blue water and white sand blend with rice paddies and wheat fields. The surrounding mountains are densely wooded with tall conifers. Throughout the year the pines are green, elegant, and quiet, giving the impression of not being of this mundane world. To the northwest of Yŏngch'ŏn County are Sunhŭng Town and Chukkye Valley. A stream flows from Mount Sobaek and the fields here are broad. The mountains are small and the water and rocks are clear and clean. On the upper stream is the Paegundong Confucian School, which offers a sacrificial ceremony to An Yu[244] (Munsŏnggong). The school was built when Deputy School Inspector Chu Se-bung of the era of King Myŏngjong first arrived at P'unggi County, and it became the first local Confucian school in this country. There is a pavilion in front of the school that has a commanding view of all the scenic spots of the village. These two villages are on a par with the famous villages of Andong in terms of stream and mountain scenery and productivity of the soil. It is said that the area below Mount T'aebaek and Mount Sobaek and the upper reaches of the Hwang River are really desirable places for the scholar-gentry to live.

Next after these areas come Chujulch'ŏn in Yongdam County to the south of Mount Chŏktŭng, Chamwŏnch'ŏn in Kŭmsan County, Changgye in Changsu County, and Chugye in Muju County. These four places have beautiful streams and mountains and excellent soil from which to produce cotton or rice. The fields are well irrigated and their harvest never fails. These places are therefore much superior to areas below Mount T'aebaek and Mount Sobaek and near the Hwang River. In these four villages there are three scenic islands: Chŏndo, Hudo, and Chukto. Although the villages have beautiful streams and mountains, the fields are small and far from homesteads. This is no small disadvantage. These villages, however, have high mountains and deep valleys to the east and west, which provide the villagers with the best refuge from war. Further north the stream bends to the east and enters Okch'ŏn County to become [a stream called] Ch'aehagye in Yangsan and Kuryonggye in Isan. Although known by different names in different places, it is really the upper stream of the Chŏktŭng. Along the banks of the stream are many tiered rocks and splendid cliffs. To the northwest it is blocked by high mountains and to the southeast it broadens into a deep, clear, and quiet watercourse. The mountains are high and splendid and do not have a harsh, menacing aspect. Even though big boats from the lower stream cannot sail up here, small boats can sail where the water is deep. This place is as beautiful as Tosan and Hahoe. The stream bends toward the east. When it is close to Mount Hwangak and Mount Tŏgyu it can provide refuge in time of war. Since there are few paddy fields, villagers engage solely in the cultivation of cotton. The profit from trading cotton is ample compensation for the poor rice crops. The economic situation of the local people is no worse than that of the above four villages. It is a suitable place for prominent people to live.

Next come three streams known as Anp'yŏnggye, Kŭmgye, and Yong-hwagye, which are located between the Hwaryŏng and Ch'up'ungnyŏng Mountain Ranges. At the point of junction of the three counties of Sangju, Yŏngdong, and Hwanggan, the three streams provide beautiful scenery and the advantage of irrigation. Rice paddies here are most fertile and there are many cotton fields as well. Since it is situated between the Ho-nam and Yŏngnam regions, the area is not too isolated and merchants gather for the exchange of goods. Furthermore, the soil here is mostly very fertile. In terms of economic conditions, it is better than many other places. But the plain is not wide, and it does not have the clear and bright atmosphere of places to the north of Hwangji, Mount Yang, and Mount Yi. This area joins Mount Songni to the north, where Chŭnghang and Mount Tojang are located. To the south it joins Mount Hwangak, which is surrounded by high mountains and low valleys. In short, the whole area provides good refuge from war and is truly an auspicious place.

Next comes Pyŏngch'ŏn in Mun'gyŏng, which has scenic places like Kaŭn, Pongsaeng, Ch'ŏnghwa, and Yongyu. To the north Pyŏngch'ŏn joins Sŏnyudong, where the streams and mountains have extraordinary scenery. The place has fertile rice paddies and rich soil for persimmons and chestnuts. Within a radius of one hundred *ri*, this location provides good hiding places from war and makes an auspicious place for retreat. It is, however, remote and has malevolent energy. It may be a good place for getting away from the vanities of the world or for Buddhist or Taoist meditation but not for ordinary living during peaceful times.

Next comes Koet'an of Koesan County in the upper stream of the Talch'ŏn to the north of Mount Songni. Kosanjŏng on the stream used to be the country home of the late minister Yu Kŭn (Sŏgyŏng). When Zhu Zhifan came to Korea as an envoy he sent an artist to draw the scenery of this area; he composed a poem and hung the poem in a frame on the wall. Though the area is located in the middle of a narrow valley, the streams and mountains here are clear and clean. There are fields to be tilled and harvested. To the east is Mount Hŭiyang, which is a good place to take refuge during times of war.

Moving south along the stream, one can find villages like Ch'ŏngch'ŏn, Kwiman, Yonghwa, and Songmyŏn lying north of Mount Songni. To the south over Yulch'i is Pyŏngch'ŏn of Mun'gyŏng County. Mountains to the north are very high and many villages face the stream that runs by these high mountains. The hills and fields are verdant and the plants and trees aromatic; the scenery is simply out of this world. Situated as it is in a mountainous area, this locality is not threatened by rough, dangerous peaks and so is a good place for retreat. The area has large fields as well as has small rice paddies, but the soil is barren, yielding little. It is not as good as either Pyŏngch'ŏn or Koet'an.

Next to these settlements comes the area of the Chuch'ŏn River in Wŏnju. Although situated in a very narrow valley, the fields are wide and open. The mountains are not high and the water is extremely clear and blue. The only shortcoming is the lack of rice paddies, [so that] people have to live on millet. To the west, Mount Chŏgak stands tall in the sky and blocks this locale from the outside world. It is a good place for eschewing war or other worldly troubles. Compared with the areas of the rivers Ch'ŏngch'ŏn and Pyŏngch'ŏn, however, it is very barren and remote.

One can easily lose count of all the streamside settlements in the plain away from the mountain passes. Kapch'ŏn Village in Kongju, however, should be counted as the best of the settlements, Yuldam of Chŏnju the second, Chakch'ŏn of Ch'ŏngju the third, Kamch'ŏn of Sŏnsan County the fourth, and Kuman of Kurye County the fifth. Speaking of Kapch'ŏn, its plain is extremely broad and the surrounding mountains are clear and beautiful. Three big streams converge in the middle of the plain and the water can be used for irrigation. The whole area yields good harvests, producing one *chong* in one *myo*, and is also suitable for cotton cultivation. It is not far from Kanggyŏng, and it has a big trading center in front. With the advantage of having a water channel leading to the sea, it is a good place for many generations to live. Yuldam is situated in an area where high hills rise to the east and rich fields lie to the west. A big stream flows to the south and the rice paddies yield one *chong* in one *myo*. Since the villagers can fish and till the land and reap the crops, this area is as good as Kapch'ŏn. Its proximity to Chŏnju City ensures public amenities.

To the west along Chakch'ŏn are villages such as Changmyŏng, Kŭmsŏng, Chajŏk, and Chŏngjwa. Numerous streams along the valleys enable the villagers to irrigate the land, and many wealthy households have lived here. Kamch'ŏn originates from Mount Hwangak and the adjacent valleys are all irrigated and have rich paddies. Never having experienced famine, the villagers have been comfortably well-off for generations and are good-natured, kind, and warm-hearted.

Mount Chiri has several branches to the east but only one to the west, which terminates abruptly at Kuman County. The rippling stream flows as if embracing the mountains, and Mount Obong is seen facing the south. Situated between two provinces, Kuman has become an important transportation center for the region and its wide fields are fertile. On a night when the stars are few and the moon is bright, small boats without boatmen are seen floating around by themselves on the river. People say it is because immortal beings from Mount Obong wander around Mount

Chiri. Compared with other streamside settlements, the village of Kuman generally has better living conditions. Since it is close to the South Sea, however, the water and soil are not as good as those of the settlements in the north. These five villages have better scenery and economic conditions than Tosan and Hahoe villages. But. as they are situated a little too far from a mountain pass, people can only live here in peaceful times and cannot find refuge from war. This is the reason they are not as good as various villages to the north of the Hwang River. Since Kuman Village has Mount Chiri to the east, people can live here in peace and war.

As for the province of Ch'ungch'ŏng, there are localities to look at: Ch'ŏngnadong in Poryŏng County, Kwangch'ŏn in Hongju County, Murŭngdong in Haemi, and the stream, Hwagye, in Namp'o are all populated by numerous rich families who have resided there for many generations. Compared to other adjacent towns these villages have easy access to sea routes. All of the scholar-gentry of Seoul regard these places highly because of the benefits that derive from the goods transported through them. It is true they are not situated in deep mountains or grand valleys, but because they are out of the way and tucked back in a corner near the sea, they are not disturbed by warfare. For this reason, [the area] is known as a most auspicious site for settlement. In Chŏlla Province, Yoch'ŏn Village in Namwŏn, Changyŏn Village in Hŭngdŏk, and Pongyŏn Village in Changsŏng are all famous settlements, having fertile soil, and many landlords have lived there for several generations.

In Kyŏngsang Province, the villages of Kŭmho in Taegu, Kach'ŏn in Sŏngju, and Ponggye in Kŭmsan have wide fields and fertile rice paddies. Their population has not decreased since the Silla dynasty. They have good geomantic and economic conditions for people to live there for many generations. Only the villages of Kach'ŏn and Ponggye have mountain passes nearby and are habitable places in times of both peace and war. In Kyŏnggi Province, the soil of the basins of Obich'ŏn in Yongin and Ch'ŏngmich'ŏn in Ŭmjuk is as fertile as that of the three southern provinces and thus [makes for] desirable places to live. In Kangwŏn Province, the whole of Anch'ang Stream in Wŏnju and both sides of Hoengsŏng Stream have beautiful scenery, but the soil is far less fertile than that of the three southern provinces. In Hwanghae Province, only the areas of Chukch'ŏn in Haeju and Suhoech'ŏn Village in Songhwa are both beautiful and not so barren. The West Sea provides the advantage of fishing and salt production. These areas are therefore really good places in which to live.

P'yŏnggang, which lies between Hwanghae and Kangwŏn Provinces, has the Chŏngjayŏn area, where the Hwang clan has resided for many generations. To the north of Ch'ŏrwŏn a gently sloping hill circles around in the middle of a great plain and a big stream flows to the southwest from Sambangch'i in Anbyŏn. Upon reaching the front of the village it becomes deep enough for small boats. The rock cliffs on the riverbanks are like screens, whereupon are pavilions, tall terraces, and deep forests.

To the west is Kwangbokch'on, which is located to the north of Ich'ŏn (伊川). The stream from Anbyŏn and Yŏngp'ung becomes wider here and deep enough for boats. The ground is covered with white stones and bright sands, and the settlement there is enveloped in a wondrous atmosphere. The town has only small rice paddies. Only Kwangbok Village draws water for irrigation and the soil there is extremely fertile. Because the north is blocked by Komit'an and Mount Kŏm, it is a desirable place to live during both peace and war. The only shortcoming is that the area is too remote for the scholar-gentry so only wealthy commoners live there. Upon reaching the front of the town of Ich'ŏn, the water of Kwangbokch'on expands and becomes a river. Every spring and summer when the water level rises, ships laden with tribute are dispatched to the capital. In Anhyŏp the river meets Komit'an, passes through T'osan, and reaches Chingp'ado in Sangnyŏng. The scenery here is splendid and sweeping, and one can see pavilions, terraces, and multistoried summer houses built by the scholar-gentry of Seoul.

Beautiful scenery induces a cheerful and bright mood. If a dwelling place is lacking in this, one becomes uncivilized. Many locales with good scenery, however, may have living conditions that are too poor for places of habitation. One cannot survive in the wild, living like a turtle or an earthworm. It stands to reason, then, that one should choose a wide plain with fertile soil and build a house where the geomantic conditions are favorable. One may afterward buy a good scenic spot around ten *ri* or half a day's walking distance away so that one can go there whenever one wishes to rid oneself of depression or even stay the night before returning home. Zhuzi liked the scenery of Mount Wuyi and wrote beautiful poems at every stream and mountain peak; however, he did not keep a house there. He once said, "When I go there in spring, I enjoy the sight of red blossoms amid the green foliage." Lovers of streams and rivers who come later can take this saying as a guide.

Conclusion

Master Yi remarks that[245] lying outside China, our country was not included when surnames were given and recorded in "Yugong" (Tribute of Yu).[246] We are the people of an eastern country. The descendants of Kija, however, took the surname of Sŏnu and those of Koguryŏ became the Ko clan. The kings of Silla took three surnames: Pak, Sŏk, or Kim. The Kim house of the state of Karak decided on the surname Kim for themselves and other noble families. From the late Silla period, contact with China was established and the practice of taking surnames was introduced. This was only prevalent among government officials and the gentry, however. Commoners still had no surnames. When the Three Han States were unified by Koryŏ, the Chinese clan system started to be imitated. Surnames were given to the people in all eight provinces of the country and everybody came to have a surname. Before this, various clans and their branches adopted the same surname according to their places of birth. People from different places, even though they shared a surname, were not regarded as members of the same clan. Thus, marriage was not prohibited between a prospective couple of the same surname if they were from different places of origin. This is because, although their surnames were the same, their ancestors were different. Under these circumstances, the surnames bestowed by the Koryŏ dynasty had little hereditary basis, so it is really perplexing why scholar-gentry should nowadays try to differentiate people on the grounds of their surnames.

The Chosŏn dynasty was founded to uphold Confucianism. At present the scholar-gentry's family names are highly prestigious because they are given special consideration when official appointments are made. People are classified into many grades in terms of social status. Descendants of the royal family and scholar-gentry serve as high-ranking officials at court. Below the scholar-gentry class come officials of several ranks posted in the countryside, such as *chungjŏng*[247] and *kongjo*.[248] Below these come educated commoners, military officers, translators, accountants, doctors, and *hansanin*[249] from the countryside. Then comes the group consisting of petty local officers, soldiers, and good civilians. Below these come private and public slaves. The lowest class consists of slaves up to petty local officials outside the capital, while farmers and their offspring, artisans, and tradespeople make up the middle class. Officials of various ranks and the scholar-gentry are called *yangban*, even though officials make up one class and the scholar-gentry another.

Even among the scholar-gentry, the Great Households and the Famous Households are differentiated. These and many other titles make intermingling altogether impossible. Social status is bound to wax and wane, though. Scholar-gentry may move down to become commoners and those who have been commoners for a long time may move up to the scholar-gentry class. That is why the Sŏnu family, which used to have high-ranking officials among them at P'yŏngyang, have now ceased to be scholar-gentry. The Sŏk and Ko clans have vanished from the scholar-gentry class. As the descendants of princes, only the Pak and Kim clans of Silla and the Kims of the state of Karak are as prosperous as ever, and these two surnames make up the foremost families in our country.

Many Chinese people who have come over to Korea over the centuries have left descendants. Some followed Kija and Wiman here, and others came here following the queens and princesses of the Koryŏ dynasty. When the Koryŏ and Yuan dynasties became one country, people moved about without restriction and some people from China came to settle in Korea. The Koryŏ dynasty did not give surnames, and the family trees of those other than prominent people are not clear. The following are the families that came from China and rose to high government posts: the Maeng clan of Onyang, Yi of Yŏnan and Yŏju, Hong of Namyang, Wŏn of Wŏnju, O of Haeju, Nam of Ŭiryŏng, Sin of Kŏch'ang, and Hwang of Ch'angwŏn. Others received their surname from the Koryŏ court.

When the genealogies of the scholar-gentry are examined one can see that most of their progenitors received surnames from the Koryŏ dynasty. But things can change over a long period of time. More than eight hundred years have passed since the beginning of the Koryŏ dynasty. Some commoners have become noblemen and have retained their nobility for many generations. Their merits and good deeds are illustrated in history and have been recorded in historical annals. Then how can one say that they are inferior to the descendants of the Ch'oe, No, Wang, and Sa families?

The Chosŏn dynasty is culturally more advanced than Koryŏ. The Great King Sejong, who possessed saintly qualities, assumed the role of king and teacher and reigned over the country with decorum and high morals. As a result, every scholar acquired the highest levels of scholarship and morality. For this reason, those with no talent or poor scholarship came to be known as boorish. Those who made even a small error in marriage were treated as barbarians. Even the slightest defect in behavior marred one's relationship with friends. Soldiers and merchants, even though they may have originated from scholar-gentry families, are regarded as unworthy company. To become a scholar, one must study the [Confucian] Classics, strive for exemplary behavior, cultivate oneself, and see that the entire household comes up to the same standard. Only then can one command respect and be revered by society. Each advancement or retreat, speech or silence, comes under the surveillance of the people around oneself.

For two hundred years from King Sejong to King Sŏnjo, there have been ups and downs and not every scholar has achieved perfection. Hence, debates have arisen on a large scale. Once started, these debates make it difficult for the virtuous to exercise their influence and easy for the unworthy to hide behind arguments. Therefore, it has become even more difficult for a scholar to deal with the world and make his name. Although the government has treated the scholar-gentry favorably in general, it has also punished them readily by execution. When an ignoble character assumes power, he may abuse the dispensing of official punishments to achieve personal revenge. Several purges of scholar-officials have occurred over the years. Those without fame are looked down upon and cast aside and the famous are envied. Once envied, one is doomed to be killed. It is therefore difficult for the scholar-gentry to serve this country. When the country is in decline, the divisions increase, and when the number of arguments increase, resentment and grievances deepen. When grudges deepen, people start to kill one another. Alas! In the past when the scholar-gentry were not appointed to government posts, they used to retreat to the hills and forests. This should apply to both the past and the present, but it has changed now. The criminals who revolted in the year of *musin* were actually scholar-gentry who started their seditious activities in the countryside.[250] Even after they were purged, the court worried that brigands might haunt the deep forests. If the court does not suspect a scholar to be an outright brigand then it names him a dubious character. If one such scholar wants to serve in government, there is no end to the factional strife awaiting him there, which may well end up in bloody murder. If one wishes to retreat and hide in the forest, one cannot easily settle even in deep mountains. Where, then, can the scholar-gentry retreat safely in the future? It is not the high-ranking officials or the middle class of the lowest grade, but always the scholar-gentry who not only find it impossible to retreat to the forest, but also find their every word and action being examined with suspicion. It makes no difference whether they receive government appointments and promotion or enjoy obscurity in the forest, there is nowhere for them to be accommodated. Thus, they come to regret having become scholar-gentry by assiduous application and self-cultivation and they rather envy the status of farmers, craftsmen, and traders. In the past the scholar-gentry complacently placed themselves above these classes. This is truly a case where things develop in the opposite direction when they come to an extreme. In this whole wide world there is no place for the so-called scholar-gentry! If one were to discard the status of scholar-gentry and live as a farmer, craftsman, or trader, would one be safe and able to keep one's dignity? No!

The pernicious effect of the present factional strife applies not only to the scholar-gentry. Everybody, from officials of rank to the middle class and lowly servants such as sedan-chair bearers, has a special relationship with certain people that cannot pass unnoticed by others. Even farmers, craftsmen, and traders have their friends. Unlike trees, stones, or beasts, humans must socialize. One cannot avoid mixing with others. Acquaintance leads to amicability, but estrangement develops into preference or hatred. Friendliness and preference lead to association and union, while estrangement and hatred result in alienation and betrayal. Once support or betrayal is manifested, the boundary between the groups is drawn, and it is impossible for those belonging to different groups to cross over this boundary. Even if one wants to stand in the middle and act to one's own advantage, one cannot do so. This is the boundary that encircles human beings. It is not as concrete as a mountain range or a river, yet it has a definite position. No one can escape it. This is the condition of factional strife. It started among the scholar-gentry but has ended up depriving all people of their capacity for mutual tolerance. An old saying goes, "Fire is born out of wood: when fire flourishes, it eventually destroys the wood."[251] Subsequently, one cannot live in the east or the west or the south or the north; there are no places to live. If there are no habitable places, there will be no distinction in the four directions of the north, south, west, and east. When there is no differentiation in the directions, then the world becomes a veritable Diagram of the Great Absolute in which things are not differentiated. Under such circumstances, there will be neither scholars nor farmers, craftsmen nor traders; neither will there be any desirable place to live. Such a world is called a land that is not a land. Thus, I have written on desirable abodes for the scholar-gentry.

Epilogue

Because he did not have the opportunity to realize his political ideas, Confucius resorted to editing the *Spring and Autumn Annals*[252] to advocate the rule of the benevolent monarch. He embodied his views in his evaluation of historical events, taking care in his choice of words to commend virtue and condemn vice.

The author's epilogue is not contained in the Chosŏn Kwangmunhoe edition. But I have entered here the translation based on the postscript found in *Tongguk p'aryŏkchi*, one of the early-period *T'aengniji* manuscripts. The entry in the manuscript is as follows: 昔孔子以道不行 托魯史假以行王道 襃貶善惡此將實 以寓意也 莊子不欲出於世 著諸篇 爲宏「勝大之言 齊萬物 一彭殤 混凡聖此將虛 以寓意也 虛實雖殊 寓意卽同 昔余在黃山江上 夏日無事 登八卦亭消暑 偶有所論 著 是將我國山川人物風俗政教沿革治否得失美惡 而編次而記之耳 古人曰 禮樂 豈玉帛鐘鼓云乎 是欲擇可居處 而恨無可居耳 活看者求之於文字之外可也 噫實 卽關石和勻 虛卽芥子須彌 後必有卞之者矣 白羊初夏上浣 靑華山人書

Zhuangzi, a recluse who was never involved in worldly affairs, wrote magnificent articles in which he set forth the notion that the myriad of things, whether they be longevity or premature death, mediocrity or wisdom, are all reducible to one and the same. He thus expressed himself through abstractions. Though their means were different, the two sages achieved the same end of self-expression. Once when I was staying on the Hwangsan River in summer, there was nothing for me to do. I would climb up to the P'algwaejŏng (Eight-Trigram Pavilion) and spend my days there enjoying the cool mountain air. Now and then I would write. [These writings turned out to be] chronological notes on our mountains and rivers, well-known personalities and customs, political changes and their successes and failures, losses and gains, vices and virtues. An ancient saying goes, "How can the rites be confined to the exchange of jade and silk, and music to the playing of bells and drums?"[253] I [have written that I] wish to find a habitable place to live in but, much to my regret, an [ideal] abode does not exist. An intelligent reader will seek meanings beyond the words. In practical terms, this book is about tolls, taxes, and revenues.[254] Meanwhile, it also deals with the hidden meanings behind practical concerns, just as [something as big as] Mount Sumeru can be contained within an [infinitesimally small] mustard seed.[255] I am certain that someone of a later generation will be capable of appreciating this.

> Ch'ŏnghwa sanin wrote [this] at the start of
> early summer [in the year of the] white sheep.

Notes

Translator's Introduction

1. *Sadaebu* (scholar-gentry, Ch. *shi dafu*) is a combination of the terms *dafu* (grand master) and *shi* (serviceman). *Dafu* denoted the group of officials below *qing* (lord) and above *shi* during the Zhou dynasty. Once the nine-rank system was established, *dafu* came to designate officials of the fifth rank and above and *shi*, those of the sixth rank and below. In the Chosŏn dynasty, officials of the fifth rank and below were called *sa* and those of the fourth rank and above were called *taebu*. But the term *sadaebu* was also used in reference to scholars as well as ranked officials, the highest class in the Chosŏn dynasty.

2. Korean society of Yi Chung-hwan's time had distinctive class divisions: *yangban* (literally meaning civil and military camps) referring to the scholar-gentry class was the highest; *chungin* (middle people) were hereditary functionaries including medical officers, interpreter-translators, accountants, and petty clerks; next were commoners, that is, farmers, artisans, merchants, butchers, entertainers, and shamans; last were slaves, the lowest group.

3. I-sop Hong, "Yi Chung-hwan's Geographical Thought," 42.

4. Yu Wŏn-dong, "Ch'ŏngdam Yi Chung-hwan," 131–132.

5. Inshil Choe Yoon, "Study and Translation of *T'aengniji*," 85.

6. Yi Chung-hwan's focus on the scholar-gentry is also seen in his separation of "the characteristics of commoners from that of scholar-gentry." For further discussion in this regard, see Inshil Choe Yoon, "Study and Translation of *T'aengniji*," 85–89. For a recent attempt to read the *T'aengniji* by focusing on the keyword scholar-gentry, see Rim Young-gul, "*T'aengniji* tasi ilkki," 75–97.

7. Mok Hoe-gyŏng's postscript is entered in the *T'aengniji* (Kyujanggak collection, ko 4790–55).

8. The *T'aengniji* existed mainly in the form of handwritten classical Chinese manuscripts in a variety of recensions under various titles until the beginning of the twentieth century. Including "P'aryŏkchi" (Treatise on eight districts), "Tongguk chirihae" (Notes on the geography of Korea), "Tongguk sansurok" (Record of Korean scenery), "Sadaebu kagŏch'ŏ" (Habitable places for scholar-gentry), and "Ch'onghwa" (Trades and commodities). Thirty-two titles for the book were discovered in libraries in Korea and overseas (Inshil Choe Yoon, "Early Period *T'aengniji* Manuscripts," 226). Among the titles, "T'aengniji," with the final syllable appearing as either the character 志 or 誌, is by far the most frequent of the text's various titles, followed by "P'aryŏkchi" and "Chinyusŭngnam" (Survey of

Korea). Considering the fact that *T'aengniji* manuscripts are found not only in libraries but also in private collections, old bookstores, and internet auctions, it is likely that numerous *T'aengniji* manuscripts have been created over the years. For the latest bibliographical study of *T'aengniji* manuscripts, see Lee Do-hun, Kim Se-ho, and Yim Young-gil, "*T'aengniji ibongo*," 99–134. Full printed versions of the *T'aengniji* were published in 1910 (*P'aryŏkchi*) and 1912 (*T'aengniji*). Before this, a version partly translated into Japanese was published in 1882 in Tokyo as *Chosen hachiikichi* (Treatise on eight districts of Korea). A version translated into Chinese based on the Japanese translation was published in Shanghai in 1885 under the title "Chaoxian dili xiaozhi" (Abridged geographical treatise of Korea).

9. Ch'oe Nam-sŏn's "Editor's Note" in Yi Chung-hwan, *T'aengniji* (1912). Ch'oe Nam-sŏn took the lead in establishing Chosŏn Kwangmunhoe (Korean Association for Cultural Enlightenment) in 1910 and published reprints of over twenty volumes of Korean classics, including the *T'aengniji*, until 1914.

10. Lee Chan, "Hanguk chirihaksa," 705.

11. Han Woo-keun, "Kaehoesa," 126.

12. Choi Wan Gee, *Han'guk sŏngnihak ŭi maek*, 131.

13. Yi Sŏng-gye (King T'aejo) was supported in the founding of the Chosŏn dynasty not only by the military powers of the Koryŏ dynasty (918–1392) but also by scholars who aspired to see the country governed according to Confucian morality with an added philosophical dimension. Upholding Neo-Confucianism gave the dynasty a new identity and the philosophical grounds to reject Buddhism. Formally accepted as the national philosophy of the Koryŏ dynasty, Buddhism had been practiced by people of all classes. It however failed to influence leaders to actively engage in social service and welfare, especially in the late Koryŏ dynasty. During this time the dynasty was faltering from attacks from the north and problems within such as hereditary aristocrats with uncontrolled privileges of owning land but not paying taxes. Officially suppressed in the Chosŏn dynasty, Buddhism was still practiced. For background on how Buddhism survived in and contributed to the Chosŏn dynasty, consult Buswell, "Buddhism under Confucian Domination."

14. Neo-Confucianism was introduced to the Koryŏ dynasty by An Hyang (1243–1306) in the late thirteenth century and was initially studied by Yi Che-hyŏn (1287–1367), Yi Saek (1328–1396), and then Chŏng Mong-ju (1337–1392) and Chŏng To-jŏn (1342–1398). Among these men, Chŏng Mong-ju is considered one of the exemplary Neo-Confucian scholars in Korea. He was well known not only for his profound understanding and teaching of Neo-Confucianism and applying its guidelines in his administration, but also for pursuing righteousness, even at the cost of his life, to defend the Koryŏ dynasty. Although Chŏng Mong-ju wished to see the reformation of the ailing dynasty, he did not cooperate with the growing force determined to overthrow it. He was murdered by Yi Pang-wŏn, the fifth son of Yi Sŏng-gye and a central figure of the emerging power to establish the new dynasty. For more information on its introduction to Korea and the formation of Korean Neo-Confucianism, consult Deuchler's introduction in her *Confucian Transformation of Korea*, 14–24.

15. "Meritorious elite" denotes those who assisted or accepted the usurpation of the throne by King Sejo (r. 1455–1468), accomplished by murdering his nephew King Tanjong (r. 1452–1455). Scholar-gentry, newly appointed during the reign of King Sŏngjong (r. 1469–1494), challenged the meritorious elite's accumulation of wealth at the expense of the rural community. The meritorious elite counter-attacked the scholar-gentry, many of whom were students of Kim Chong-jik (1431–1492), when a paper titled "Lament for the Righteous Emperor" was discovered in the draft for the *Annals of King Sŏngjong*. Composed by Kim Chong-jik, the paper metaphorically criticized King Sejo's deeds. Having established that Kim Il-son, one of Kim Chong-jik's pupils, had inserted the composition in the draft of the annals, a group of meritorious elites incited King Yŏnsan (r. 1494–1506) to execute Kim Il-son and his associates, the result of which was the death or banishment of over fifty people in 1498.

16. They later split into two further factions: Southerner (Namin) and Northerner (Pugin) from the former and Old Doctrine (Noron) and Young Doctrine (Soron) from the latter, and so forth. While the Ministry of Rites administered the government service examinations, the Ministry of Personnel (Ijo) took charge of the appointment of successful candidates to civil posts and the Ministry of Military Affairs (Pyŏngjo) was responsible for the appointment of military posts. The latter two ministries were called selecting offices (銓曹 *chŏnjo*) and the senior fifth- and senior sixth-rank officials (郎官) of the ministries were called selection secretaries (銓郎 *chŏllang*), an abbreviation of 銓曹郎官 (*chŏnjo-nanggwan*). There were three senior fifth officials and three senior sixth-rank officials in each office. As court official posts in the Chosŏn dynasty were graded into nine ranks and each rank had senior and junior positions, the rank of selection secretaries was not considered to be high rank. For a detailed account of the development of literati factional politics in the Chosŏn dynasty, see the section on "Social Characteristics" in the translation in this book and the secondary sources cited there.

17. See Yi Chung-hwan, *T'aengniji* (1912), 44.

18. 今吾家 輝祖集成一書 縷縷 數千言 欲得士大夫可居處 其間 山脈水勢 風氣 氓俗 財賦之産 水陸之輸 井井有別 余未「見也 See "T'aengnijisŏ" in Yi Ik, *Sŏngho Sŏnsaeng chŏnjip*, pt. 49.

19. Inshil Choe Yoon, "Study and Translation of *T'aengniji*," 144–150.

20. The Kunlun Mountains in western China were regarded by ancient Chinese as the backbone of the world.

21. For example, in the fifty-volume *Tongguk yŏji sŭngnam* (Survey of Korean geography) and fifty-five-volume *Sinjŭng tongguk yŏji sŭngnam* (Newly augmented survey of Korean geography), after the cities of Seoul and Kaesŏng are discussed, the closest province to Seoul (Kyŏnggi) is then covered, followed by three southern provinces (Ch'ungch'ŏng, Kyŏngsang, Ch'ŏlla) and finally the northern provinces (Hwanghae, Kangwŏn, Hamgyŏng, and P'yŏngan).

22. *Chiri* (地理) is the term entered in the Chosŏn Kwangmunhoe edition and all of the *T'aengniji* manuscripts. In Yi Chung-hwan's time, *chiri* was used to mean both geography and *p'ungsu* (wind and water, Ch. *fengshui*). *P'ungsu* is a systematic way of examining the physical environment based on the belief that vital en-

ergy flows underground and human beings can benefit from it. In this book, I have used the term "geomancy" instead of *chiri* and *p'ungsu*. This art of evaluating appropriate landforms for dwellings and gravesites has been widely used in Korea since the Koryŏ dynasty. It was believed that certain sites transmitted vital energy to the people who occupied them.

23. An auspicious site, supported by its main mountain (主山 *chusan*) located closely behind it (to the north), is expected to have an homage mountain (朝山 *chosan*) and a table mountain (案山 *ansan*) in front of it (to the south). While the table mountain is low lying and closer to the auspicious site, the homage mountain is higher and lies further south. The table mountain serves as a table (案) between the master (主), who sits on the highest ground, and visitors or officials paying homage (朝) to him. In the case of Seoul, Mount Nam is the table mountain of the auspicious site of Kyŏngbokkung with Mount Paegak its main mountain and Mount Kwanak its homage mountain. This kind of layout is found in traditional settings for important ceremonies. In the case of ancestral memorial services, the ancestral tablet is kept on a high table, and a lower table laden with food is placed between the tablet and the offspring who are there bowing to the ancestors. For the idealized auspicious landscape and landscape terms, see Hong-key Yoon, "Human Modification of Korean Landforms," 246–247.

24. Water flow is to the south of an auspicious site and looks as if it is bowing toward the site.

25. Yi Ik, *Sŏngho Sŏnsaeng chŏnjip*, pt. 49.

26. His "Hyanggŏsoji 鄉居小誌" (A short treatise on living in a country) is entered after his abridged *T'aengniji*. See Choe Inshil, "*T'aengniji* ch'ogip'ilsabon ch'ujŏng ŭl wihan sŏjijŏk koch'al," 168.

27. Sim No-sung, a member of Old Doctrine, compiled *Taedong p'aerim* in 1821. Containing fifty-one different works of unofficial history in 125 volumes, it served as the original manuscript from which *P'aerim* (Miscellaneous collection) was copied. *P'aerim* stored at Yeungnam University has eighty-nine works in 191 volumes and is thought to have been compiled after the enthronement of King Kojong in 1863. On the other hand, *Taedong p'aerim* is found to have copied the compiled works of Kim Ryŏ (1766–1822). See Ahn Dae-Hoe, "*P'aerim* kwa Chosŏn hugi yasa ch'ongsŏ ŭi paltal," 20, 299–326.

28. 其文優有可觀 論城內卜居之地 山川風土人心謠俗 鑿鑿如指掌 又及黨論本末 文章言議 平定不偏....異趣之書 余亦多見 此可蔽之. See "Sanhaep'ilhŭi 山海筆戲" (Brush play among mountains and sea), the fortieth episode recorded in the *kapcha* (1834) year, and quoted in Sim No-sung, *Nunmul iran muŏsin'ga*, 287.

29. There are two forewords and six postscripts to the *T'aengniji*, and some *T'aengniji* manuscripts contain one or more of these. For example, *Sadaebu kagŏch'ŏ* (National Library, ko 2700–105) has Chŏng Ŏn-yu's foreword (written in 1753) and postscripts by Yi Chung-hwan (1751), Mok Sŏng-gwan (1752), Mok Hoe-gyŏng (1752), and Yi Pong-hwan (1753). Yi Ik's foreword (1751) is found in his *Sŏngho chŏnjip*, chap. 49, as is his postscript in chap. 55. Chŏng Yag-yong's postscript is in his *Tasan simunjip*, chap. 14.

30. Inshil Choe Yoon, "Study and Translation of *T'aengniji*," 46–48.

31. Inshil Choe Yoon, "Study and Translation of *T'aengniji*," 48–50.

32. 夫衣食乏則不可處 士氣歇則不可處 武力競則不可處 侈風勝則不可處 猜嫌多則不可處. See "Foreword to the *T'aengniji*," in Yi Ik, *Sŏngho chŏnjip*, chap. 49.

33. 宜先視水火 其次五穀 其次風俗 其次山川之勝. See "Postscript to the *T'aengniji*," in Chŏng Yag-yong, *Tasan simunjip*, chap.14.

34. 君看擇里志 生理最稱佳, in "Kwijŏnsich'o 歸田詩草," in Chŏng Yag-yong, *Tasan simunjip*, chap. 7.

35. 夫子曰 里仁爲美 擇不處仁 焉得知也 世人以此爲藉口 擇里之說所由起也 然今所謂擇里者 非擇里之仁 惟利之是圖也…. 擇里之書 李重煥創著 人多被惑 其弊無窮 故亦爲之辨爾. The whole text of "T'aengni pyŏnjŭngsŏl 擇里辨證說" can be found in Yi Kyu-gyŏng, "T'aengni pyŏnjŭngsŏl 擇里辨證說" (On selecting settlements), "Ch'ŏnjip'yŏn" (Heaven and earth), *Ojuyŏnmun changjŏnsango* 五洲衍文長箋散稿 (Random expatiations), *Hanguk kochŏn chonghap DB* (Comprehensive database of Korean classics), accessed July 7, 2017, http://db.itkc.or.kr/search/group?q=query†%E6%93%87%E9%87%8C%E8%BE%A8%E8%AD%89%E8%AA%AA.

36. After a comprehensive covering of Chinese works and Korean works such as *Tongguk yŏjiji* (Geographical description of Korea), *P'alto chiji* (Geographical description of the eight provinces), *Yŏji sŭngnam* (Augmented geographical survey of Korea), and other works, Yi Kyu-gyŏng listed the *T'aengniji*—together with Yi Ik's *Sŏngho sasŏl* (Miscellaneous discussion of *Sŏngho*) and several other works—as a work worthy of referencing when discussing regional surveys of Korea. See "Chiji pyŏnjŭngsŏl 地誌辨證說" (On geographical description), *Ojuyŏnmun changjŏnsango Hanguk kochŏn chonghap DB*, accessed July 7, 2017, http://db.itkc.or.kr/imgviewer/item?itemId=BT#imgviewer/imgnode?grpId=&itemId=BT&dataId=ITKC_BT_1301A_0140_010_0150.

37. See Jeong Myunghyun, "*Imwŏn kyŏngjeji* sabondŭl e taehan sŏjihakchŏk kŏmt'o," 206. *Imwŏn kyŏngjeji* is also known as *Imwŏn simnyukchi* (Sixteen treatises on rural life management). Written and compiled by Sŏ Yu-gu (1764–1845) with quotations from 852 publications in Korea and China, it is a practical guide to the lifestyle of scholar-gentry in retirement.

38. This *P'aerim*, selected works of unofficial history in forty-five volumes, is stored in Yonsei University library. Works by twenty-three authors, including Yi I (1536–1584) and Song Si-yŏl (1607–1689) are entered in the collection. The most recent work in the collection is that of Yi Ŭi-ch'ŏl (1703–1778). As records from the reign of King Yŏngjo are also included, the collection is thought to have been compiled after the reign of King Chŏngjo (r. 1776–1780).

39. Edited by Hong Chung-in (1677–1752), the *Aju chamnok* is a collection of abridged writings mainly on literati factional politics from the time of King Sŏnjo (r. 1567–1608). The full collection of 107 chapters in forty-seven volumes is stored in Jangseogak.

40. Edited by Hwang Tŏk-kil around 1800, *Choyasinp'il* is a multivolume collection on literati factional politics beginning with the emergence of the two factions in 1575 and is stored in Kyujanggak (kyu 15580 v. 2).

41. For the entire contents, see Yi Wŏn-sun, *Hwahae hwip'yŏn*.

42. Based on unofficial historical records written in Korea, the *Yŏllŏsil kisul* is

regarded to have objectively described major events from the start of the Chosŏn dynasty up until the era of King Sukchong.

43. Ch'oe Nam-sŏn's "Editor's Note" in Yi Chung-hwan, *T'aengniji* (1912).

44. *Chosen hachisikichi* (The eight provinces of Korea) was translated by Kondo Sinsuki, and *Chaoxian dili xiaozhi* (Abridged geography of Korea) was translated by Jian Jinggui.

45. Lautensach, *Korea*, 37. For the original publication, see H. L. Lautensach, *Korea, eine Landeskunde auf Grund eigener Reisen und der Literatur* (Leipzig: Koehler-Verlang, 1945).

46. Lautensach, *Korea*, 38. This is Lautensach's concluding remark after his survey of a series of modern scholars' evaluations on geographical writings in Korea, including published works and unpublished manuscripts such as Sin Kyŏng-jun's (1712–1781) "*Pal-to yuk-taero ko* (Examen des six grandes routes de la Coré)." Among them, a fifty-five-volume geographical work explained to have been "printed in 1537" was translated as "the fifty-five-volume *Tongguk yŏji sŭngnam* (Survey of Korean geography)." *Tongguk yŏji sŭngnam* was completed in 1481 in fifty volumes. I think what Lautensach intended to mention is the fifty-five-volume *Sinjŭng tongguk yŏji sŭngnam* (Newly augmented geographical survey of Korea), which was published in 1530.

47. Yi Chin-hyu (1657–1710) held many posts, including chief royal secretary, governor of Ch'ungch'ŏng province and Hamgyŏng province, magistrate of Andong, and vice minister of Rites.

48. See "Kangwŏn Province" in the translation in this book.

49. Inshil Choe Yoon, "Study and Translation of *T'aengniji*," 52.

50. Johann Heinrich von Thünen (1783–1850) proposed how land would be used in his "Isolated State," with the type of farming that made the most profit located closest to the city, which is at the center of the state and the least profitable farming activity on the periphery, hence the creation of four rings of different farming patterns around the city. The band of intensive farming including the cultivation of vegetables and fruit and dairy being located closest to the city, activities for securing firewood and timber in the second closest band, extensive crop farming in the third band, and animal husbandry for the production of meat in the farthest band. This agricultural land-use model is based on the hypothesis that the "isolated state" is self-sufficient; it assumes a topographically uniform plain without natural barriers such as mountains or rivers and a climate and soil fertility that are the same throughout. At its center is a large town that will "supply the rural areas with all manufactured products"; the town, in turn, "obtains all its provisions from the surrounding countryside." See *Von Thünen's Isolated State: An English Edition of Der isolierte Staat*. Part 1 of this book was originally published in 1826 and section 1 of part 2 was published in 1850. Alfred Weber theorized the optimum location of industries to maximize profit. For detailed hypothesis and discussions, see Weber, *Theory of the Location of Industries*.

51. The following are the selected articles and theses on geographic features of the *T'aengniji*: Rho Do-yang, "*P'aryŏkchi* 'kagŏji' haesŏl"; Sŏ Su-in, "*T'aengniji*

yŏn'gu sŏsŏl"; Hong-key Yoon, "*T'aengniji*: A Korean Settlement Geography"; I-sŏp Hong, "Yi Chung-hwan's Geographical Thought in *T'aengniji*"; Hong-key Yoon, "*T'aengniji*: A Classical Cultural Geography of the Korean Settlement"; Park Young-han, "Ch'ŏngdam Yi Chung-hwan ŭi chiri sasang e kwanhan yŏn'gu"; Lee Chan, "*T'aengniji* e taehan chirihakchŏk koch'al"; Choe Young-jun, "*T'aengniji*: Hangukchŏk inmun chirisŏ."

52. See the "Scenery" section of the translation in this book.

53. The members of the offices of the Inspector General and the Censor General.

54. See Yi Hong-ryŏl, "Taegan chedo ŭi pŏpchesa chŏk koch'al," 34.

55. I-sŏp Hong, "Yi Chung-hwan's Geographical Thought," 41–42.

56. I-sŏp Hong, "Yi Chung-hwan's Geographical Thought," 44.

57. Jung Doo Hee, "Yi Chung-hwan," 129.

58. Suematsu Yasukazu, "Hachiikishi ni tsuite," 6.

59. See the sections on "Kangwŏn Province" and "Social Characteristics" in the translation in this book.

60. See "Kangwŏn Province" in the translation in this book.

61. The prime minister (*yŏngŭijŏng*), the first deputy prime minister (*chwaŭijŏng*), and the second deputy prime minister (*uŭijŏng*).

62. The ministers of the offices of Personnel, Taxation, Rites, Military Affairs, Punishments, and Works.

63. Court official posts in the Chosŏn dynasty were graded into nine ranks: each rank had senior and junior positions, starting from senior first rank (high chief state councilors) and ending with junior ninth rank. The prime minister and the two deputy prime ministers are senior first rank, and the six ministers are senior second in the ranking system of the Chosŏn dynasty.

64. The Office of the Inspector General (Sahŏnbu) investigated the alleged wrongdoings of government officials and royal families. This office, made up of six inspectors and twenty-four bailiffs, was headed by the inspector general, who was junior second rank, and had inspectors' posts of junior third rank and below. The Office of the Censor General (Saganwŏn) advised kings on their speech and actions and commented on wrong governance, appointments, sentencing of notorious criminals, etc. Having become an independent office, the Office of the Censor General was made up of five members, with the censor general, a senior third-rank officer, as the head and four censors of junior third-rank status and below.

65. The Office of the Censor General was made independent in 1401, during the reign of King T'aejong (r. 1400–1418).

66. The three offices of law (*Samsa*): the Office of the Inspector General, the Office of the Censor General (as discussed in the preceding notes) and the Office of Special Advisers (Hongmun'gwan). The main duty of the Office of Special Advisers was to look after historical records in the royal archives, correctly enter court documents, and give royal lectures, as well as to advise the kings when asked.

67. See the early part of the section "Social Characteristics" in the translation in this book.

68. Quoted from the early part of "Social Characteristics" in the translation in this book.

69. See *Annals of King Sŏngjong* on the sixth day in the first month of 1494.

70. Song Ch'an-sik, "Chosŏnjo sarim chŏngch'i ŭi kwŏllŏk kujo," 120–140.

71. Song Ch'an-sik professed that he acquired, through the *T'aengniji*, the knowledge that selection secretaries played pivotal roles in leading public opinion of the Three Remonstrative Offices. See Song Ch'an-sik, "Chosŏnjo sarim chŏngch'i ŭi kwŏllŏk kujo," 120–122.

72. Chŏng Man-jo, "Chosŏn sidae ŭi sarim chŏngch'i."

73. See Yi Hong-ryŏl, "Taegan chedo ŭi pŏpchesa chŏk koch'al," 10–37.

74. Quoted from the latter part of "Social Characteristics" in this book.

75. Yi Kyu-bo showed his literary talent at an early age and produced many writings of diverse genres. One of his most famous writings is "Tongmyŏngwang-p'yŏn (Saga of King Tongmyŏng)," on the founder of the Koguryŏ kingdom (37 BCE–CE 668) of Korea. Written at the age of twenty-six, it is an epic poem covering legendary tales from before the birth of Chumong and the succession of his son, King Yuri. While working at the Koryŏ court, Yi Kyu-bo wrote many diplomatic letters, especially during the Mongol invasions. His "Petition to the Emperor" ("Chinjŏngp'yo," Ch. "Chenqingbiao") proved to be effective in appeasing the Mongol's outrageous demands on the Koryŏ dynasty. "Yi Kyu-bo," "Yŏlchŏn" (Biographies), vol. 102, chap. 15, *Koryŏsa*, accessed October 10, 2016, http://db.history .go.kr/KOREA/item/level.do?itemId=kr&bookId=列傳&types=o#articleList/kr _102_0010_0020.

76. Yi Ŏn-jŏk was "canonized" and initiated into the National Shrine to Confucius at the Royal Confucian Academy in Seoul. He is one of the eighteen Korean Confucian sages, a number that includes Ch'oe Ch'i-wŏn (857–?), Chŏng Mong-ju (1337–1392), Yi Hwang (1501–1570), and Yi I (1536–1584). Having passed the civil service examination in 1514, Yi Ŏn-jŏk rose to the position of censor in 1530. He opposed the reappointment of Kim An-no, who once wielded power as the father-in-law of Princess Hyohye, a daughter of King Chungjong. This led to his forced resignation from the court and return to his hometown. Later, he accepted appointments to posts such as judge in the State Tribunal. He was implicated in an incident that followed the literati purge in 1545 and was banished in 1547 to Kanggye, a northern town in P'yŏngan Province. In one of his petitions he emphasized that the king's attitude is the most important in the monarchy and wrote ten clauses for King Chungjong to heed. In another petition he listed eight items necessary for a king's learning and training. In the period after his resignation and during his banishment, Yi wrote several books, emphasizing the superiority of *i* (principle/plan) over *ki* (matter/material). Yi Hwang also pursued this line of study.

77. Yi Ik, "Yi Hwijo Myogalmyŏng" (The tombstone inscription of Yi Hwijo [Chung-hwan]), in his *Sŏngho Sŏnsaeng munjip*, chap. 44.

78. The Mok family played an important role in Yi Chung-hwan's life after marriage. It was his association with Mok Ho-ryong, a relative of Mok Im-il, that led to Yi Chung-hwan's banishment from public life. The fact that both Mok

Sŏng-gwan (1691–1772) and Mok Hoe-gyŏng (1698–?), who were also related to Yi Chung-hwan by marriage, wrote postscripts to the *T'aengniji* indicates that he maintained a close relationship with the Mok family even after his banishment. For a detailed genealogy of Yi Chung-hwan and the Mok family, see Kim Chŏng-sim, "Yi Chung-hwan ŭi *T'aengniji* e kwanhan yŏn'gu," 3–4; Koishi Akiko, "Ri Ju-kan to *Takurishi*," 76–77; Lee Moon-Jong, "Yi Chung-hwan ŭi saengae wa *T'aengniji* ŭi sŏngnip," 124–127.

79. The civil service examination was the most prized among government service examinations. Apart from the civil service examination, there were military service examinations and miscellaneous examinations for technical subjects such as interpretation, penal codes, medicine, astronomy, and geomancy. These technical subjects were not as highly valued by *yangban* scholars due to the Confucian perspective on jobs. Therefore, these posts were often taken by commoners.

80. Senior ninth rank was the second lowest rank, as court official posts in the Chosŏn dynasty were graded into nine ranks with each rank having senior and junior positions.

81. For the background on the political changes covering the period of the reign of King Kyŏngjong and the early part of King Yŏngjo's reign that is relevant to the arrest and banishment of Yi Chung-hwan, see Haboush, *Confucian Kingship in Korea*, 29–33.

82. Having no heir either from Queen In'gyŏng (1661–1680) or from Queen Inhyŏn, King Sukchong made his son born of Lady Chang the crown prince in 1690 amidst severe opposition from the Old Doctrine Faction. Having entrapped Queen Inhyŏn in order to dethrone her, Lady Chang, as the new queen, then had an exorcism performed by shamans aimed at causing the death of the newly deposed queen. When this was discovered, Lady Chang was sentenced to death and executed in 1701.

83. *Kyŏngjong sillok* and *Sŭngjŏngwŏn ilgi*, eleventh day, fifth month, 1723. O Myŏng-hang's accusation was based on hearsay, which he claimed to have been widespread. As the king considered O Myŏng-hang's request appropriate, Yi Chung-hwan must have stepped down straight away, as it was customary that the accused stay away from his office while he was being investigated, even if the allegations were only based on rumor. The arrest of Yi Chung-hwan was ordered in the following month. See *Kyŏngjong sillok* and *Sŭngjŏngwŏn ilgi*, sixth day, sixth month, 1723.

84. *Kyŏngjong sillok*, eleventh day, sixth month, 1723.

85. *Kyŏngjong sillok*, second day, ninth month, 1723.

86. Being the leader of the Old Doctrine Faction at the time, Min Chin-wŏn, the second deputy prime minister and the highest-ranking official present in the state tribunal, persistently accused Yi Chung-hwan of cooperating with Mok Ho-ryong in the 1722 incident.

87. The day after two interrogations with thirty beatings each, Mok Ho-ryong was found dead. See *Ch'uan kŭp Kugan*, ninth day, twelfth month, 1724.

88. *Ch'uan kŭp Kugan*, twenty-eighth day, fourth month, 1725.

89. *Ch'uan kŭp Kugan*, first, second, and seventh day, fifth month, 1725.

90. Yi Cham (1660–1706) was awarded the post of second inspector in the Office of the Inspector General, a junior third rank, in the second month of 1723. The award of a posthumous post was an act of vindication of Yi Cham's honor. The post, however, was revoked in 1725.

91. See *Yŏngjo sillok*, twenty-first day, seventh month, 1725.

92. *Yŏngjo sillok*, twentieth day, twelfth month, 1726.

93. See *Yŏngjo sillok*, twentieth and twenty-second day, twelfth month, 1726.

94. *Yŏngjo sillok*, fourth day, seventh month, 1727.

95. *Yŏngjo sillok*, eleventh day, seventh month, 1727. The chief of the Correction Tribunal was of junior first rank.

96. *Yŏngjo sillok*, sixth day, tenth month, 1727.

97. *Yŏngjo sillok*, seventh day, twelfth month, 1727.

98. See the section on "Scenery" in the translation in this book.

99. Running to the east of Mount Inwang, in present-day Ch'ŏngundong, the stream of Ch'ŏngp'unggye was one of the most scenic spots in Seoul during the Chosŏn dynasty. One day in 1620, seven scholars and high-ranking officials, including Yi Sang-ŭi, the minister of military affairs, and Yi Kyŏng-jŏn, (1567–1644) the minister of punishment, assembled at the stream and wrote poems and sketched scenes of their gathering. Later, they put the poems and drawings into albums and shared them among themselves. To commemorate this, 120 years later, their descendants gathered at the same spot. Yi Ik wrote that he could not attend the meeting but Yi Chung-hwan and others from his family did. Quoted in Lee Moon-Jong, *Yi Chung-hwan kwa "T'aengniji,"* 115.

100. See Yi Ik, "Yi Hwijo Myogalmyŏng," in *Sŏngho Sŏnsaeng munjip,* chap. 44.

101. Lee Moon-Jong, "Yi Chung-hwan ŭi saeng'ae wa *T'aengniji* ŭi sŏngnip," 137.

102. Chŏng To-jŏn, a scholar and military official, was given the power to set out the political and administrative structures of the new dynasty. With the ideal of having balanced power between the throne and officials, he completed *Chosŏn Kyŏnggukchŏn* (Code of governance of Chosŏn) in 1394. The code suggested a comprehensive norm for governance and served as the basis for government-initiated codes such as *Kyŏngje yukchŏn* (Six codes of governance), promulgated in 1397, and eventually *Kyŏngguk taejŏn* (National code), which started to be implemented in 1485. For more information on Chŏng To-jŏn, consult Chai-sik Chung, "Chŏng Tojŏn."

103. The highest administrative organ in the Chosŏn dynasty, led by the prime minister and two deputy prime ministers.

104. The ministries of Personnel, Taxation, Rites, Military Affairs, Punishments, and Public Works.

105. Being the organs representing public opinion, the freedom of speech of members of the Three Remonstrative Offices was guaranteed. These offices were first installed in the court during the reign of King Sŏngjong in the Koryŏ dynasty.

106. As for the exercise of their political powers, see the beginning of the "Social Characteristics" section in this book.

107. The role of the offices of the Inspector General and the Censor General expanded during the twenty-five years of King Sŏngjong's reign. The king, who was enthroned at the age of twelve and was guided by his grandmother Queen Chŏnghŭi for the first seven years, was willing to listen to the advice of these two offices, later to his dismay. (For an explanation of the increase in their activities, see Wagner, *Literati Purges*, chap. 2.) During the reign of King Yŏnsan (who did not take their advice and criticism well) there was discovered, in the draft of the *Annals of King Sŏngjong*, a poem, "Lament for the Righteous Emperor," that metaphorically criticized King Sejo for usurping the throne and killing young King Tanjong. Incited by a group of meritorious elite, King Yŏnsan executed Kim Il-son, who had inserted the draft of the annals, along with his associates and many officials of the Three Remonstrative Offices and banished many others in 1498. Like the following two purges, the first purge is regarded as having been a blow by the then king against the Three Remonstrative Offices.

108. For a detailed explanation of their education and the civil service examinations, see Yi Sŏng-mu, "The Influence of Neo-Confucianism."

109. For more information on social hierarchy and the kinship system in Korea, consult Deuchler, "The Contours of Korean Society in Late Chosŏn," in Deuchler, *Confucian Transformation of Korea*, 6–14.

110. Keum Jang-tae, *Han'guk Sirhak sasang yŏn'gu*, 14–15.

111. When King Kyŏngjong died suddenly in the fourth year of his reign, Prince Yŏning ascended to the throne and executed Old Doctrine accusers, including Kim Il-gyŏng and Mok Ho-ryong, who belonged to Young Doctrine Faction. The new king at the same time tried to embrace the Young Doctrine Faction and appointed its members to high government offices. Radical members of the Young Doctrine Faction, who were left out of these appointments, spread rumors attributing the old king's sudden death to the new king and, in the *musin* year (1728), they staged a revolt against him with some members of the Southerner Faction.

112. King Yŏngjo implemented new measures such as the Equalized Tax Law (Kyunyŏkpŏp). After the period of the Hideyoshi invasion (1592–1597), commoners between sixteen and sixty years of age had been expected to pay taxes in clothing material in lieu of army service. This tax provided considerable income to the court but was a great burden on the poor. With the implementation of the new law, the burden was halved.

113. In the Koryŏ and Chosŏn dynasties, compilation of one's writings and subsequent printing thereof were mostly carried out by one's descendants or pupils. Apart from manpower, considerable funding as well as agreement from one's community were required for printing. The descendants of Yi Chung-hwan might not have had the financial means to publish his work. There is no record that all of his works were ever compiled.

114. I found no manuscript containing a postscript by either Yi Ik or Chŏng Yak-yong among the aforementioned *T'aengniji* manuscripts.

115. For the verification of the order of contents, see Inshil Choe Yoon, "Early Period *T'aengniji* Manuscripts."

116. See Inshil Choe Yoon, "Early Period *T'aengniji* Manuscripts." For the verification of its copy date, see Huh Woong, "Kungmunp'an *T'aengniji* ŭi ŏnŏ punsŏk." The manuscript is stored in the National Library of France. Its content, however, can be found in *Aesan hakpo* 3 (1983): 75–163.

117. As the *T'aengniji* manuscripts were hand copied over the period from 1751 to the 1930s, I have divided the 180 years into three periods and provisionally named the ones that would have been copied during the first sixty-year period "early *T'aengniji* manuscripts."

118. See Choe Inshil, "*T'aengniji* ch'ogip'ilsabon ch'ujŏng ŭl wihan sŏjijŏk koch'al."

119. See Inshil Choe Yoon, "Early Period *T'aengniji* Manuscripts." For more and detailed examples of common features in the "Geomancy" section, see Inshil Choe Yoon, "Geomantic Ideas in *T'aengniji* Manuscripts."

120. The last emperor of the Ming dynasty (1368–1644).

121. Koishi Akiko, "Ri Ju-kan to *Takurishi*," 83.

122. Inshil Choe Yoon, "Study and Translation of *T'aengniji*," 21.

123. For the full translation of Yi's postscript, see Yi Chung-hwan's "Epilogue" section of the translation in this book.

124. Inshil Choe Yoon, "Study and Translation of *T'aengniji*," 20–21.

125. Based on the fact that the part of the Naktong River that flows in front of Yangsan in Kyŏngsang Province is named the Hwangsan River on *Taedongyŏjido* (map of Taedong created by Kim Chŏng-ho), Koishi Akiko ("Ri Ju-kan to *Takurishi*," 82) has claimed that the Hwangsan River is a part of the Naktong River. Arguing that there is no P'algoejŏng on that part of the river, Lee Moon-Jong ("Yi Chung-hwan ŭi saeng'ae wa *T'aengniji* ŭi sŏngnip," 149) posits, on the other hand, that the part of the Kŭm River that flows around Hwangsanch'on in Kanggyŏng, where P'algoejŏng stood, would have been called the Hwangsan River. Song Si-yŏl, a famous Neo-Confucian scholar, had P'algoejŏng built facing the Kŭm River and taught his students there.

126. Ch'ŏnghwa sanin is one of Yi Chung-hwan's pseudonyms.

127. Koishi Akiko attempts to explain the reason why Suematsu interpreted *paek* (white) *yang* (sheep) as the year of the dog. See Koishi, "Ri Ju-kan to *Takurishi*," 84; Inshil Choe Yoon, "Study and Translation of *T'aengniji*," 21–24.

128. Inshil Choe Yoon, "Study and Translation of *T'aengniji*," 21–24.

129. Inshil Choe Yoon, "Study and Translation of *T'aengniji*," 23–24.

130. Yi Chung-hwan, *T'aengniji* (1971), 9–10; Nishikawa Takao, "*Takurishi* no imyonitsuite" (On various names of *T'aengniji*), 130.

131. Yoon, Inshil Choe, "A Study and Translation of *T'aengniji*," 32–34.

132. Yoon, Inshil Choe, "A Study and Translation of *T'aengniji*," 22.

133. 其中一局是吾家人所著 向者 諸家作序 改其標題 爲擇里志. See Kim Yaksŭl, "Sŏngho susabon *T'aengniji* e taehayŏ," 71.

134. Inshil Choe Yoon, "A Study and Translation of *T'aengniji*," 23.

135. See Koishi Akiko, "Ri Ju-kan to *Takurishi*," 85.

136. Inshil Choe Yoon, "Study and Translation of *T'aengniji*," 29–32.

137. Formally called *kwŏnsuje* (the title at the start of the book) it appears mainly at the beginning of an author's writing.

138. In the twelve manuscripts, I did not include *T'aengniji* (Ilsa Ko 915.1-Y58t) in Kyujanggak. At the beginning of the main text of this manuscript, under the inner title *T'aengniji*, it is indicated that "the original title is Sadaebu kagŏch'ŏsŏ 士大夫可居處序, not Sadaebu kagŏch'ŏ 士大夫可居處."

139. *Wayurok* is a private collection of Kim Young-jin.

140. Lee Do-hun, Kim Se-ho, and Yim Young-gil, "*T'aengniji* ibongo," 113; Ahn Dae-hoe," *T'aengniji* ŭi kujŏnjisik panyŏng kwa chiyŏkchŏnsŏl sŏsul ŭi sigak," 48. Together with three other *T'aengniji* manuscripts this manuscript is grouped into the early-manuscript group in "*T'aengniji* ibongo."

141. Kim Young-jin, "Chosŏn hugi *Wayurok* ibon yŏn'gu," 243.

142. Choe Inshil, "*T'aengniji* ch'ogip'ilsabon ch'ujŏng ŭl wihan sŏjijŏk koch'al," 159.

143. Choe Inshil, "*T'aengniji* ch'ogip'ilsabon ch'ujŏng ŭl wihan sŏjijŏk koch'al," 168–169.

144. Kim Yak-sŭl, "Sŏngho susabon *T'aengniji* e taehayŏ," 71.

145. 向者 諸家作序 改其標題 爲擇里志 又取其錯誤十餘 改擇 有刪正 未知渠信受否耳.

146. See the "Scenery" section of the translation in this book.

147. Inshil Choe Yoon, "Study and Translation of *T'aengniji*," 122. See the location of the Outer City Wall of P'yŏngyang in Plate 2, map of P'yŏngyangbu (City of P'yŏngyang) in P'yŏngan Province.

148. Inshil Choe Yoon, "Study and Translation of *T'aengniji*," 117–142.

149. For the contents of the entries, see Pak Hyŏn-kyu, "Kwanghaegunjo yugu seja sagŏng wa chŏlmyŏngsi kamsang," 266.

150. Pak Hyŏn-kyu, "Kwanghaegunjo yugu seja sagŏnkwa chŏlmyŏngsi kamsang," 257–277; Kim Tong-uk, " 'Yuguguk seja' iyagi ŭi yubyŏn yangsang," 153–154.

151. Ahn Dae-hoe, "*T'aengniji* ŭi kujŏnjisik panyŏng kwa chiyŏkchŏnsŏl sŏsul ŭi sigak," 59.

152. Yun Hyu (1617–1680) wrote that Yi Sun-sin had metal chains cast, whereby he cut through the entrance of a harbor. See Yun Hyu, "T'ongjesa Yi Ch'ungmugong yusa" (Memorabilia of Commander-in-Chief Yi Sun-sin), in *Paekhojip,* chap. 21. Quoted in from Ahn Dae-hoe, "*T'aengniji* ŭi kujŏnjisik panyŏng kwa chiyŏkchŏnsŏl sŏsul ŭi sigak," 59–61.

153. Ahn Dae-hoe, " *T'aengniji* ŭi kujŏnjisik panyŏng kwa chiyŏkchŏnsŏl sŏsul ŭi sigak."

154. It is thought that the translation was based on the Chosŏn Kwangmunhoe edition of *T'aengniji* and a ten-page explanation was written by the translator. Pak Yong-su, "*T'aengniji* hangŭl kugyŏk pon," accessed July 4, 2016, http://san .chosun.com/site/data/html_dir/2012/03/30/2012033001547.html.

155. Yi Chung-hwan, *T'aengniji* (1969), 20.

156. Yi Chung-hwan, *P'aryŏkchi* (1910).

157. For example, in his translated version of *T'aengniji* (1977), Rho Do-Yang demonstrates that his translation was based on the Chosŏn Kwangmunhoe edition of *T'aengniji* by attaching its full text.

158. Ch'oe Pŏm-sŏ, *Sosŏl T'aengniji*.

159. Sin Chŏng-il, *Tasi ssŭnŭn T'aengniji*; Kŏri Munhwa Simin Yŏndae, *Taegu sin T'aengniji*; Han Sam-gŏn, *Ulsan T'aengniji*; Sin Chŏng-il, *Saero ssŭnŭn T'aengniji*; No Chu-sŏk, *Seoul T'aengniji*; Sŏul Sin *T'aengniji* Saŏptan, *Ch'ŏngnyŏn, sŏul ŭi maŭl ŭl t'amhada*; Kang Che-yun, *Sŏm T'aengniji*.

160. Yi Chung-hwan, *T'aengniji* (2011); Yi Chung-hwan, *T'aengniji: Urittang e taehan kamdongjŏgin pogosŏ* (2012).

161. See Suematsu Yasukazu. "*Hachiikishi* ni tsuite," 1–2.

162. Nishikawa Takao, "Takurishi no imyo ni tsuite," 119.

163. This refers to *Yi Chung-hwan's T'aengniji: The Korean Classic for Choosing Settlement*, translated with an introduction and notes by Inshil Choe Yoon (Sydney: Wild Peony, 1998).

164. Inshil Choe Yoon, "Early Period *T'aengniji* Manuscripts," 246.

165. The beginning part of the conclusion is missing and phrases revealing the relationship between Korean and Chinese dynasties are entered differently from those used in other manuscripts. See Bae Woo-sung, "*T'aengniji* e taehan yŏnksahakchŏk tokpŏp," 213–214.

166. See Choe Inshil, "*T'aengniji* ch'ogibon ŭi t'ŭksŏng," 143; Inshil Choe Yoon, "Early Period *T'aengniji* Manuscripts," 237–242.

167. For a detailed explanation of early-period *T'aengniji* manuscripts, see Inshil Choe Yoon, "Early Period *T'aengniji* Manuscripts," 225–249.

Translation

1. In "Sadaebu kagŏch'ŏ" in *Wayurok, Tongguk chirihae*, and other early-period *T'aengniji* manuscripts, a phrase "Yija wal" (Master Yi remarks that) appears prior to this. The missing phrase in this text is thought to have been inserted by Yi Chung-hwan to indicate his authorship in an indirect way. The initially circulated *T'aengniji* manuscripts had no name or pseudonym of the author.

2. A legendary emperor of ancient China, said to have been a peasant. He became the son-in-law of Emperor Yao and eventually succeeded to the throne. He is known to have thoroughly surveyed his kingdom and organized it into twelve regions. He oversaw various tribes, standardized measurements, and collected fair taxes. With his fine achievements and his filial piety toward his malicious father, he is hailed as an examplar of a benevolent ruler with high moral standards, especially in Confucian literature.

3. Refers to the Xia, Shang, and Zhou dynasties. Xia, the first dynasty in Chinese legend, started around the twenty-first century BCE and lasted until the sixteenth century BCE. The Shang dynasty is recorded to have existed between

the sixteenth and eleventh century BCE and was succeeded by the Zhou dynasty (eleventh century–256 BCE).

4. A collection of ancient Chinese poetry including folk songs of the Zhou dynasty. It is the earliest remaining record of ancient Chinese songs.

5. A classic on ancient Chinese historical records.

6. The first unified Chinese dynasty.

7. A legendary emperor of ancient China who ruled the country with righteousness and devotion. His exemplary achievements include bringing floods under control. While he was said to have peacefully passed on his throne not to his son but to Shun and thus was praised by Confucius and his followers, other records reveal the succession to Shun to have been neither peaceful nor voluntary.

8. Ceremonies for the coming of age, marriage, funeral, and sacrifices to ancestors.

9. In this final paragraph the author is thought to have intended to present the three basic elements he covers in the *T'aengniji*: the universe-time (heaven), place (earth), and people.

10. One of the most famous and longest mountain ranges in western China, stretching about two thousand kilometers from the Pamirs in the west across Qinghai Province. It borders the Tibetan plateau along its southern edge and Tarim basin along its northern edge. With high peaks reaching seven thousand meters, it was considered by the ancient Chinese to be the backbone of the world; from it, four ranges branch off in four directions: the southern into China proper, the eastern into Korea, and the western and northern ranges into the wilderness. Zhu Xi (1130–1200) regarded it as the ancestor of all the world's mountains.

11. A mountain range north of Liaodong Peninsula, stretching southwest to northeast.

12. A peninsula in China northwest of Korea.

13. The highest mountain in Korea, 2,750 meters above sea level, forming one of Korea's two volcanic landforms and situated on the border between Manchuria and Korea. Koreans tend to call a group of mountains by the name of its most famous summit.

14. An ancient Chinese book describing areas in China, its surroundings and faraway lands. It contains most ancient Chinese mythologies and information on not only locally found animals, plants, minerals, and treasures, but also imagined creatures and local products. Out of the extant eighteen chapters, the five chapters on mountains describe areas in China proper in the simplest way by listing a mountain, its local products and their functions, and then lists religious sacrificial rites at the end of each chapter. Assigning each chapter to the five directions of south, west, north, east, and central, they are thought to be the earliest creation, possibly dating to the fourth century BCE. The way the other chapters present areas is more varied; many descriptions of places and their local products are non-realistic. Mount Buxian is recorded in the chapter "Great Remote North."

15. A *ri* is a traditional Korean measure of distance equivalent to four hundred meters.

16. A place in Jilin Province, Manchuria, where six brothers of the first Qing emperor resided.

17. Early capital of the Qing in Manchuria and where many Koreans were taken during the Manchu invasion (1636–1637). Yun Chip, O Tal-che, and Hong Ik-han, three famous Korean scholars who opposed surrendering to the Qing army, were also taken there and killed.

18. People who lived in Manchuria and established the Jin (K. Kŭm, 1115–1234) dynasty in China. As descendants of Tungus, they were known as Malgal (Ch. Mohe) during the Tang dynasty and Jurchen during the Song and Ming dynasties. Those who belonged to southern Tungusic tribes and were called Manchu established the Qing dynasty.

19. Chinhan, Pyŏnhan, and Mahan were the Three Han States in the southern part of the Korean Peninsula before the establishment of the Silla and Paekche kingdoms. What comprised the territories of the three states is controversial but has generally been understood as follows: Chinhan is thought to have occupied most of Kyŏngsang Province, the territory of Pyŏnhan extends from the Naktong River basin to the eastern area of Chŏlla Province, and that of Mahan occupied Kyŏnggi Province, Ch'ungch'ŏng Province, and most of Chŏlla Province.

20. The Paekche kingdom developed from one of the city-states of Mahan. *Samguk sagi* (History of the Three Kingdoms) introduces Paekche as having been established in Hanam wiryesŏng in 17 BCE by King Onjo, a son of Ko Chumong, the first king of the Koguryŏ kingdom. Hanam wiryesŏng is thought to be around Namhansansŏng (Namhan Mountain Fortress) in the Han River basin. The Paekche kingdom was destroyed by Silla and Tang armies in 660 CE.

21. The most ancient Korean state, which spread from Liaodong in the west to the northwestern region of the Korean Peninsula. In *Samguk yusa* (Memorabilia of the Three Kingdoms) Old Chosŏn is introduced as having been founded by Tan'gun Wanggŏm. See "Kojosŏn (Wanggŏm Chosŏn)," Kii (Wonder) 1, chap. 1, in *Samguk yusa*. Archeological remains confirm that the kingdom was well established before the fourth century BCE. See Lee Ki-baik, *A New History of Korea*, 13–16.

22. Having been a kingdom with strong military power confronting Han commendaries, Koguryŏ is thought to have been well established by the first century CE. Its territory covered present-day Liaoning Province in China, the northern part of the Korean Peninsula, and the southern Manchurian region. It eventually was defeated by the allied forces of Silla and Tang and collapsed in 668 CE.

23. An ancient Korean tribe that lived in the eastern part of Korea. Yemaek is thought to have arisen in the area of the Amnok River and its tributary region by the fourth century BCE. Its population of 280,000 in the second century BCE is mentioned in the histories of the Han and Later Han dynasties. People of Yemaek are thought to have settled in northeastern China and the middle and eastern regions of the Korean Peninsula, becoming the residents of Puyŏ, Koguryŏ, Okchŏ, and Tongye.

24. The Three Hans usually refers to the ancient Korean states of Pyŏnhan,

Chinhan, and Mahan. In this case, however, it seems to have meant the three kingdoms of Koguryŏ, Paekche, and Silla.

25. Wu County, which belongs to Jiangsu Province, was also referred to as the northern part of Zhejiang Province.

26. Nine different ethnic groups in the northeast of China, many of whom were related to ancient Korean tribes. The term means "many different people," not necessarily nine tribes, the number nine being important in China to connote multitudes.

27. Known as a Chinese intellectual and court official at the end of the Shang dynasty who fled to northern Korea.

28. Wiman is said to have been a Chinese general of the state of Yan during the Warring States period (475–221 BCE). Wiman reportedly defected to Korea and was entrusted by the Korean king with defending the Korean-Chinese border in Manchuria. He later deposed the king and assumed the throne himself (r. 194–180 BCE). After becoming king he used the Korean name Chosŏn for the kingdom.

29. The first king of the Silla kingdom as recorded in *Samguk sagi* and *Samguk yusa*. His birth is described as him emerging from a large egg in a glow of light. When he grew to be a teenager, new settlers with Old Chosŏn origins made him their king. His birth and life are portrayed by mystical events, as is the case with the founding myths of many countries.

30. The founder of Koguryŏ, who established its capital in Cholbon along a northern branch of the Amnok River, was depicted in *Samguk sagi* and *Samguk yusa* as being related to the sun. He is depicted to be an extraordinary born leader, as seen in his conception by sunlight that shone on his mother and his consequent birth by emerging from a large egg. His mystical birth resembles the myth of Pak Hyŏkkŏse, the first king of the Silla kingdom.

31. Kungye was the founder of the Later Koguryŏ kingdom; Kyŏn Hwŏn was the founder of the Later Paekche kingdom.

32. A man from the Later Zhou dynasty (951–960), Shuang Ji became a naturalized Korean during the Koryŏ dynasty; he suggested to King Kwangjong (r. 949–975) that there should be a civil service examination, which was instituted in 958. See the entry "Great King Kwangjong Muo (Ninth) year" in *Koryŏsa chŏryo*, chap. 2.

33. The author used P'aesu to indicate the Taedong River, which runs through P'yŏngyang, the largest city in P'yŏngan Province. In the Chosŏn dynasty the heart of P'yŏngyang was on the plains along the Taedong River south of the Ch'ŏngch'ŏn River. Both the Yesŏng and Imjin Rivers flow to the south of Hwanghae Province, which lies to the south of P'yŏngan Province. P'aesu is an old Korean word for river, indicating one of the following rivers: Amnok, Ch'ŏngch'ŏn, Taedong, Yesŏng, or Imjin (see Chŏn Yong-sin, *Han'guk kojimyŏng sajŏn*, 276). In his major geographical work, *Taedong sugyŏng*, Chŏng Yag-yong (1762–1836) acknowledged P'aesu as being one of many names for the Amnok River but designated P'aesu as the name of what is now known as the Taedong River (Yang Bo Kyung, "Chosŏn sidae ŭi chayŏn insik ch'egye," 88–91). Considering that Yi

Chung-hwan and Chŏng Yag-yong, who both had in-depth knowledge of Korean geography, used the name P'aesu for the Taedong River, it would appear that P'aesu was the established name for that river in the late Chosŏn period.

34. One of the most important outposts and fortresses of the Koguryŏ dynasty in Manchuria and scene of fierce battles between the Tang Chinese and the Koguryŏ Korean armies in 645. Led by Yang Man-ch'un, Korean soldiers withstood several attacks and a lengthy siege of the area before the fortress eventually fell to the Chinese army in 668.

35. Khitan refers to the Mongolian ethnic group that established the Liao dynasty. They invaded Koryŏ in 993, 1010, and 1018 but were defeated each time.

36. Pavilions were built for permanent use in Korea at scenic spots or at places such as palaces, city gates, monasteries, and Confucian schools. Pillars were made from the trunks of trees, the floor of wooden boards, and the roof of clay tiles. Today, the most commonly found type of pavilion is a single-story structure, often with supporting columns under the floor. A term that refers to these pavilions is a word ending with the last syllable *jŏng* or *chŏng*; the term that refers to the bigger, most often two-storied, pavilions has as its last syllable *lu, nu,* or *ru;* and the term that refers to the pavilions built on terraced high grounds has the last syllable *dae or tae.*

37. This couplet and the episode before and after its composition are entered in chap. 2 of Yi In-no's *P'ahanjip.* It is recorded in *P'ahanjip* and other sources, however, that the pavilion where Kim Hwang-wŏn wrote this poem was Pubyŏngnu, which is much smaller than Yŏn'gwangjŏng, though situated close by.

38. Refers to Huang Taiji (1592–1643), who established the Qing dynasty in 1636 and declared himself its first emperor.

39. Hagok is the cognomen of Hŏ Pong (1551–1588), who served as an envoy to China and was famous for his poetry and prose.

40. Female artist-entertainers.

41. The "five grains" literally denote rice, Italian millet, beans, barley, and broomcorn millet. This expression usually refers, however, to various grains, starting with rice, that are primarily consumed both in Korean people's daily life and on special occasions.

42. *Myo* is a unit used to measure area initially introduced during the Zhou dynasty, though the exact measurement has changed over time. From King Sejong's reign to the late Chosŏn dynasty, one *myo* meant around 260 square meters. One *chong* was equivalent to 2,160 or 2,880 liters of grain. Yielding one *chong* from one *myo* is regarded as a good harvest. The expression of harvesting "one *chong* for every *myo*" here is found neither in *Tongguk chirihae* nor *Tongguk p'aryŏkchi.*

43. A tribal state on the middle part of the Yalu River at the beginning of the Koguryŏ dynasty.

44. Referring to the measurements of traditional Korean buildings, *kan* has been used as a unit of both length and area: one *kan* denotes the length between two columns and also an area covered by one column width squared. As the main frame of buildings were built with tree trunks, the length of columns was limited.

In the case of ordinary Korean-style houses, one *kan* usually measures 2.4 meters (approx. eight feet) in length, and in the case of palaces, public buildings, and temples, it means 2.7–3 meters (approx. 9–10 feet). Nowadays, *kan* is pronounced *k'an*.

45. The grand-scale measurement used in this sentence indicates that it includes buildings other than Kangsŏllu. Although Kangsŏllu was known for its vast scale, it alone did not exceed three hundred *kan*, which is around 2,700 square meters.

46. The third capital of Koguryŏ for two hundred years, presumed to be near the middle part of the Yalu River on the Manchurian side.

47. Refers to the counties of Yŏyŏn, Chasŏng, Much'ang, and Uye, which, to defend against the Jurchen, were established in the northernmost area of the province to the south of the Amnok River. Yŏyŏn was established in 1416 during the reign of King T'aejong, and the other three counties were created during the reign of King Sejong. While they served important roles, the court found their maintenance difficult and costly. The three counties of Yŏyŏn, Much'ang, and Uye were disestablished by 1455 and Chasŏng was also closed in 1459. All residents of these counties were forced to evacuate to Kanggye County.

48. Yi Sŏng-nyang is the father of Li Rusong, a Ming general who fought for Korea against Japan in the Hideyoshi invasion of 1592–1598.

49. The attack was aimed at Ming China, the then newly arising dynasty of the time after the defeat of the Yuan.

50. King Ch'ang (r. 1388–1389), who was enthroned at the age of nine by Yi Sŏng-gye after his father was forced to abdicate, was also killed by Yi Sŏng-gye's men.

51. The thirty-fourth and last Koryŏ king, who reigned from 1389 to 1392.

52. "Qing soldiers" entered in the Chosŏn Kwangmunhoe edition of *T'aengniji* is an error. In most other *T'aengniji* manuscripts, including *Tongguk chirihae*, "Han soldiers" appears in its place.

53. *Boehmeria nivea*, a perennial grass from which thread for weaving fabric (*mosi*) is produced. Being fine and delicate, ramie fabric has traditionally been the most valued for summer clothes.

54. A tribal state of Yemaek whose territory lay around the Hamhŭng Plain in Hamgyŏng Province from around the second century BCE until subjugated by Koguryŏ in 56 CE.

55. Ch'ŏllyŏng was regarded as one of the most important mountain passes. Being surrounded by high mountain ranges, it was the only overland route by which people and commodities from the farthest northern province could be transported to the south and to Seoul.

56. A hunter-gatherer tribe that lived along the Sungho River in the northeast of Manchuria. It was annexed by King Kwanggaet'o during the Koguryŏ dynasty.

57. One of the four commandaries of Emperor Wu of the Han dynasty. It was established in the northern part of Korea in 107 BCE, after the conquest of the Wiman Chosŏn kingdom, and was pushed further north in 75 BCE due, it is thought, to local resistance to Han power. See Lee Ki-baik, *A New History of Korea*, 22–23.

58. The location of Chŏngp'yŏng City is indicated in the Chinese characters for Chŏngp'yŏngbu in the bottom/left corner of the map [see Plate 3].

59. A state established in northern Manchuria by the Jurchen in the beginning of the twelfth century. It was conquered by the Yuan dynasty.

60. The posthumous title of King Sejong.

61. The six garrisons are Kyŏngwŏn, Kyŏnghŭng, Puryŏng, Onsŏng, Chongsŏng, and Hoeryŏng.

62. Sansŏng denotes a walled mountain fortress.

63. The eighth emperor (r. 1100–1125) of the Northern Song dynasty.

64. The ninth emperor (r. 1125–1127) of the Northern Song dynasty. Emperors Huizong and Qinzong and their family members were taken hostage by the Jurchen after they sacked Kaifeng, the capital city. With this, the Northern Song dynasty came to an end.

65. The Korean name for the sea that lies to the east of Korea. It is nowadays also known as the Sea of Japan.

66. The first emperor (r. 1127–1162) of the Southern Song dynasty.

67. A lake west of the city of Hangzhou in Zhejiang Province in China.

68. Entering 宣化 (Xuanhua; K. Sŏnhwa) in the Kwangmunhoe edition as the name of the emperor's tomb is an error. The correct name is 宣和 (Xuanhe; K. Sŏnhwa), the era name of Emperor Huizong.

69. In *Tongguk chirihae* and many other *T'aengniji* manuscripts, "our tenth ancestor" is preceded by Kyŏnghŏn'gong, his posthumous title and name. Posthumous titles are given to kings, queens, scholars, and officials based on their achievements.

70. In Jingzhou 荆州 in China, no one who passed the local civil service examinations went on to succeed in the examinations at the capital. People called this lack of success tianhuang, which means "heavenly barrenness." So, when Liu Tui finally succeeded, people called it po tianhuang (K. p'ach'ŏnhwang), "breaking through the heavenly barrenness."

71. Kunja River (Kunjaha) is another name for Sŏngch'ŏn River (Sŏngch'ŏn'gang). "Chiri chŏn'go" (Gazetteer of authentic precedent) and "Pyŏljip" (Separate collection), in Yi Kŭng-ik, *Yŏllŏsil kisul*.

72. A wife of King T'aejo who bore the princes Pangbŏn and Pangsŏk, the king's seventh and eighth sons.

73. Kongjŏng 恭定 is a posthumous title bestowed on King T'aejong. He was the fifth son of King T'aejo, called Prince Pangwŏn before he ascended to the throne. T'aejong is a temple title that was bestowed on him before his tablet was installed in Chongmyo, the royal ancestral shrine.

74. The revolt in 1398 led by Prince Pangwŏn against his younger half-brother, Crown Prince Pangsŏk, and Chŏng To-jŏn. It is also called "the revolt of Prince Pangwŏn." At the end of the Koryŏ dynasty, Yi Pangwŏn, the fifth son of Yi Sŏng-gye, contributed greatly in his father's establishment of the Chosŏn dynasty by having, with the help of Chŏng To-jŏn, Chŏng Mong-ju killed and King Kongyang abdicate. With the creation of the new dynasty Chŏng To-jŏn and his fellow

meritorious servants came to exercise great power in structuring the new order of governance, while Prince Pangwŏn's contributions were overlooked. King T'aejo installed Prince Pangsŏk, his youngest son out of eight, as crown prince and appointed Chŏng To-jŏn to take care of him. Forced to give up his own warriors under the new regulation, Prince Pangwŏn had Chŏng To-jŏn and his associates killed. He deposed Crown Prince Pangsŏk and had him and Prince Pangbŏn killed.

75. Kongjŏng 恭靖 is a posthumous title bestowed on King Chŏngjong. He was the second son of King T'aejo. When read in Korean, the Chinese character 靖 in his title and the Chinese character 定 in the title given to King T'aejong have the same pronunciation: jŏng.

76. Seoul was the capital of the Chosŏn dynasty and was called either Hanyang or Hansŏng.

77. The story of Pak Sun, which starts from "Queen Sindŏk" and is three paragraphs long, is missing in *Tongguk chirihae*. This story was most likely added to the *T'aengniji* manuscripts at a later stage, long after Yi Chung-hwan passed away. See Choe Inshil, "*T'aengniji* ch'ogibon ŭi t'ŭksŏng," 143; Inshil Choe Yoon, "Early Period *T'aengniji* Manuscripts," 239.

78. Those who had gathered at the first meeting after the Buddha died.

79. A deep pit that is often made by the force of waterfalls.

80. The family name of the royal family of the Koryŏ dynasty.

81. The old name of Pukchŏng in Hamgyŏng Province.

82. The old name of Yangju County in Kyŏnggi Province.

83. The old name of Myŏrak. After the collapse of military rule (1170–1270) during the Koryŏ dynasty, the name Myŏnak (綿岳 Cotton Hill) was changed to Myŏrak (滅惡 Destroying Evil).

84. P'ae River (浿江 P'aegang) here denotes the Taedong River.

85. Ledebouriella seseloides, a perennial grass about one meter tall. Many small flowers bloom at the end of the stem like the spokes of a wheel. Its young shoots were eaten and the roots were used for medicine.

86. During the reign of Chengdi (33–7 BCE), the twelfth emperor of the Han dynasty, Wang Mang was in charge of the military. When the next emperor, Aidi (r. 7–1 BCE), died without a son, Wang enthroned the nine-year-old prince Pingdi (r. 1 BCE–6 CE) and held the reigns of power. Some years later, he poisoned the emperor and established the Xin dynasty (9–25 CE). As its first emperor, he initiated reforms in several areas, including land systems, which created more social turmoil. He was finally killed in 23 CE in Xi'an during a revolt led by the Liu family. Liu Xiu established the Later Han dynasty (25–220 CE) and its capital in Luoyang.

87. A measuring unit for grain: one *mal* is eighteen litres.

88. As the ninth emperor of the Yuan dynasty, he reigned from 1329 to 1332.

89. The eleventh and the last emperor of the Yuan dynasty, who reigned from 1333 to 1370. Shundi is the posthumous epithet of the Ming dynasty.

90. An old name for the Yesŏng River.

91. The insignificant changes along the steep eastern shores of the Korean

Peninsula caused by the tide are pointed out here compared to the big tidal changes made to the gently sloped western shores.

92. Kwandong (關東) here denotes the area to the east (東) of Taegwallyŏng (大關嶺), which is a mountain pass on the T'aebaek Mountain Range. It is also used as another name for Kangwŏn Province.

93. The "two capitals" denote Hansŏng (Seoul) and Kaesŏng.

94. A *tu* is a traditional Korean measure of volume equivalent to eighteen litres, same as *mal*.

95. Imgyeyŏk (Imgye Station) in Kangnŭng, one of the small stations, was where horses were kept for transportation. Imgye County, where Imgyeyŏk was located, was also called Imgyeyŏk County. It has belonged to Chŏngsŏn since 1906.

96. When Yi Sŭng-hyu (1224–1300) was dismissed from the court in 1280 on account of his remonstrance of the mistakes and wrongdoings of the king and his aides, he retreated to Mount Tut'a in Samch'ŏk County and wrote *Chewang un'gi* (Rhymed record of emperors and kings), a set of epic poems of the history of China and Korea. Earlier, the year after passing the civil servant examination in 1252, Yi Sŭng-hyu (1224–1300) visited his mother in Samch'ŏk County. As the roads were blocked due to a Mongol invasion, he remained there, engaged in growing grains and vegetables and looking after his mother, Kudong, on Mount Tut'a. His frank advice and admonition while serving at the Koryŏ court are well documented. He chose to voluntarily retire at around the age of seventy and rejected further offers of court posts.

97. Having ascended to the throne at the age of twelve as the sixth Chosŏn king, Tangjong was forced to abdicate and pass the throne to one of his uncles, later King T'aejong (r. 1455–1468). In the following year, six officials attempted the restoration of the abdicated king, but the plot was uncovered and they were all killed. As a result, the former king was demoted and, given the title Prince Nosan, he was exiled to Yŏngwŏl. In the ninth month of 1456, Prince Kŭmsŏng, his other uncle, who was also in exile, planned to restore him to the kingship. When the plan was found out, Prince Nosan was demoted to the status of commoner and was killed the next month.

In *T'aengniji, pyŏngja* (1696) is introduced as the year when King Tanjong's title was posthumously restored. In *Sukchong sillok*, however, it is recorded that 1698 is the year when King Sukchong granted the late Prince Nosan the posthumous title and elevated his grave to become a tomb, naming it Changnŭng. See *Sukchong sillok* (Veritable record of King Sukchong), 24th year, 11th month.

98. Sŏng Sam-mum, Pak P'aeng-nyŏn, Yi Kae, Ha Wi-ji, Yu Sŏng-wŏn, and Yu Ŭng-bu, were put to death in 1456, their attempt to reinstate the former king to the throne having been found out.

99. Yi Cha-hyŏn passed the civil servant examination and was assigned to a junior eighth-rank post. But he resigned and went into seclusion on Mount Ch'ŏngp'yŏng. His grandfather Yi Cha-yŏn had three daughters, who became consorts of King Munjong (r. 1046–1083).

100. Usuju, also called Uduju, is a name of Ch'unchŏn given during the Sil-

la dynasty. In "Shihuo zhi" (Treatise on food and commodities) in *Hanshu* and "Pingzhun shu" (Treatise on the balanced standards) in *Shiji* (Historical records), it is recorded that Peng Wu established Canghai County in order to destroy Chosŏn. The exact location of Canghai County is not clear. Some understood it to be Usuju.

101. Great King of Kongjŏng (恭定) refers to King T'aejong (r. 1400–1418), the third king of the Chosŏn dynasty.

102. Yan Ling refers to Yan Guang, who in his youth was a study companion of the future emperor Guangwu (r. 25–57), the first emperor of the Later Han dynasty. When Guangwu ascended to the throne, Yan Guang went into hiding. When the emperor searched for him and appointed him as his advisor, Yan Guang declined and retired to hermitage on Mount Fuchun. From his pseudonym, Ziling, he came to be called Yan Ling.

103. Huan Rong was poor but kept studying from his youth and became a famous teacher with many students, including a prince, who later became Emperor Ming (r. 57–75) of the Later Han dynasty. Huan Rong accepted a succession of high government positions, including as one of the three highest court officers, which Emperor Guangwu had offered.

104. The blue dragon (青龍 *ch'ŏngnyong*) and the white tiger (白虎 *paekho*) are mountains that support an auspicious site both to the left and to the right. For more a comprehensive description of the requirement for an auspicious site, see n. 23 of my introduction regarding the homage mountain.

105. The translation of this sentence is based on the text of the Kwangmunhoe edition. In this edition, 地利 (chiri, benefit of the land) is entered. However, 地理 (chiri, geomancy) is used in most other *T'aengniji* manuscripts. I think 地理 is the correct word in this context. Therefore, a more accurate translation would be "The area is the best in terms of geomancy."

106. Refers to Yi Hang-bok (1556–1618), whose earnest handling of political affairs and diplomacy, especially during the Hideyoshi invasion, earned him the post of prime minister. He was also well known for his humor and friendship since his youth with Yi Tŏk-hyŏng, who also became prime minister. Many benefited from his impartiality and commitment to good causes. His objection to the deposition of Queen Dowager Inmok, however, resulted in his exile to Pukch'ŏng, one of the most remote areas in Hamgyŏng Province, and his death there.

107. After serving as the governor of Ch'ungch'ŏng Province and chief of the Royal Secretariat, Yi Chin-hyu (1657–1710) was appointed governor of Hamgyŏng Province in 1703. From Yi Chung-hwan's description of his father's journey to Kangnŭng, Yi Chin-hyu could have been appointed magistrate of the Special City of Kangnŭng before his appointment as governor of Hamgyŏng Province.

108. *Ch'i* is a traditional measurement. One *ch'i* is about 3.03 centimeters.

109. Refers here to *p'ungsu* (Ch. *fengshui*). It is the art of finding auspicious sites by evaluating the surrounding mountains and watercourses and the layout of locales. It originated in ancient China and became important in locating residences, palaces, cities, and grave sites in East Asia.

110. Those knowledgeable about geomancy who were consulted when determining the location of residences or grave sites.

111. A mountain with its summit having the appearance of a gently rolling hill. It is called a water-type star mountain because the shape represents waves.

112. Sangju was called Sangnak (上洛) and *tong* (東) means east. This might be the reason for the explanation that the Naktong (洛東) River, which flows to the east of Sangju, means "east of Sangju."

113. Kyŏngsang Province was divided into a left side and a right side along the Naktong River in 1519 during the reign of King Chungjong. Naming the eastern part of the river Kyŏngsang Chwado (left side of the province) and the western part Kyŏngsang Udo (right side of the province) reflects the capital-centered orientation of directions.

114. Kyerim is an old name for Kyŏngju. The whole name, Kyerim kunjaguk, referred to Korea (Silla) as a kingdom of honored gentlemen.

115. A geomantic term for a landform in which a mountain range hooks around on itself, with the end of the hook facing the main range from which it originated.

116. Area to the south of the pass of Choryŏng. This area denotes Kyŏngsang Province.

117. The queen referred to is Queen Chinsŏng (r. 887–897), the last of the three queens of the Silla dynasty.

118. This could mean the extensive Gobi Desert, which spreads from central Asia to the northeastern border of Manchuria. The northern part of Manchuria was a wilderness roamed by hunters and nomads, while eastern Manchuria was swampland. This description is essentially correct in human terms but not in terms of physical geography: between the boundry of the Silla kingdom and the Gobi Desert lay Manchuria, which is not a desert but poorly vegetated plains. Even though not a sandy desert, Manchuria could have been perceived as an extension of the great desert.

119. The four great Korean Neo-Confucian scholars were Yi Hwang (1501–1570), Yi Ŏn-jŏk, Chŏng Ku, and Chŏng Il-tu.

120. This seems to refer to the Manchu invasions of 1627, 1634, and 1636.

121. Third rank in the nine-rank civil service system of the Chosŏn dynasty's central government. Each rank consisted of senior and junior ranks. Third-rank officials of the six ministries of the central government were normally third ministers, a rank under the ministers (senior second rank) and vice-ministers (junior second rank).

122. The place that King Gong (?–128 BCE) of the Lu state had built in the city wall of Qufu, the capital of the state.

123. Guan Yu (K. Kwan U), a Chinese general of the Three Kingdoms (220–280), is deified and worshiped in many shrines in Korea. He is most popularly called Kwan Wang (King Guan) in Korea.

124. It is said that King Sŏnjo had it constructed after dreaming of Kwan U, who was anxious at not having a place in which his spirit could reside.

125. He also adopted Kwiraejŏng as his pseudynym.

126. In the Kwangmunhoe text, Kongsan (Mount Kong) is entered in the place of P'algongsan (Mount P'algong).

127. The commonly used phrase "ten-thousand-men-high mountain" is used to express considerable height; it is not meant to be an accurate measure of height. If this expression were translated literally, the height of the mountain would be more than twenty thousand meters. Korea's highest mountain, Mount Paektu, is 2,750 meters high.

128. Tongnae is now part of present-day Pusan. During most of the Chosŏn dynasty, however, Tongnae was a much more important port than Pusan.

129. A special residential and commercial quarter for Japanese people set up by the Korean government in an effort to control their activities and access to Korean shores.

130. A title given to King Tanjong (1452–1455), the sixth king of the Chosŏn dynasty, after he was dethroned.

131. A Confucian faction that was hived off from the Northerners Faction in 1599 by Hong Yŏ-sun and his followers.

132. A temporary government post granted to people who organized armies of volunteers when Korea was faced with foreign invasions.

133. Another name for Chŏlla Province. Honam means south of the lake; Yi Ik interpreted the lake in question to be Pyŏkkolche in Kimje County, Chŏlla Province. The lake was made during the Silla dynasty. See Song Ch'an-sik, "Sŏngho Yi Ik ŭi 'Saengjae' [Generating wealth] p'yŏn," 203.

134. Great King of Kongjŏng (恭靖) refers to King Chŏngjong (r. 1398–1400), the second king of the Chosŏn dynasty.

135. After Yi Sŏng-gye became the first Chosŏn king, he bestowed the posthumous title King Mokcho on his great-great-grandfather.

136. This explanation for the origin of the place-name is questionable. Sŏsi (Ch. Xi Shi) was a Chinese beauty who lived in the Spring and Autumn period (770–476 BCE). Known as one of the four ancient beauties of China, Xi Shi is said to have been born in present-day Zhuji in Shaoxing Prefecture in Zhejiang Province. Rho Do-yang pointed out that in *Tongguk yŏji sŭngnam* it was written as Sŏjip'o not Sŏsip'o. See Yi Chung-hwan, *T'aengniji* (1969), 107. This suggests that the entry of Sŏsip'o and its explanation as the birthplace of Sŏsi is based on popular hearsay. This entry is not confined to the Chosŏn kwangmunhoe version of *T'aengniji* but also found in a *T'aengniji* manuscript titled Chinyusŭngnam (Sangbaek ko 915.1-J563) in the Kyujanggak collection.

137. A mountain whose sharp pointed summit and steep slopes give it the shape of a flame.

138. A Tang poet who gathered volunteers to defeat rebels led by Huang Chao in southeast China.

139. A style of classical Chinese writing that contrasts with pre-Han style. Each phrase consists of either four or six characters in couplets. It was popular during the Six Dynasties period and the Tang dynasty.

140. The *liwen* style, commonly called parallel prose, is the same as four-six-style prose.

141. Better known as Samjiwŏn or Samgiwŏn. According to Yi Haeng, *Sinjŭng tongguk yŏji sŭngnam*, Samgiwŏn is to the west of Haenam County. The last syllable, wŏn, denotes a lodge built by the government in strategic transportation locations for those traveling on official missions.

142. The great victory won by Admiral Yi Sun-sin in front of the Pyŏkp'ajŏng in Chindo took place in 1597, during the second invasion by the Japanese army. By attracting Japanese warships through a narrow strait with rapid sea currents between Chindo and the land, Yi Sun-sin defeated the Japanese navy, which had more than ten times the number of his thirteen warships. Before the fallen city of P'yŏngyang was recaptured in 1592, an event mentioned in the text, Yi Sun-sin won a series of battles, the first great victory won at Hansando. He used fast-moving "turtle ships," whose metal covering over the deck had the appearance of a turtle.

143. A Ming envoy who attempted to establish a truce with Hideyoshi's Japanese army during the invasion.

144. The commanding officer of the Ming army dispatched to help Korea resist the Hideyoshi invasion between 1592 and 1598.

145. A Ming general who fought for Korea during the Hideyoshi invasion.

146. The title bestowed by the court on Sima Guang (1019–1086), a famous historian of Song China.

147. The old name for Fujian Province in China and also the name of the people who lived there.

148. The governor's headquarters in Ch'ungch'ŏng Province was shifted to Kongju in 1598 from Ch'ungju, which since 1395 had been the provincial governor's seat. The move was precipitated by the almost total destruction of the headquarters during the Hideyoshi invasion. Kongju was the capital of Paekche for sixty years until Puyŏ became the new capital in 538.

149. The Tang established a commandery in Ungjin, a part of present-day Kongju, in 660.

150. The two invasions are called *imjin waeran* and *pyŏngja horan* in Korea, as Japanese troops invaded Korea in the year of *imjin* and the Manchu invasion occurred in the year of *pyŏngja*.

151. Hwaryang is present-day Chihwari in Namyang County.

152. Refers to the downstream of the Kŭm River before it flows into the Yellow Sea (West Sea).

153. Yusŏng, Kyŏngch'ŏn, Iin, and Yugu were under the jurisdiction of Kongju in the Chosŏn dynasty.

154. Mount Wŏlsŏng is to the east of Kongju.

155. "Sipsŭnggi" (Writings on ten excellent places for refuge) listed ten places where one could lead a safe life during times of war in Korea. "Namsago sipsŭng posingi" (Nam Sa-go's writings on ten excellent places for refuge and safekeeping), one of the versions entered in "Tongguksansurok" (in Yu Chung-nim, *Chŭngbo sallim kyŏngje*, Ilsa ko 630.2 J572 v.16), ranked them as follows: the first, Kŭmgyech'on in P'unggi; second, the sunny side of Mount T'aebaek in Hwasan;

third, below Mount Songni in Poŭn; fourth, Unbongdong in Tongchŏmch'on; fifth, Kŭmdanggok in Yech'ŏn; sixth, between the streams of Yugu and Magok in Kongju; seventh, the upper stream to the direct east from Yŏngwŏl; eighth, Mup'ung in Muju; ninth, Pyŏnsan in Puan; and tenth, Mansudong on Mount Kaya in Hapch'ŏn.

156. Yi Kwal was one of the major contributors to the success of the Injo Restoration in 1623 and was positioned in the northern frontier to defend Chosŏn against the rising Later Jin, which became the Qing dynasty. Some among the meritorious retainers of the restoration accused Yi Kwal's son Chŏn and others of conspiracy in the first month of 1624. Although the accusation was revealed to be false, Yi Chŏn was ordered to be sent under escort to Seoul. Fearing for his son's life and subsequently learning of his death in Seoul, Yi Kwal beheaded the court's messenger bringing word of his son's death and started a revolt. His army quickly advanced southward and occupied Seoul. Soon after, his army was defeated by the government's army and he was killed on the fifteenth day of the second month of 1624. King Injo, who fled to Kongju, returned to Seoul a week later.

157. T'ongjŏng Taebu 通政大夫 is a third level of a major government post of the civil servants' ranks.

158. Pseudonym and better-known name of Su Shi (1037–1101), a Song-dynasty poet. His "Ode to the Red Cliff" (Chibifu) is one of his most famous poems.

159. The text, 蘇仙赤壁今蒼壁 廋亮南樓是北樓, is contained in chap. 2 of *Sŏgyŏng sijip* (Collection of Yu Kŭn's poetry). The manuscript is stored in the libraries of Keimyung University and Yonsei University (Kosŏ [I] 811.98 Yu Kŭn sŏ-p'an-[V1–3]).

160. This explanation is made because the second Chinese character for Kongbungnu means north.

161. Xu Ning, a poet during the era of the Tang emperor Xianzong (r. 805–820), wrote a poem on Lu Shan Falls. Although people praised it as a beautiful stanza, Su Dongpo commented that the poem was badly composed.

162. For this river, the name 赤江 (Chŏkgang) appears in the Chosŏn Kwangmunhoe version of *T'aengniji* and in *Tongguk p'aryŏkchi*. This is meant to be 赤登江 (Chŏktŭnggang), which appears in the explanation of its being the source of the Kŭm River in both these versions as well as in the *Tongguk chirihae*.

163. A short-lived political party at the end of the Ming dynasty made up of Chinese scholars and officials. Founded by Gu Xiancheng in 1604, this party intended a restoration of Confucian values and called for moral vigilance in the public sphere. Although its members held important posts in the Ming government at the beginning of emperor Tianqi's reign (r. 1620–1627), when attacked by opposite powers, its members were purged and it ceased to exist once Emperor Chongzhen (r. 1628–1644) ascended to the throne.

164. A scholar-official and poet at the end of the Ming dynasty and the beginning of the Qing dynasty. He was one of the important members of Donglin Dang.

165. Jingzhou County (靖州), in present-day Hubei Province in China.

166. Yuzhou County, in present-day Henan Province in China.

167. Korean zither with twelve strings played with both hands. According to *Samguk sagi*, the *kayagŭm* was created by King Kasil of a Kaya kingdom. On the king's request, Urŭk composed twelve songs for the *kayagŭm*. When the Kaya kingdom was in turmoil, he surrendered to the Silla king Chinhŭng (r. 534–576). Urŭk is recorded to have stayed at present-day Ch'ŏngju and continued his composition and teaching. See "King Chinhŭng" in *Samguk sagi*, chap. 4.

168. Changhŏn is the posthumous title of King Sejong (r. 1418–1450).

169. The place that is referred to is the fortress of Namhansansŏng.

170. Kanghwado lies to the northwest of Inchŏn and has an area of 302 sq km. Both sizable and close to the shore and the capitals, the island had been used as a hiding place for royals during several foreign invasions. In the second Mongol invasion in the thirteenth century, the Koryŏ court withdrew to Kanghwado from Kaesŏng. Kanghwa served as the capital for ten years and was successful in defending the throne. During the first Manchu invasion in 1627, King Injo withdrew to Kanghwado from Seoul and succeeded in defending against the Qing soldiers. In the second Manchu invasion, however, the island where the crown prince and other royals were hiding fell to the Qing soldiers. Upon hearing that the Kanghwado had fallen and the crown prince captured, King Injo, who was hiding in the Namhansansŏng, left the fortress and agreed on a peace treaty with the Qing emperor.

171. The river here means the strait between the mainland and Kanghwado.

172. Tondae is a small wall often built atop castle walls.

173. In *Tongguk chirihae* and other manuscripts, "the emperor's court" is entered in place of "the Ming court."

174. An island belonging to Ch'ŏlsan County in North P'yŏngan Province.

175. This clause is found only in the Chosŏn kwangmunhoe version of *T'aengniji*. In most of the manuscripts, including *Tongguk chirihae*, "as our court paid tribute to the Ming court" is entered instead.

176. The crown prince was with King Injo and could not escape to Kanghwado. His two brothers did, however.

177. One *sŏm* is equivalent to about 180 liters.

178. Having been appointed the resident commander of Kanghwa in 1741, Kim Si-hyŏk contributed in building the outer fortresses in Kanghwado. On account of his contribution, he was promoted, in 1744, to the position of chief magistrate of Seoul and then to the inspector general (*taesahŏn*). Therefore, the year of pyŏngin (1746) in the text is incorrect.

179. In geomancy mountains are grouped into five types based on their shapes: water, wood, fire, earth, and metal. Water-type mountains have a summit with the appearance of rippling water; wood-type mountains are tall and narrow; fire-type mountains have a summit in the shape of a flame; earth-type mountains have a flattish top; and metal-type mountains have the appearance of an upturned metal rice bowl.

180. The Chinese character 李 for the surname Yi means plum.

181. Qian Jin means one thousand *kŭn*. One *kŭn* is six hundred grams.

182. *T'ongp'yŏn* denotes *P'yŏnnyŏn t'ongnok* (Abridged chronological history), which Kim Kwan-ŭi compiled during the reign of King Ŭijong (1146–1170). The text itself no longer exists but its content is contained as quotations in "Koryŏ segye" (Genealogical record of Koryŏ) in *Koryŏsa*. In "Koryŏ segye" a more elaborate story of a pig is included. The story goes that Chakchegŏn kept a pig while he was living at Taejŏng (大井 Great Well) but the pig refused for a year to enter the pigsty. One day he said to the pig, "If this place was not a desirable place to live, I would follow where you would go in the future." The next morning, the pig strolled to the southern slope of Songak and laid himself down. Chakchegŏn finally built a house there. "Koryŏ segye," *Koryŏsa*, accessed July 7, 2017, http://db.history.go .kr/KOREA/item/level.do?itemId=kr&bookId=고려세계&types=o#detail/kr _$s02_0070.

A story of finding an auspicious place after following a pig also is found in *Samguk sagi*. According to this story, King Yuri (r. 19 BCE–18 CE) of Koguryŏ ordered a subject named Sŏlchi to follow a runaway sacrificial pig. Reaching Winaam in Kungnaesŏng (present-day Jian), the pig was caught. Having penned it in a local house in Kungnaesŏng, Sŏlchi, who was in charge of sacrificial service, returned to the king and reported the place where he had found the pig. He described it as having a deep and rugged landscape, fertile fields for grains, and a rich supply of deer and fish, and suggested that the capital be moved there not only because of the material benefit for this king's people but also for safety from war and strife. In less than two years, King Yuri shifted the capital (which had been Cholbon) to Winaam in Kungnaesŏng. See *Samguk sagi*, chap. 13.

183. According to "Koryŏ segye" in *Koryŏsa*, Tosŏn said "in the field where non-glutinous millet is to be planted, hemp is planted" when he saw the house that Sejo (the father of Wang Kŏn, the founder of the Koryŏ dynasty) had newly built. On Sejo's request Tosŏn prescribed the way a house was to be built to benefit from the auspiciousness of the site and prophesized Sejo's having a son the following year, to be named Wang Kŏn. Kim Kwan-ŭi is quoted by Yi Che-hyŏn (1237–1367) to have said that "[the two terms] non-glutinous millet and king are similar in vernacular Korean." See Yi Che-hyŏn's writing at the end of "Koryŏ segye," in *Koryŏsa*, accessed July 7, 2017, http://db.history.go.kr/KOREA/item /level.do?itemId=kr&bookId=고려세계&types=o#detail/kr_$s02_0100. For more information on Tosŏn's comments and activities in relation to the founding of the Koryŏ dynasty, see Byŏng-hŏn Choi, "Tosŏn's Geomantic Theories and the Foundation of Koryŏ Dynasty."

184. Emperor Xuanzong (r. 846–859) of the Tang dynasty.

185. Shiliu Yuan (Sixteen Palaces) was built in the massive Xiyuan (West Garden) in Luoyang during the reign of Emperor Yang in the Sui dynasty (581–618).

186. According to Yi Haeng, *Sinjŭng tongguk yŏji sŭngnam*, Kwangmyŏngsa well is the well that the princess of the Sea God and her little daughter entered to go to the water palace. Yi Haeng, *Sinjŭng tongguk yŏji sŭngnam* quotes "Koryŏ segye" in *Koryŏsa* as follows: When Chakchegŏn and a princess of the Sea God settled on Mount Songak, the princess asked him to promise not to look at her

when she visited the water palace. One day Chakchegŏn secretly watched his wife and little daughter enter a well and transform into yellow dragons. When his wife returned home, she said in anger that she could no longer live there because he had not kept his promise. She and the daughter changed into dragons, entered the well and never came back. See chap. 4, "Kaesŏngbu," in Yi Haeng, *Sinjŭng tongguk yŏji sŭngnam*.

187. The time that spans over fifty years between the collapse of the Tang dynasty in 907 and the establishment of the Song dynasty in 960. During this period the Later Liang, Later Tang, Later Jin, Later Han, and Later Zhou kingdoms rose and fell.

188. The last emperor of the Tang dynasty.

189. King U (r. 1374–1388) was enthroned by Yi Sŏng-gye as the thirty-second Koryŏ king. He was said to have been born of King Kongmin (r. 1351–1374) and one of Sin Ton's maids. King U's son, Ch'ang, became the thirty-third king of the dynasty in 1388.

190. A former monk who served for several years as advisor to King Kongmin, the thirty-first king of the dynasty. With his talent and the king's trust, Sin Ton implemented several radical policies. He was severely criticized by the courtiers not only for his use of political power but also his indulgence in women and alcohol. He was finally sentenced and executed in 1371.

191. King Kongyang (r. 1389–1392) was made the thirty-fourth Koryŏ king after the abdication of King Ch'ang. Under pressure from Yi Sŏng-gye, he had King U and King Ch'ang killed. He later abdicated and Yi Sŏng-gye rose to the throne as the founder of the Chosŏn dynasty.

192. Wang Jian (452–489) and Chu Yuan (435–482) were officials during Emperor Ming's reign in the fifth-century Song kingdom (420–479) during the Southern dynasties. Both men helped General Xiao Daocheng, who assassinated the successor of Emperor Ming, allowing Emperor Shun to finally take over the throne and found the Qi kingdom (齊 479–502). Because of their contributions to the formation of the kingdom, Chu Yuan was appointed to the position of presiding minister of the state and Wang Jian yielded great power in the new cabinet.

193. The text, 一聲柔櫓滄波外 借問山僧奈爾何 (*ilsŏngyunoch'angp'aoe, ch'amunsansŭngnaeiha*), is entered in chap. 7 of Nam Hyo-on's *Ch'ugangjip*. Nam Hyo-on (1454–1492) is one of "six loyal subjects" (*saengyuksin*). The text is also contained in Hŏ Pong (1551–1588), *Haedong yaŏn*.

194. The Chinese characters of the family names of Ma (馬), Chŏn (全), and Ok (玉) contain the radical of Wang (王).

195. Chancellor was the title of the highest minister of state in the Koryŏ dynasty.

196. Chingsa is a title for those who were called to the court to serve in a government post.

197. The Buddhist sutra inscribed on palmyra palm leaves. It is regarded as the first Buddhist scripture.

198. An homage mountain, which is expected to be situated to the south of an auspicious site, symbolizes a servant paying homage to a king. The homage

water flow is a river in front of an auspicious site that looks as if it is bowing toward the site.

199. The entry of 水氣 (*sugi*, water energy) in the Chosŏn Kwangmunhoe edition is an error. This is the only appearance of *sugi* in this edition. In early-period manuscripts such as "T'aengniji" in *P'aerim* and *Tongguk chirihae*, 風氣 (*p'unggi*) is entered instead. Literally meaning "wind energy," *p'unggi* is used several times in varying contexts in *T'aengniji* manuscripts and can be translated as civilization, energy, spirit, vigor, atmosphere, scenery, climate, or the wholesome energy of a place. See Inshil Choe Yoon, "Geomantic Ideas in *T'aengniji* Manuscripts," 364–366.

200. 水中 (*sujung*, in the water) is found not only in this Chosŏn Kwangmunhoe edition but also in several late-period *T'aengniji* manuscripts. This is an apparent error. In the early-period manuscripts, including "T'aengniji" in *P'aerim* and *Tongguk chirihae*, 山中 (*sanjung*, in the mountain) is entered. See Inshil Choe Yoon, "Geomantic Ideas in *T'aengniji* Manuscripts," 367.

201. In the early-period manuscripts such as "T'aengniji" in *P'aerim*, the two sentences below follow after this statement:

> An established geomantic theory prescribes that the house site that faces to the left-hand side should have a watercourse that flows in the direction of *chŏng-ohaeng* (correct five elements) or *ssangsan-ohaeng* (parallel mountains' five elements) and the house site that faces to the right-hand side should have a watercourse that flows in the direction of *chin-ohaeng* (true five elements). The orientation of the house, together with the direction of the incoming water, should also be in accordance with the principle of *chŏngyang-chŏng'ŭm* (clean yang and clean yin) to become very auspicious.

At a later stage of the hand-copying of the *T'aengniji* mansuscripts, the above two sentences are found to have been replaced with the sentence "This is not discussed here in detail because there are geomancers' books [on the subject]," as in the text above. The paragraph that starts with "However, house sites are" in this translation was also added at a later stage of hand-copying. See Inshil Choe Yoon, "Early Period *T'aengniji* Manuscripts," 235–237; Inshil Choe Yoon, "Geomantic Ideas in *T'aengniji* Manuscripts," 362–364. Water, wood, earth, metal, and fire are explained in the *Book of Documents* to be the five elements (K. *ohaeng*; Ch. *wuxing*) that make up the universe. The "correct five elements," "parallel mountains' five elements," and "true five elements" are three of the many ways of combining the five elements with yin-yang forces and the twenty-four directions to prescribe the auspiciousness or inauspiciousness of a location. For the functions of the yin-yang forces and the five elements and their relation to geomancy, consult chap. 4, "Yin-Yang Theory and Geomancy," in Hong-key Yoon, *Culture of Fengshui in Korea*, 57–65.

202. This person also helped the host by serving guests, etc.

203. The specified procedure in the text is for a bridegroom to go to the bride's house, greet her, and bring her to his home for the wedding ceremony.

204. The ancient legendary Chinese emperor who was born with the body of a man and the head of a bull. He is especially revered for making a tool for cultivating crops and teaching people about agriculture.

205. The prime minister and the two deputy prime ministers. They are senior first rank in the Chosŏn ranking system.

206. The ministers of the offices of Personnel, Taxation, Rites, Military Affairs, Punishments, and Works. They are senior second in the ranking system.

207. The three offices of law are the offices of Inspector General, Censor General, and Special Advisers. The Office of Special Advisers looked after the books and the historical records in royal archives and administered royal documents. Its members also advised the king when so requested. When a king did not heed the advice given by the offices of the Inspector General and Censor General, these two offices would invite the Office of Special Advisers to give the king a final censoring. The members of the three offices were highly respected, especially among scholars, for their role in advising and censoring kings.

208. The senior fifth- and senior sixth-rank officials of the ministries of Personnel and Military Affairs were called selection secretaries. The title comes from the fact that these officials were responsible for administering the selection of candidates to government posts. The number of selection secretaries differs from time to time. Three fifth major-grade official posts and three senior sixth-rank posts were assigned to each of the two ministries during the reign of King T'aejong (1400–1418). These posts and their general roles are described in "Central posts" (Kyŏnggwanjik), "Personnel code" (Ijŏn), in *Kyŏngguk taejŏn* (National code), which was published in 1485.

209. Sim Ŭi-gyŏm was a brother of Queen Insun, wife of King Myŏngjong (r. 1545–1567).

210. Queen Inmok, wife of King Sŏnjo and mother of Crown Prince Yŏngch'ang (1606–1614). Born to a concubine of King Sŏnjo, Prince Kwanghae succeeded King Sŏnjo, killed Crown Prince Yŏngch'ang, and, removing Queen Inmok from the throne, placed her under house arrest.

211. One who passed the first licentiate examination of the civil service examinations during the Chosŏn dynasty.

212. Officials of the senior third rank and below.

213. Burying a coffin in such a way that it can be reached by tunnels through which seasonal offerings can be transported to be laid by the coffin.

214. Illegitimate sons were barred from promotion to higher ranks during most of the Chosŏn dynasty.

215. While Kim Ch'ang-jip was prime minister, Yi I-myŏng was first deputy prime minister, Yi Kŏn-myŏng was second deputy prime minister, and Cho T'aech'ae was the first minister-without-portfolio.

216. This term seems to have been used as the mid-point between the beginning of the Chosŏn dynasty and the time in which the author lived.

217. As two of the five elements (K. *ohaeng*; Ch. *wuxing*), water and fire are mutually incompatible.

218. Literally, "[Korea] is a small country that can be compared to a small dot in a corner [of the world]."

219. An inaccurate description of the landform around Hamhǔng, which is on a plain.

220. The western region of the middle part of Korea, comprising the whole of Kyǒnggi Province, the southern part of Hwanghae Province, and the northern part of Ch'ungch'ǒng Province.

221. Known to be the last king (r. 1775–1763 BCE) of the Xia dynasty.

222. Refers to Yanxi, Zhongxing, and Zhenhu. When Duke Mu (Mu Gong, r. 659–621 BCE) of the Qin state (?–598 BCE) died and was buried, these three officers were buried alive along with many others. It is said that they were sons of Ziju, and people of the kingdom mourned their immolation by composing a poem. The poem, "Huangniao" (Oriole) has three verses, one each for Yanxi, Zhongxing, and Zhenhu. The first verse, 交交黃鳥 止于棘 誰從穆公 子車奄息 維此奄息 百夫之 特 臨其穴 惴惴其慄 彼蒼者天 殲我良人 如可贖兮 人百其身, translates as follows:

> Warbling and warbling, an oriole sat on a thornbush.
> Who followed Duke Mu to his death?
> It is Ziju's Yanxi.
> This person, Ziju's Yanxi, was better than one hundred men.
> When he came across the grave, he was terrified and he trembled.
> Oh, blue heaven, there, you are wiping out our good men.
> Could he have been redeemed should one hundred lives be given? (Yu Chǒng-gi, Happon sasǒ samgyǒng, 353)

223. King Xuan of the Wei state (魏, 403–225 BCE) during the Zhou dynasty had a son called Ji. The king took Ji's wife and she bore him two children, Shou and Shuo. When Shuo and his mother made false accusations against Ji, King Xuan sent Ji out as an envoy with the intent that a robber would kill him on the way. Having stolen Ji's documents, Shou instead of Ji went out and was killed by the robber, who mistook him for Ji. Ji followed, and when he encountered the robber and protested that it was he and not Shou that King Xuan had ordered killed, the robber killed Ji as well. "The two royal princes" are the two sons of King Xuan—Ji and Shou—who were killed by the robber. The poem, "Erzi Chengzhou" (Two sons in a boat) is contained in "Beifeng," Shijing: 二子乘舟 汎汎其景 願言思子 中心 養養 二子乘舟 汎汎其逝 願言思子 不瑕有害. It translates as follows:

> A boat with two sons on board is sailing far away.
> My thoughts are on them, my heart is pounding.
> A boat with two sons on board has sailed away.
> With worrying heart, I wish they come to no harm.

See Yu Chǒng-gi, *Happon sasǒ samgyǒng*, 311.

224. In all of the hand-copied *T'aengniji* manuscripts that have this part, as

well as the Chosŏn Kosŏganhaenghoe edition printed in 1910, this is entered differently: "Therefore, from olden days Korea has been loyal to China."

225. The sentence as it appears in all hand-copied *T'aengniji* manuscripts that have this part as well as the Chosŏn Kosŏganhaenghoe edition is different: "But Korea alone has only maintained its boundaries and served China with her utmost sincerity."

226. The sixteenth and last emperor of the Ming dynasty.

227. A well-known poet and calligrapher whose pseudonym was Pongnae.

228. Pongnae denotes Mount Kŭmgang in summer while P'ungak is the mountain's name in autumn. The eight Chinese characters mean "the autumn scenery of Mount Kŭmgang is the transformation of a heavenly residence."

229. Tanwujie seems to refer to the Chinese pilgrim 曇無竭. The entry of the last Chinese charcter, 偈, in the Kwangmunhoe version is an error.

230. According to Buddhist tradition, the seven golden mountain ranges surround Mount Sumeru, which is considered to be the center of the universe.

231. This mountain is said to be located near Dunhuang in western China.

232. Avataṃsakasūtra (Ch. Huayan jing).

233. Mount Kŭmgang is in Korea, beside the East Sea. It lies in a northeasterly direction from India.

234. The waterfall at Lushan, one of China's five sacred mountains, is in Jiujiang City, Jiangxi Province.

235. *Sarira* are the small bead-like remains from the cremation of a Buddhist monk.

236. Korea's three southern provinces: Ch'ungch'ŏng, Kyŏngsang, and Chŏlla.

237. Zhu Xi built a study on a mountain in Fujian Province in China and changed the mountain's name to Mount Yungu.

238. This famous poem is found in several collections, among them *Chibong yusŏl* by Yi Su-gwang (1563–1628), *Ubokchip* by Chŏng Kyŏng-se (1563–1633), and *Sŏngho sasŏl* by Yi Ik.

239. The Buddhist term *sangwang* (elephant king) refers to all enlightened people.

240. In ancient China, constellations were understood to have connections with regions on earth. A record of the division of China proper and adjacent lands into twenty-eight areas appears during the Warring States period. Being to the east of China, Korea is thought to have been connected to the eastern quarter of the celestial globe. Belonging to the area of the fourth star of the quarter, which was believed to be in charge of the god of horses, Chejudo was used as a horse-breeding ground.

241. Anbyŏn belonged to Hamgyŏng Province during the Chosŏn dynasty.

242. Fortified walled fortress that Dong Zhuo (139?–192), a tyrannical general at the end of the Han dynasty, had built in Mei County, his fiefdom near Chang'an.

243. The text, 田園歸路三千里 帷幄思深四十年 (*chŏn-wŏn-gwi-ro-sam-ch'ŏn-ri, yu-ak-sa-sim-sa-sip-nyŏn*), is the first half of the full poem, with the second part be-

ing 立馬渡迷回首望 終南山色故依然 (ip-ma-do-mi-hoe-su-mang, chong-nam-san-saek-ko-ŭi-yŏn) (As I stop the horse at Tomi stream and look back, / The color of Mount Chongnam is still the same.) Mount Chongnam is one of many names of Mount Nam in Seoul. This poem is in "Sŏae Sŏnsaeng yŏnbo" (Chronology of Sŏae), the eleventh month in 1598, in Yu Sŏng-nyong, *Sŏaejip*, 2:78.

244. A scholar of the last period of the Koryŏ dynasty who is credited with having introduced Neo-Confucianism to Korea from China.

245. In this final part in most *T'aengniji* manuscripts, after "Master Yi remarks that," the following is entered:

> how can Korea have "scholar-gentry"? As for the Chinese, apart from the descendants of the five nomadic barbarians from the north, all are the descendants of emperors and sages and thus cultivated the laws of Yao, Shun, King Wen, King Wu, Zhougong, and Confucius. Therefore, they are the real scholar-gentry. The so-called scholar-gentry in our country are all descendants of Korean people.

246. A section of the *Book of Documents (Shujing)* on geography, tribute, and taxes of the territory during Emperior Shun. It is said that during the reign of Emperor Yao there were nine years of floods. Emperor Yao ordered Gun, his servant, to take flood control measures, but Gun was unsuccessful. But on the order of Emperor Shun, the successor of Emperor Yao, Gun's son Yu inspected nine states and established their boundaries and conferred land and surnames on feudal lords.

247. Originating during the Wei kingdom (220–265) of China, this term refers to officials at the county level who evaluated the ability of local candidates and assigned them appropriate grades. These grades were then reported to the central government and were the basis for appointment to official positions.

248. Originated during the Han dynasty, it refers to county-level government officials appointed from among locals. They were responsible for recommending talented people among the locals, recording the appointees' achievements, offering sacrifices, and performing ceremonies.

249. Highly trained military people without government positions.

250. Yi In-jwa was a member of the Young Doctrine Faction who was ousted from power, infiltrated Ch'ŏngju, and led a revolt against the capital in 1728. He was defeated in Ansŏng by government forces and executed in Seoul.

251. The quotation is a translation of 火生於木 火發必尅 (hwasaengŏmok hwabalp'ilgŭk) of the Kwangmunhoe text. The quotation is thought to come from 火生於木 禍發必尅 姦生於國 時動必潰 (hwasaengŏmok hwabalp'ilgŭk kansaengŏguk sidongp'ilgwe), which translates, "Fire is born out of wood and is bound to defeat wood at the time of disaster; disloyal subjects are born in a country and are bound to destroy the country when the tide serves." In "Huangdi yinfu jing jizhu" (Collected notes on the Book of Hidden Code by Emperor Huang) in *Yinfu jing*, the phrase is explained by replacing 禍 (K. hwa, disaster) with 火 (K. hwa, fire): 火生

於木 火發而木焚, which translates as "Fire is born out of wood: fire flourishes and burns the wood." See *Yinfu jing*, 4.

252. In the text, as in n. 251 above, The History of Lu 魯史 (Ch. Lushi), another name of the Spring and Autumn Annals (Chunqiu), is entered.

253. The quotation 禮樂豈玉帛鐘鼓云乎 in the text is from 禮云禮云 玉帛云 乎哉 樂云樂云 鐘鼓云乎哉 in "Yang Huo" in *Analects of Confucius* (Ch. *Lunyu*; K. *Nonŏ*). In ancient China, precious presents such as jade and silk were exchanged when countries formed friendships and offered when feudal lords paid tribute to the sovereign state. A translation of the part is as follows: "When I keep saying 'Ritual! Ritual!' do you think I'm just ranting about jade and silk? And when I keep saying 'Music! Music!' do you think I'm just ranting about bells and drums?" (Confucius, *Analects*, 135).

254. The phrase kwansŏk hwagyun 關石和勺 in the epilogue originates from kwansŏk hwagyun 關石和鈞 (using measuring scales appropriately), which appears in "Songs of Five Sons" (Wuzizhige, K. Ojajiga) in "Annals of the Xia dynasty (Xiashu)" of the *Book of Documents*. Sŏk denotes 120 *kŭn* and *kyun* denotes thirty *kŭn*. As one *kŭn* is six hundred grams, they are, respectively, seventy-two kilograms and eighteen kilograms. The whole phrase connotes that tolls and taxes should be appropriately levied and collected.

255. Buddhist cosmology places Mount Sumeru at the center of the world. As a metaphor, the mustard seed (芥子 K. *kaeja*) and (Mount) Sumeru (須彌 K. Sumi) in the *T'aengniji* text represent interfusion, the integral concept of the *Flower Garland Sūtra*: The realms in the cosmos are mutually interdependent and contain each other. In *Vimalakīrtinirdeśasūtra* 維摩詰所說經 (K. *Yumahil sosŏlgyŏng*) this metaphor is used to express the state of the inconceivable liberation: those who attain the state can put Mount Sumeru into a mustard seed without altering the volume of either 諸佛菩薩有解脫名不可思議 若菩薩住是解脫者 以須彌之高廣 內芥子中 無 所增減 (不思議品 K. Pulsaŭip'um, or The Inconceivable Liberation). The full text can be found at http://kb.sutra.re.kr/. Similar expressions with references to the mustard seed and Mount Sumeru in sutras such as *Annotation of Vimalakīrtisūtra* 維摩經疏 (J. *Yuimagyō shō*) and *Summary of Vimalakīrtisūtra* 維摩經抄 (J. *Yuimagyō sho*) can be found at http://21dzk.l.u-tokyo.ac.jp/SAT/ddb-sat2.php.

Bibliography

Works by Yi Chung-hwan

HAND-COPIED MANUSCRIPTS OF *T'AENGNIJI* (MANUSCRIPTS IN PRIVATE COLLEC-
TIONS INCLUDE THE NAME OF THE COLLECTION; MANUSCRIPTS HELD BY LIBRAR-
IES INCLUDE THE NAME OF THE LIBRARY FOLLOWED BY THE LIBRARY CATALOGUE
INFORMATION.)

Chinyusŭngnam 震維勝覽. Jangseogak, B15AB 16; Korea University, B10 A3F;
National Library of Korea, Ko 2700-98; National Library of Korea, Han Ko
Cho 60-70; National Library of Korea, Han Ko Cho 60-74; National Library
of Korea, Ko Kwi 2700-11; Kyujanggak, Sangbaek Ko 915.1 J563; Kyujanggak,
Kyu 7732; Kyujanggak, Ko 4790-38.

Chŏbyŏkt'onggi 鰈域通志. Korea University, Ayŏn B10A3N.

Ch'onghwa 總貨. Jangseogak, K2-4189.

Ch'ŏnghwa mannok 青華慢錄. National Library of Korea, Ko 2701-5.

Ch'ŏnghwa sanin p'aryŏkchi 青華山人八域誌. National Library of Korea, Han Ko
Cho 60-17.

Ch'ŏnghwa sanin p'aryŏkchich'o 青華山人八域志抄. Kyujanggak, Sangbaek Ko
915.1-Y58c; Sookmyung Women's University, CL 915.1 Yi Chung-hwan
Ch'ŏng.

Chosŏnjiri 朝鮮地理. Yonsei University, Kosŏ Mugyongsil 915.1 Chosŏnji.

Chosŏnp'alto kag ŏji 朝鮮八道可居誌. Soongsil University, 915.1 Yi 7769 Cho.

Chosŏnp'alto pokkŏron 朝鮮八道卜居論. Yonsei University, Kosŏ (III) 4299.

Haedong p'aryŏkchi 海東八域誌. Yonsei University, Kosŏ (I) 915.1 Yi Chung-
hwan Hae.

Kangsanji 江山誌. Lee Hae-jun collection.

Kibang Pokkŏsŏl 箕方卜居說. National Library of Korea, Ko 2701-8.

Kuuji 邱隅誌. National Library of Korea, Ko 2709-3.

Pakchongji 博綜誌. Jangseogak, Kwi K2-4180; Kyujanggak, Kyu 3742.

P'altosansugi 八道山水記. Kyujanggak, Ko 4790-11.

P'aryŏkchi 八域誌. Dankook University, Ko 981.1 Yi 861木; Konkuk University, 915.1 Yi57교; Korea University, Mansong B10 A3J; Korea University,
Ayŏn B10A3M; Korea University, Ayŏn B10A3M; National Library of Korea, Ko 2107-165; National Library of Korea, Ko 2107-11; National Library
of Korea, Han Ko Cho 60-50; Seoul National University, Ilsŏk 915.1 Y58pp;
Chon'gyonggak, B16AB-0015; Chon'gyonggak, B16AB-0015a; Yonsei Uni-

versity, Kosŏ (III) 3779; Asami Collection, University of California, Berkeley. P'aryŏk kagŏji 八域可居志: Kyujanggak, Kyu 7492.

P'aryŏk kagŏji 八域可居誌. Korea University, Mansong B10 A3K; National Library of Korea, Ko 2700-122; Yonsei University, Kosŏ (III) 1841.

P'aryŏkki 八域記. National Library of Korea, Han Ko Cho 60-67.

P'aryŏk Yoram 八域要覽. Korea University, Sinam B10 A3H.

Pokkŏsŏl 卜居說. Dankook University, Ko 915.1 Yi 861 ㅂ; National Library of Korea, Sŭnggye Ko 2701-4; National Library of Korea, Han Ko Cho 60-28; Yonsei University, Kosŏ (Yi Wŏn-ch'ŏl) 915.1 Yi Chung-hwan T'aek Ka.

Sadaebu kagŏch'ŏ 士大夫可居處. In Nam Ha-haeng 南夏行, *Wayurok* 臥遊錄. Kim Yŏng-jin collection.

Sadaebu kagŏch'ŏ 士大夫可居處. National Library of Korea, Ko 2700-105; Jangseogak, MF35-332~337; Jangseogak, in *Ajujamnok* 鵝洲雜錄 K3-650.

Sohwaji 小華誌. National Library of Korea, Sŏngho Ko 2700-81.

T'aeksŭngji 擇勝誌. National Library of Korea, Han Ko Cho 60-29.

T'aengniji 擇里誌. Catholic University, T 133.323 ㅇ887ㅌ; Dongguk University, 911.51 Yi 77 ㅌ 2; Dongguk University, D 981.1 Yi 77 Ka; Jangseogak, K2-4190; Jangseogak, K2-4192; Jangseogak, B15AB 2B; Jangseogak, B15AB 2A; Korea University, B10 A3; Korea University, B10 A3La; Korea University, B10A3A; Korea University, B10 A3B; Korea University, B10 A3C; Korea University, B10 A3E; Korea University, Sinam B10 A3A; Korea University, Yuktang B10 A3L; Korea University, Yuktang B10 A3La; National Library of Korea, Ko 2700-12; National Library of Korea, 2700-37; Keimyung University, (Ko) 910.22 Yi Chung-hwan ㅌ; Kyonggi University, K102182; Kyujanggak, Ko 915.1-Y58t v. 1–2; Kyujanggak, in *Choya sinp'il* 朝野信筆 Kyu 15580; Chon'gyonggak, B16 AB 0007a; Yonsei University, Kosŏ (Kim Chun-sŏk) T'aengnigi 擇里記: Dankook University, Ko 912.51 Yi 861ㅌ. 0660.

T'aengniji 擇里志. Jangseogak, K2-4191; Kyujanggak, Ilsa Ko 915.1-Y58t; Kyujanggak, Ko 4790-55; Waseda University, ru 04 01674; Waseda University, ru 04 02488; Yonsei University, in *P'aerim* 稗林 951.508 [冊 28]; Yonsei University, Kosŏ (III) 4301; Yonsei University, Kosŏ (I) 915.1; Yonsei University, Kosŏ (III) 4297.

T'aengnijich'o 擇里誌. National Library of Korea, Ko 2700-90.

Tongguk chirihae 東國地理解. National Library of France.

Tongguk ch'onghwarok 東國總貨錄. Kyujanggak, Kyu 15737.

Tongguk p'aryŏkchi 東國八域志. Yonsei University, Kosŏ (III) 4294.

Tongguk sanch'ŏnpyŏllok 東國山川別錄. Jangseogak, K2-4346; Yonsei University, Kosŏ K2-4346.

Tongguk sansuji 東國山水誌. Korea University, Sinam B10 A3G;

Tongguk sansurok 東國山水錄. Dankook University, 915.1 Yi 861ㅌ; Kyujanggak, Kyu 11638; Kyujanggak Sangbaek Ko 915.1 D 717; Jangseogak, in *Chŭngbo Sallimgyŏngje* 增補山林經濟 v 11; Kyujanggak, in *Chŭngbo Sallimgyŏngje* 增補山林經濟 Ilsa Ko 630.2 J572; Kyujanggak, in *Chŭngbo Sallimgyŏngje* 增補山林經濟 Ko 9100 10; Kyujanggak, in *Chŭngbo Sallimgyŏngje* 增補山林經濟 Ko

9100 1; Kyujanggak, in *Chŭngbo Sallimgyŏngje* 增補山林經濟 Ko 9100 1A; Kyu-janggak, in *Chŭngbo Sallimgyŏngje* 增補山林經濟 Kyu 7676; Kyujanggak, in *Chŭngbo Sallimgyŏngje* 增補山林經濟 Kyu 12688.

Tongguk sansuron kagŏji 東國山水論可居地. Korea University, Sinam B10 A3G.

Tongyŏhwiram 東輿彙覽. Jangseogak, B15AB 9.

Tongyurok 東維錄. Yonsei University, Kosŏ (I) 915.1 Tongyurok P'il.

PUBLISHED WORKS BY YI CHUNG-HWAN (LISTED CHRONOLOGICALLY)

————. *Chosen hachiikichi* (The eight provinces of Korea). Japanese translation by Kondo Sinsuki. Tokyo: Nisshusya, 1882.

————. *Chaoxian dili xiaozhi*. (Abridged geography of Korea). Chinese translation by Jian Jinggui. Shanghai: Osa Kanin, 1885.

————. *P'aryŏkchi*. Copy edited by Shakuo Shunjo. Seoul: Chosŏn Kosŏganhaeng-hoe, 1910.

————. *T'aengniji*. Copy edited by Ch'oe Nam-sŏn. Seoul: Chosŏn Kwangmunhoe, 1912.

————. *T'aengniji*. Korean translation by Yun Sŏk-wŏn. P'yŏngyang: Sahoegwaha-kwŏn Ch'ulp'ansa, 1964.

————. *T'aengniji*. Korean translation by Rho Do-Yang. Seoul: Chayugyoyangsa, 1969.

————. *T'aengniji*. Korean translation by Yi Ik-sŏng. Seoul: Ŭryu Munhwasa, 1971.

————.*T'aengniji*. Translated by Rho Do-Yang; Pak Che-ga. *Pukhagŭi*. Translated by Yi Sŏk-ho. Seoul: T'aeyangsŏjŏk, 1972.

————. *T'aengniji*. Korean translation by Yi Yŏng-t'aek. Seoul: Samjungdang, 1975.

————. *T'aengniji*. Korean translation by Rho Do-YangYang. Seoul: Myŏngji Tae-hakkyo Ch'ulp'anbu, 1977.

————. *T'aengniji*. Translated into Japanese as *Takurishi* by Kajii Noboru. Tokyo: Seeko Shoboo, 1983.

————. "Tongguk chirihae" (Notes on the geography of Korea). *Aesan Hakpo* 3 (1983): 75   163.

————. *T'aengniji*. Korean translation by Rho Do-YangYang. Seoul: Samgyŏngdang, 1985.

————. *T'aengniji*. Korean translation by Yi Ch'an. Seoul: Taragwŏn, 1985.

————. *T'aengniji*. Korean translation by Yi Ik-sŏng. Seoul: Hangilsa, 1992.

————. *T'aengniji*. Korean translation by Ch'a Ch'ang-yong. Seoul: Sŭlgisaem, 1994.

————. *T'aengniji*. Korean translation by Hur Geong-jin. Seoul: Hanyang Ch'ul-p'an, 1996.

————. *Yi Chung-hwan's T'aengniji: The Korean Classic for Choosing Settlement*. Translated with an introduction and notes by Inshil Choe Yoon. University of Sydney East Asian Series 12. Sydney: Wild Peony, 1998.

————. *T'aengniji*. Korean translation by Yi Ik-sŏng. Seoul: Ŭryu Munhwasa, 2002.

————. *T'aengniji*. Korean translation by Yi Min-su. Seoul: P'yŏnghwa Ch'ulp'ansa, 2003.

————. (Chŏngsonyŏn ŭl wihan) *T'aengniji* (*T'aengniji* for youth). Korean translation by Kim Hŭng-sik, P'aju: Sŏhae Munjip, 2006.

————. *T'aengniji*. Translated into Japanese as *Takurishi* by Hiraki Minoru. Tokyo: Heibonsya, 2006.

————. *T'aengniji*. Korean translation by Hur Geong-jin. P'aju: Sŏhae Munjip, 2007.

————. *T'aengniji*. Edited by Chŏn Kŭn-wan and illustrated by Kim Kang-sŏp. P'aju: Juniŏ Kimyŏngsa, 2008.

————. *T'aengniji*. Edited by Yi Chong-ran and illustrated by Kwŏn O-hyŏk. Seoul: Kyowŏn, 2011.

————. *T'aengniji: Uri ttang e taehan kamdongjŏgin pogosŏ* (Moving report on our land). Edited by Pak Se-gyŏng and illustrated by Pak Su-min. P'aju: P'aran Chajŏngŏ, 2012.

————. *T'aengniji Manhwa* (Yi Chung-hwan's *T'aengniji* as a cartoon). Edited by Chŏn Kŭn-hwan and with cartoons by Kim Kang-sŏp. P'aju: Junior Kimyŏngsa, 2012.

————. *T'aengniji*. Korean translation by Yi Min-su. Seoul: Oljae, 2013.

Other Sources

Ahn Dae-Hoe. "*P'aerim* kwa Chosŏn hugi yasa ch'ongsŏ ŭi paltal" (*P'aerim* and the flourishing of unofficial history series publication). *Nammyŏnghak yŏn'gu* 20 (2005): 299–326.

————. "*T'aengniji* ŭi kujŏnjisik panyŏng kwa chiyŏkchŏnsŏl sŏsul ŭi sigak" (The inclusion of local legends and orally transmitted knowledge in *T'aengniji*). *Taedong Munhwa Yŏn'gu* 93 (2016): 41–74.

————. "*T'aengniji* wa Chosŏn hugi chibang ihae ŭi hyŏksin" (*T'aengniji*, a new approach to understanding geography in the late Chosŏn period). *Han'guk hanmunhak yŏn'gu* 53 (2014): 69–102.

Bae Woo-sung. "*T'aengniji* e taehan yŏnksahakchŏk tokpŏp — p'ilsabon pigyo yŏn'gu rŭl chungsimŭro" (A historical rereading of *Taengniji*: A comparison of written texts). *Hanguk Munhwa* 33 (2004): 213–246.

Buswell, Robert E., Jr. "Buddhism under Confucian Domination: The Synthetic Vision of Sŏsan Hyujŏng." In *Culture and the Stage in Late Chosŏn Korea*, ed. JaHyun Kim Haboush and Martina Deuchler, 134–159. Cambridge, MA: Harvard University Asia Center, 1999.

————, ed. *Religions of Korea in Practice*. Princeton Readings in Religions. Princeton, NJ: Princeton University Press, 2007.

Ch'a Chu-hwan. *Han'guk togyo sasang yŏn'gu* (A study of Taoism in Korea). Seoul: Seoul Taehakkyo Ch'ulp'anbu, 1986.

Chang Tŏk-sun. *Hanguk sŏrhwa munhak yŏn'gu* (A study of oral literature in Korea). Seoul: Seoul Taehakkyo Ch'ulp'anbu, 1984.

Cho Myŏng-gi et al. *Han'guk sasang ŭi simch'ŭng yŏn'gu* (An in-depth study of Korean thought). Seoul: Usŏk, 1986.

Cho Tong-gŏl et al., eds. *Han'guk ŭi yŏksaga wa yŏksahak* (Korean historians and historical studies). Seoul: Ch'angjak Kwa Pip'yŏngsa, 1994.

Ch'oe Ch'ang-jo. *See* Choi Chang-jo.

Ch'oe Hang et al. *Kyŏngguk taejŏn* (National Code). Academy of Korean Studies, Hangukhak Haksulchŏngbogwan, K2–2062. http://aks.koreaa2z.com /viewer.php?seq=55&cateUrl=246&hidSearchText=경국대전.

Ch'oe I-don. *See* Choi Edon.

Choe Inshil. "Chosŏn Kwangmunhoebon *T'aengniji* wa Chosŏn Kosŏganhaehoebon *P'aryŏkchi*" (Chosŏn Kwangmunhoe edition of *T'aengniji* and Chosŏn Kosŏganhaehoe edition of *P'aryŏkchi*). *Proceedings Summary of the 2014 Annual Conference of the Association of Korean Cultural and Historical Geographers*, 1–9. Seoul: Sungshin Women's University, 2014.

———. "*T'aengniji* ch'ogibon ŭi t'ŭksŏng" (The characteristics of early *T'aengniji* manuscripts). In *Proceedings of the 2011 Geography Conference*, ed. Korean Geographical Society, 142–151. Sŏngnam: Academy of Korean Studies, 2011.

———. "*T'aengniji* ch'ogip'ilsabon ch'ujŏng ŭl wihan sŏjijŏk koch'al" (A bibliographic approach toward the identification of early *T'aengniji* manuscripts). *Sŏjihakpo* 40 (2012): 155–174.

———. "*T'aengniji* chŏsul, chŏnsa, pŏnyŏgedaehan il koch'al" (An appraisal of handwritten copies and translations of *T'aengniji*). *The Third International Conference on Korean Language, Literature and Culture*, 204–215. Seoul: Yonsei University, 2009.

Ch'oe Pŏm-sŏ. *Sosŏl "T'aengniji"* (*T'aengniji*, a novel). 3 vols. Seoul: Kirinwŏn, 1995.

Ch'oe Pyŏng-hŏn. "Tongyang pulkyosa sang ŭi hanguk pulkyo" (The position of Korean Buddhism in the history of Buddhism in the East). *Hanguksa simin kangjwa* 4 (1989): 14–42.

———. "Tosŏn ŭi saeng'ae wa namal yŏch'o ŭi p'ungsu chirisŏl: Sŏnjong kwa p'ungsu chirisŏl ŭi kwan'gye rŭl ctungsim ŭyo" (The life of Tosŏn and geomancy during the period of the end of Silla and the beginning of Koryŏ: The relationship between Sŏn Buddhism and geomancy). *Hanguksa Yŏn'gu* 11 (1975): 101–146.

Ch'oe Wan-gi. *See* Choi Wan-gee.

Ch'oe Wŏn-sŏk. *See* Choi Won Suk.

Ch'oe Yŏng-sŏng. *Ch'oe Ch'i-wŏn ŭi sasang yŏn'gu* (A study of Ch'oe Ch'i-wŏn's thought). Seoul: Asea Munhwasa, 1990.

Choe Young-jun. "Chosŏn hugi sirhakcha tŭl ŭi p'ungsu chiri" (Geomancy as discussed by Sirhak scholars in the late Chosŏn dynasty). *Hanguk Munhwa* 11 (1990): 469–504.

———. *Kukt'o wa minjok saenghwalsa* (The history of the territory and daily life of Koreans). Seoul: Hangilsa, 1997.

———. "P'ungsu wa *T'aengniji*" (Geomancy and *T'aengniji*). *Hanguksa simin kangjwa* 14 (1994): 98–122.

———. "*T'aengniji*: Hangukchŏk inmun chirisŏ" (*T'aengniji*: A book of Korean human geography). *Chindan Hakpo*. 69 (1990): 165–189.

————. *Yŏngnam daero* (The great Yŏngnam road). Seoul: Koryŏ Taehakkyo Minjok Munhwa Yŏn'guwŏn, 1990.

Choi, Byŏng-hŏn. "Tosŏn's Geomantic Theories and the Foundation of the Koryŏ Dynasty." *Seoul Journal of Korean Studies* 2 (1989): 65–92.

Choi Chang-jo. *Hanguk ŭi p'ungsu sasang* (Geomantic thought in Korea). Seoul: Minumsa, 1984.

————. "P'ungsu, the Korean Traditional Geographic Thoughts." *Korea Journal* 26, no. 5 (1986): 35–45.

————. "Study of How Koreans View and Utilize Nature." *Korea Journal* 32, no. 4 (1992): 26–45.

Choi Edon. "16 segi nanggwangwŏn ŭi hyŏngsŏng kwajŏng" (Formation process of the selection secretaries' right in the sixteenth century). *Hanguk sahak* 14 (1986): 3–50.

————."16 segi nanggwangwŏn ŭi sŏngjang kwa pungdang chŏngch'i" (Expansion of the selection secretaries' power and factional politics in the sixteenth century). *Kyujanggak* 12 (1989): 31–58.

————. "16 segi sarimp'a ŭi ch'ŏngje kanghwa undong" (Reinforcement movement of the recommendation system by the sixteenth-century literati group). *Hanguk Hakpo* 15, no. 1 (1989): 89–146.

————. "Sŏngjongdae sarim ŭi hun'gu chŏngch'i pip'an kwa sae chŏngch'i mosaek" (Criticizing politics by the *hun'gu* group and seeking new politics by the literati group during the reign of Sŏngjong). *Hanguk Munhwa* 17 (1996): 113–132.

Choi Wan Gee. *Hanguk sŏngnihak ŭi maek* (Lineage of Neo-Confucianism in Korea). Seoul: Nŭt'inamu, 1989.

Choi Won Suk. "Hanguk esŏ chŏn'gaedoen p'ungsu wa pulgyo ŭi kyosŏp." (Fengshui's interaction with Buddhism in Korea). *Taehan chirihakhoeji* 44, no. 1 (2009): 77–88.

Chŏn Yong-sin, ed. *Han'guk kojimyŏng sajŏn.* (Dictionary of old place-names of Korea). Seoul: Koryŏ Taehakkyo Minjok Munhwa Yŏn'guso, 1995.

Chŏng Chae-sŏ, trans. *Shanhai jing* (Classic of mountains and seas). Seoul: Minumsa, 1985.

Chŏng Ch'i-yŏng. *See* Jung Chi-Young.

Chŏng Man-jo. "Chosŏn sidae ŭi sarim chŏngch'i: 17 segi ŭi chŏngch'i hyŏngt'ae" (Literati politics in the Chosŏn dynasty: Types of politics in the seventeenth century), 196–244. In *Hanguksa sang ŭi chŏngch'i hyŏngt'ae* (Types of politics in Korean history), by Yi Chong-uk et al. Seoul: Ilchogak, 1993.

Chŏng Myŏng-hyŏn. *See* Jeong Myunghyun.

Chŏng Ok-cha. *Chosŏn hugi chisŏngsa* (Intellectual history in the late Chosŏn dynasty). Seoul: Ilchisa, 1991

————. *Chosŏn hugi munhwa undongsa* (The history of cultural movements in the late Chosŏn dynasty). Seoul: Ilchokak, 1988.

Chŏng To-jŏn and Hamhŏ Tŭkt'ong. *Korea's Great Buddhist-Confucian Debate: The Treatises of Chong Tojon (Sambong) and Hamho Tuktong (Kihwa).* Translated and with an introduction by A. Charles Muller. Korean Classics: Philosophy and Religion. Honolulu: University of Hawai'i Press, 2015.

Chŏng Tu-hi. *See* Jung Doo Hee.

Chŏng Yag-yong. *Tasan simunjip* (Literary anthology of Tasan). http://db.itkc .or.kr/dir/item?itemId=BT#dir/node?grpId=&itemId=BT&gubun=book &depth=2&cate1=C&cate2=&dataGubun=서지&dataId=ITKC_BT_1260A.

Chosŏn wangjo sillok (Annals of the Chosŏn dynasty). In *Hanguk kochŏn chonghap DB* (Comprehensive database of Korean classics). http://db.itkc.or.kr/dir/item ?itemId=JT#/dir/list?itemId=JT&gubun=book.

Ch'uan kŭp kugan (Interrogation records of major offenders). Translated by O Hang-nyŏng et al. Chŏnju: Heureum Ch'ulp'ansa, 2014.

Chung, Chai-sik. "Chŏng To-jŏn: 'Architect' of Yi Dynasty Government and Ideology." In *The Rise of Neo-Confucianism in Korea*, ed. Wm. Theodore de Barry and JaHyun Kim Haboush, 59–88. New York: Columbia University Press, 1985.

Confucius. *The Analects*. Translated and with commentary by David Hinton. Berkeley, CA: Counterpoint. 2014.

Deuchler, Martina. *The Confucian Transformation of Korea: A Study of Society and Ideology*. Cambridge, MA: Council on East Asian Studies, Harvard University, 1992.

———. "Neo-Confucianism: The Impulse for Social Action in Early Yi Korea." *Journal of Korean Studies* 2 (1980): 71–111.

———. "Neo-Confucianism in Early Yi Korea: Some Reflections on the Role of Ye." *Korea Journal* 15, no. 5 (1975): 12–18.

Duncan, John B. *The Origins of the Chosŏn Dynasty*. Seattle: University of Washington Press, 2000.

———. "The Social Background to the Founding of the Chosŏn Dynasty: Change or Continuity?" *Journal of Korean Studies* 6 (1988–1989): 39–79.

Ha Tong-ho. "*Tongguk chirihae sŏjigo*" (A bibliographic study of *Tongguk chirihae*). *Aesan Hakpo* 3 (1983): 55–73.

Haboush, JaHyun Kim. *The Confucian Kingship in Korea*. New York: Columbia University Press, 2001.

———. "Confucian Rhetoric and Ritual as Techniques of Political Dominance: Yŏngjo's Use of the Royal Lecture." *Journal of Korean Studies* 5 (1984): 39–62.

Han Sam-gŏn. *Ulsan T'aengniji* (Regional geography of Ulsan). Ulsan: Tosŏch'ulp'an Chong, 2011.

Han Woo-keun. "Kaehoesa" (Opening remarks). *Chindan Hakpo*, 69 (1990): 126.

———. *Sŏngho Yi Ik yŏn'gu* (A study of Sŏngho Yi Ik). Seoul: Seoul Taehakkyo Ch'ulp'anbu, 1990.

———. *Yijo hugi ŭi sahoe wa sasang* (The society and thought of the late Chosŏn dynasty). Seoul: Ŭryu Munhwasa, 1987.

Han Young-woo. *Chŏng To-jŏn sasang ŭi yŏn'gu* (A study of Chŏng To-jŏn's thought). Seoul: Seoul Taehakkyo Ch'ulp'anbu, 1989.

———. *Chosŏn chŏngi sahoe kyŏngje yŏn'gu* (A study of the social economy of early Chosŏn). Seoul: Ŭryu Munhwasa, 1991.

———. *Chosŏn chŏngi ŭi sahoe sasang* (Social thought of the early Chosŏn). Seoul: Hanguk Ilbosa, 1976.

———. *Wangjo ŭi sŏlgyeja Chŏng To-jŏn* (Chŏng To-jŏn, the architect of a dynasty). Seoul: Chisiksanŏpsa, 1999.

Hanguk Munhwayŏksa Chirihakhoe, ed. *Hanguk ŭi chŏnt'ong chirisasang* (Traditional geographic thought in Korea). Seoul: Minumsa, 1991.

Hanguk Togyosasang Yŏn'guhoe, ed. *Togyo wa hanguk munhwa* (Taoism and Korean culture). Seoul: Asea Munhwasa, 1991.

Hŏ Hŭng-sik. *Hanguk chungse pulgyosa yŏn'gu* (A study of the history of Buddhism in medieval Korea). Seoul: Ilchokak, 1994.

Hŏ Pong, ed. *Haedongyaŏn* (Unofficial stories of Korea). Kyujanggak collection, kyu 3797.

Hŏ Ung. *See* Huh Woong.

Hong Chung-in. *Aju chamnok* (Assorted records of Hong Chung-in). In *Chosŏn tangjaeng kwan'gye charyojip* (Collection of sourcebooks on factional strife during the Chosŏn dynasty), ed. Yi I-hwa. Seoul: Yŏgang Ch'ulp'ansa, 1990.

Hong Hyŏng-ok. *Hanguk chugŏsa* (The history of dwellings in Korea). Seoul: Minumsa, 1992.

Hong I-sŏp. *Chosŏn kwahaksa* (The history of science in Korea). Seoul: Chŏngŭmsa, 1946.

———. "Yi Chung-hwan's Geographical Thought in *T'aengniji*." *Korea Journal* 30 (1974): 40–44.

———. "Yi Chung-hwan ŭi sahoe kyŏngjeron" (Yi Chung-hwan's social economic view). *Yonsei ch'unch'uno* 116, December 10, 1957.

Hong Man-sŏn. *Sallim kyŏngje* (Farm management). Seoul National University, Kyujanggak collection, ko 9100 6.

Hucker, Charles O. *A Dictionary of Official Titles of Imperial China*. Stanford, CA: Stanford University Press, 1985.

Huh Woong. "Kungmunp'an *T'aengniji* ŭi ŏnŏ punsŏk" (Linguistic analysis of the Korean-alphabet version *T'aengniji*). *Aesan Hakpo* 3 (1983): 31–54.

Hwang Sŏn-myŏng. *Chosŏnjo chonggyo sahoesa yŏn'gu* (A study of the religious and social history of the Chosŏn dynasty). Seoul: Ilchisa, 1992.

Hwang Tŏk-kil, ed. *Choya sinp'il* (Trustworthy writings of scholars both in and out of government office). Kyujanggak collection, kyu 15580 v.2.

Hwang Yun-sŏk. *Ijae nan'go* (Rough drafts of Ijae). Sŏngnam: Hanguk Chŏngsin Munhwa Yŏn'guwŏn, 1997.

Im Chae-hae. *Hanguk minsok kwa chŏnt'ong ŭi segye* (Aspects of Korean folklore and tradition). Seoul: Chisiksanŏpsa, 1991.

Im Ch'ŏl-ho. *Sŏrhwa wa minjung ŭi yŏksa ŭisik* (Folk tales and people's historical awareness). Seoul: Chimmundang, 1989.

Im Tŏk-sun. *Munhwa chirihak* (Cultural geography). Seoul: Pŏmmunsa, 1992.

Im Yŏng-gŏl. *See* Rim Young-gul.

Iryŏn. *Samguk Yusa: Legends and History of the Three Kingdoms of Ancient Korea.*

Translated by Tae-Hung Ha and Grafton K. Mintz. Seoul: Yonsei University Press, 1997.

Jeong Myunghyun, "*Imwŏn kyŏngjeji* sabon tŭl e taehan sŏjihakchŏk kŏmt'o (The bibliographical investigation on copying editions of *Imwŏn kyŏngjeji*)" *Kyujanggak* 34 (2009): 205–230.

Jung Chi-Young. "Chosŏn sidae sadaebudŭl ŭi kyot'ongsudan (The literati's means of transportation in the Joseon period)," *Munhwayŏksa chiri* 25, no. 2 (2013): 74–87.

Jung Doo Hee. *Chosŏn ch'ogi chŏngch'i chibaeseryŏk yŏn'gu* (A study of political ruling powers at the beginning of the Chŏsun dynasty). Seoul: Ilchokak, 1983.

———. *Chosŏnsidae ŭi taegan yŏn'gu* (A study of censorial officials in the Chŏsun dynasty). Seoul: Ilchokak, 1994.

———. "Yi Chung-hwan." *Hanguksa simin kangjwa* 3 (1988): 119–139.

Kang Che-yun. *Sŏm T'aengniji* (Travelogue of islands), Seoul: Homi, 2015.

Kang Man-Gil. *Hanguk yugyo ŭi ihae* (Understanding Korean Confucianism). Seoul: Minjok Munhwasa, 1989.

———. "Research on Han River Merchants." *Korea Journal* 17, no. 10 (1979): 21–32.

———. "Sirhak Thought and Its Reflection in Policies." *Korea Journal* 14, no. 5 (1974): 4–13.

Kang Man-Gil et al. *Tasan ŭi chŏngch'i kyŏngje sasang* (The political economic thought of Chŏng Yak-yong). Seoul: Ch'angjak kwa pip'yŏngsa, 1990.

Keum, Jang-tae. *Confucianism and Korean Thoughts*. Seoul: Jimoondang Publishing Company, 2000.

———. *Hanguk Sirhak sasang yŏn'gu* (A study of Practical Learning thought of Korea). Seoul: Chimmundang, 1987.

Kim Chŏng-sim. "Yi Chung-hwan ŭi T'aengniji e kwanhan yŏn'gu" (A study of Yi Chung-hwan's T'aengniji). Master's thesis, Sungmyŏng Women's University, 1982.

Kim Duk Hyun. "Yugyojŏk ch'ollak kyŏnggwan ŭi ihae" (Understanding the landscape of Confucian villages), 191–214. In *Hanguk ŭi chŏnt'ong chirisasang* (Traditional geographic thought in Korea), ed. Hanguk Munhwayŏksa Chirihakhoe. Seoul: Minumsa, 1991.

Kim Hongkyung. "A Party for the Spirits: Ritual Practice in Confucianism." In Buswell, ed., *Religions of Korea in Practice*, 163–176.

Kim Ki-duk. "Koryŏ sidae kaegyŏng ŭi p'ungsujirijŏk koch'al (Examining the geographical features of the Koryŏ dynasty's Kaegyŏng in *feng shui* theoretical terms)." *Hanguksasangsahak* 17 (2001): 63–119.

Kim Pu-sik, et al., eds. *Samguk sagi* (History of the Three Kingdoms). Translated by Yi Chae-ho. Seoul: Sol, 1997.

Kim Pyŏng-wŏn. "Chosŏnjo chŏllang yŏn'gu" (A study of the selection secretaries of the Chosŏn dynasty). *Chibangchŏngbu yŏn'gu* 2 (2003): 241–261.

Kim T'ae-yŏng. *Chosŏn chŏngi t'oji chedosa yŏn'gu* (A study of the history of the land system in early Chosŏn). Seoul: Chisiksanŏpsa, 1983.

Kim Tŏk-hyŏn. *See* Kim Duk Hyun.

Kim Tong-uk. "'Yuguguk seja' iyagi ŭi yubyŏn yangsang" (A study of "Prince of Ryukyu" tales). *Hanminjok ŏmunhak* 44 (2003): 153–178.

Kim U-gi. "Chŏllang kwa samsa ŭi kwan'gye esŏ pon 16 segi kwŏllyŏk kujo" (The power structure of the sixteenth century from the perspectives of the relationship between selection secretaries and the three remonstrative offices). *Yŏksakyoyuknonjip* 13 (1990): 617–639.

———. "Chosŏnhugi sarim ŭi chŏllangjik chinch'ul kwa kŭ yŏkhal" (The advancement of late Chosŏn-period literatis to selection secretary posts and their role). *Taegusahak* 29 (1986): 75–116.

Kim Yak-sŭl. "Sŏngho susabon *T'aengniji* e taehayŏ" (On Sŏngho's handwritten *T'aengniji* manuscript). *Kukhoe tosŏgwanbo* 5, no. 4 (1968): 69–75.

Kim Yong-dŏk. *Chosŏn hugi sasangsa yŏn'gu* (A study of the history of thought in late Chosŏn). Seoul: Ŭryu Munhwasa, 1977.

Kim Young-jin. "Chosŏn hugi *Wayurok* ibon yŏn'gu" (A study of different versions of *Wayurok* during the late Chosŏn period). *Kojŏn munhak yŏn'gu* 48 (2015): 221–257.

Kim Yun-gon. "Yi Chung-hwan ŭi *T'aengniji*" (Yi Chung-hwan's *T'aengniji*) 119–139. In *Sirhak yŏn'gu immun*, ed. Yŏksahakhoe. Seoul: Ilchokak, 1973.

Ko, Donghwan. *Chosŏnhugi sŏul sangŏp paldalsa yŏn'gu* (A study of the developmental history of commerce in Seoul in late Chosŏn). P'aju: Chisiksanŏpsa, 1998.

———. "Development of Commerce and Commercial Policy during the Reign of King Chongjo." *Korea Journal* 40, no. 4 (2000): 202–226.

Koishi Akiko. "Ri Ju-kan to *Takurishi*" (Yi Chung-hwan and *T'aengniji*). *Shosen gappo* 115 (1985): 27–102.

Kŏri Munhwa Simin Yŏndae. *Taegu sin T'aengniji: Taegu ŭi chaebalgyŏn* (New regional geography of Taegu: The new discovery of Taegu), Seoul: Pukraendŭ, 2007.

Koryŏsa (History of Koryŏ). Translated by Sahoe Kwahagwŏn Kojŏn Yŏn'guso. P'yŏngyang: Sahoe Kwahagwŏn Ch'ulp'ansa 1962?–1964. Kuksa p'yŏnch'an wiwŏnhoe (National Institute of Korean History), *Hanguksa taeit'ŏbaeisŭ (Korean History Database)*. http://db.history.go.kr/KOREA/item/level.do?itemId=kr.

Koryŏsa chŏryo (Essentials of Koryŏ history). Translated by Minjokmunhwa Ch'ujinhoe. Seoul: Minjokmunhwa Ch'ujinhoe 1968–1977. Kuksa p'yŏnch'an wiwŏnhoe (National Institute of Korean History), *Hanguksa taeit'ŏbaeisŭ (Korean History Database)*. http://db.history.go.kr/KOREA/item/level.do?itemId=kj&types=r.

Kŭm Chang-t'ae. *See* Keum Jang-tae.

Lautensach, Hermann. *Korea*. Translated by Katherine Dege and Echkart Dege. Berlin: Springer-Verlag, 1988.

Lee Byung Hyoo. "Chosŏn chŏngi chibaeseryŏk ŭi kaltŭng kwa sarim chŏngch'i ŭi sŏngnip" (Conflict among the ruling powers in early Chosŏn and the establishment of literati politics). *Minjok Munhwa Nonch'ong* 11 (1990): 163–193.

———. "Chosŏn chŏngi sarimp'a ŭi silch'e wa sŏngkyŏk" (The true nature and character of the literati group in early Chosŏn). *Chosŏnsidaesahakpo* 39 (2006): 209–222.

———. "Chosŏn chungjongjo chŏngguk kongsin ŭi sŏngbun kwa tonghyang" (Characteristics and trends of meritorious officials during the reign of King Chungjong in Chosŏn). *Taegusahak* 15, no. 1 (1978): 289–317.

———. "Chosŏn wangjo 16 segi chŏngguk ŭi ch'ui wa Yŏngnamsarimp'a ŭi taeŭng" (The development of the political situation in sixteenth-century Chosŏn and responses from the Yŏngnam literati group). *Yŏksa kyoyuk nonjip* 25 (1999): 197–234.

Lee Chan. "Hanguk chirihaksa" (The history of geography in Korea) 683–735. In vol. 3 of *Hanguk Munhwasa taegye*, ed. Minjok Munhwa Yŏn'guso. Seoul: Koryŏ Taehakkyo, 1968.

———. "*T'aengniji* e taehan chirihakchŏk koch'al" (Geographical review of *T'aengniji*). *Aesan Hakpo* 3 (1983): 1–29.

Lee Do-hun, Kim Se-ho, and Yim Young-gil. "*T'aengniji* ibongo (Consideration of the different versions of *T'aengniji*)." *Taedong Munhwa Yŏn'gu*, 93 (2016): 99–134.

Lee Ki-baik. *A New History of Korea*. Translated by Edward W. Wagner with Edward J. Shultz. Seoul: Ilchokak, 1989.

Lee Moon-Jong. *Yi Chung-hwan kwa "T'aengniji"* (Yi Chung-hwan and *T'aengniji*). Seoul: Ara, 2014.

———. "Yi Chung-hwan ŭi saengae wa *T'aengniji* ŭi sŏngnip" (The life of Yi Chung-hwan and his process of writing *T'aengniji*). *Munhwa yŏksa chiri* 16, no. 1 (2004): 123–156.

Lee, Peter H., ed. *Sourcebook of Korean Civilization*. Vol. 1. New York: Columbia University Press, 1993.

Muller, A. Charles. "The Great Confucian-Buddhist Debate." In Buswell, ed., *Religions of Korea in Practice*, 177–204.

Mun Myŏng-sŏ. "*T'aengniji* yŏn'gu" (A study of *T'aengniji*). *Hong'ik sahak* 2, 1985.

Murayama Chijun. *Chosen no fusui* (Korean geomancy). Seoul: Chosen Shotofu, 1931.

Na Kyŏng-su. *Hanguk ŭi sinhwa yŏn'gu* (A study of Korean myths). Seoul: Kyomunsa, 1993.

Nam Hyo-on. *Ch'ugangjip* (Anthology of Nam Hyo-on). Kyujanggak collection, Karam ko 819.51-N15c.

Nishikawa Takao. "Takurishi no imyo ni tsuite" (On various names of *T'aengniji*). *Kan* 103 (1983): 126–129.

No Chu-sŏk. *Seoul T'aengniji* (Regional geography of Seoul). Seoul: Sodamch'ulp'ansa, 2014.

No To-yang. *See* Rho Do-Yang.

O Sŏng. "*T'aengniji* ŭi p'alto ch'ongnon kwa saengnijo e taehan koch'al" (On "Eight Provinces" and "Saengni" in *T'aengniji*). *Chindan Hakpo*, 69 (1990): 145–163.

Pae U-sŏng. *See* Bae Woo-sung.

Pak Hyŏn-kyu, "Kwanghaegunjo yugu seja sagŏnkwa chŏlmyŏngsi kamsang"

(The incident of the Ryukyu crown prince during the reign of King Kwang-hae and the appreciation of his poem composed before being killed). *Tong-bang hanmunhak* 20 (2001): 257–277.

Pak Kwang-yong. "Yi Chung-hwan ŭi chŏngch'ijŏk wich'i wa *T'aengniji* sŏsul" (Yi Chung-hwan's political status and his writing of *T'aengniji*). *Chindan Hakpo* 69 (1990): 127–143.

Pak Yong-su. "*T'aengniji* hangŭl kugyŏk pon" (Translated versions of *T'aengniji* in the Korean alphabet). Accessed July 4, 2016, http://san.chosun.com/site /data/html_dir/2012/03/30/2012033001547.html.

Palais, James B. *Confucian Statecraft and Korean Institutions: Yu Hyŏngwŏn and the Late Chosŏn Dynasty*. Seattle: University of Washington Press, 1996.

Park Young-han. "Ch'ŏngdam Yi Chung-hwan ŭi chiri sasang e kwanhan yŏn'gu (Geographical thoughts of Yi Chung-hwan, Korean human geographer in the eighteenth century)," *Naksan Chiri* 4 (1977): 25–39.

Rho Do-Yang. "*P'aryŏkchi* 'kagŏji' haesŏl'" (A Study of *Pal-yuk-ji*). *Chirihak* 1 (1963): 91–96.

Rim Young-gul. "*T'aengniji* tasi ilkki—kiwŏdŭ 'sadaebu rŭl t'onghayŏ" (Rereading *T'aengniji* by the keyword *sadaebu*). *Taedong Munhwa Yŏn'gu* 93 (2016): 75–97

Rogers, Michael C. "*P'yŏnnyŏn t'ongnok*: The Foundation Legend of the Koryŏ State." *Journal of Korean Studies* 4 (1982–1983).

Sim No-sung. *Nunmul iran muŏsin'ga* (What are tears?). Translated by Kim Young-jin. P'aju: T'aehaksa, 2001.

Sin Chŏng-il. *Saero ssŭnŭn "T'aengniji"* (*T'aengniji* newly written). 10 vols.. Ko-yang: Tosŏch'ulp'an Taŭm, 2012.

———. *Tasi ssŭnŭn "T'aengniji"* (*T'aengniji* rewritten). 5 vols. Seoul: Humanist, 2004–2006.

Sŏ Su-in. "*T'aengniji* yŏn'gu sŏsŏl" (An introduction to *T'aengniji* studies). *Chirihak* 1 (1963): 83–90.

Sŏ Yu-gu. *Imwŏn kyŏngjeji* (Writings on rural life management). Korea University, E1 A34 0–52.

Song Ch'an-sik. *Chosŏnhugi sahoekyŏnjesa ŭi yŏn'gu* (A study on the social and economic history of late Chosŏn). Seoul: Ilchokak, 1997.

———. "Chosŏnjo sarim chŏngch'i ŭi kwŏllŏk kujo (The power structure of lite-rati politics in the Chosŏn dynasty)." *Kyŏngje sahak* 2 (1978): 120–140.

———. "Sŏngho Yi Ik ŭi 'Saengjae' p'yŏn." (Yi Ik's "Saengjae") *Ch'ŏngmaek* 23 (1966) 202–208.

Sŏng Nak-hŭi. *Ch'oe Ch'i-wŏn ŭi si chŏngsin yŏn'gu* (A study of Ch'oe Ch'i-wŏn's soul of peotry). Seoul: Kwandong Ch'ulp'ansa, 1993.

Sŏul Sin *T'aengniji* Saŏptan (Seoul New *T'aengniji* Project Team), ed. *Ch'ŏngnyŏn, sŏul ŭi maŭl ŭl t'amhada* (Youth, surveying towns in Seoul). Seoul: Sŏul Tŭkpyŏlsi Munhwa Chŏngch'aek-kwa (Department of Cultural Policy, City of Seoul), 2014.

Suematsu Yasukazu. "Hachiikishi ni tsuite" (On *Paryŏkchi*). *Shyomotsu doogokai sooshi* 9, 1–8. First published in *Keijyo Teidai shigakukaishi* 14 (1939).

Vermeersch, Sem. "Buddhism as a Cure for the Land." In Buswell, ed., *Religions of Korea in Practice*, 76–85.

von Thünen, J. H. *Von Thunen's "Isolated State": An English Edition of "Der isolierte Staat."* Translated by Carla. M. Wartenberg with an introduction by Peter Hall. Oxford: Pergamon Press, 1966.

Wagner, Edward Willett. "The Civil Examination Process as Social Leaven—The Case of the Northern Provinces in the Yi Dynasty." *Korea Journal* 17, no. 1 (1977): 22–27.

———. *The Literati Purges: Political Conflict in Early Yi Korea.* Cambridge, MA: East Asian Research Center, Harvard University, 1974.

——— "Yijo sarim e kwanhan chaegŏmt'o" (Reexamination of the literati in the Chosŏn dynasty). *Chŏnbuk sahak* 4 (1980): 163–173.

Weber, Alfred. *Theory of the Location of Industries.* Translated with an introduction and notes by Carl J. Fredrich. Chicago: University of Chicago Press, 1957.

Wi Wŏn-hak. *"T'aengniji" yŏn'gu: Hanguk ŭi chŏnt'ongjŏk chiyŏk yŏn'gu* (A study of *T'aengniji*: Traditional Korean study on regions). Seoul: Sinyangsa, 1993.

Yang Bo Kyung. "Chosŏn sidae ŭi chayŏn insik ch'egye" (Epistemological system of recognizing nature in the Chosŏn dynasty). *Hanguksa simin kangjwa* 14 (1994): 70–97.

———. "Perceptions of Nature in the Joseon Period." *Korea Journal* 37, no. 4 (1997): 134–155.

Yang Junsong. *Hanlongjing* (Classic of rousing dragons). In *Jingjiao Dili zhengzong* (Meticulously proofread orthodox lineage of geomancy) ed. Jiang Guozong. Shinchu, Taiwan: Chulin Shuchu, 1967.

Yang Po-gyŏng. *See* Yang Bo Kyung.

Yang Wenhui. *Yang Renshan Jushi yizhu* (Posthumous work of Hermit Yang Renshan). Tainan Shi: Heyu Chubanshe, 1996.

Yi Ch'an. *See* Lee Chan.

Yi Chun-sŏn et al. *Hanguk yŏsa chiri* (Historical geography of Korea). Seoul: Purungil, 2011.

Yi Haeng et al. *Sinjŭng tongguk yŏji sŭngnam* (Newly augmented geographical survey of Korea). Korean translation by Kwŏn Tŏk-chu et al. Seoul: Minjok Munhwa Mungo Kanhaenghoe, 1969–1970.

Yi Hong-ryŏl. "Taegan chedo ŭi pŏpchesa chŏk koch'al (A historical survey of the institution of censorial officials). *Sach'ong* 5 (1960): 10–37.

Yi Ik. *Sŏngho chŏnjip* (Complete collection of the works of Sŏngho). http://db.itkc .or.kr/dir/item?itemId=BT#dir/node?grpId=&itemId=BT&gubun=book &depth=2&cate1=G&cate2=&dataGubun=서지&dataId=ITKC_BT_0489A.

———. *Sŏngho sasŏl* (Miscellaneous discussion of Sŏngho). http://db.itkc.or.kr/dir /item?itemId=BT#dir/node?grpId=&itemId=BT&gubun=book&depth=2 &cate1=G&cate2=&dataGubun=서지&dataId=ITKC_BT_1368A.

———. *Sŏngho Sŏnsaeng chŏnjip* (Complete collection of the works of Yi Ik). Seoul: Kyŏngin Munhwasa, 1974.

———. *Sŏngho Sŏnsaeng munjip* (Collection of the literary works of Yi Ik). 7 vols. In vols. 267–273 of *Hanguk yŏktae munjipch'ongsŏ* (Generations of Korean literary works collection series). Seoul: Kyŏngin Munhwasa, 1997.

Yi In-no. *P'ahanjip* (Jottings to break up idleness); Sŏng Hyŏn, *Yongjaech'onghwa* (Assorted writings of Yongjae). Translated with notes by Koryŏ Taehakkyo Minjok Munhwa Yŏn'guso. Seoul: Koryŏ Taehakkyo Minjok Munhwa Yŏn'guso, 1975.

Yi Ki-baek. *See* Lee, Ki-baik.

Yi Kŭng-ik. *Yŏllŏsil kisul* (Narratives of Yŏllŏsil). http://db.itkc.or.kr/search /group?q=query†%ED%8C%94%EC%97%AD%EB%B3%B5%EA%B1%B0 %EC%A7%80.

Yi Mun-jong. *See* Lee Moon-Jong.

Yi Pyong-Do. *Hanguk yuhaksa* (The history of Korean Confucianism). Seoul: Asea Munhwasa, 1989.

———. *Koryŏ sidae ŭi yŏn'gu* (A study of the Koryŏ period). Seoul: Ŭryu Munhwasa, 1948.

———. *Kuksa taegwan* (An overview of Korean history). Seoul: Pomungak, 1956.

——— "Three Kingdoms and Their Civilization." *Korea Journal* 4, no. 7 (1964): 10–15.

Yi Pyŏng-hyu. *See* Lee Byung Hyoo.

Yi Song-mu. *Chosŏn ch'ogi yangban yŏn'gu* (A study of early Chosŏn *yangban*). Seoul: Ilchokak, 1980.

———. *Chosŏn sidae tangjaengsa* (The history of the factional strife of the Chosŏn period). Seoul: Arŭmdaunnaldŭl, 2007.

———. "The Influence of Neo-Confucianism on Education and the Civil Service Examination System in Fourteenth- and Fifteenth-Century Korea." In *The Rise of Neo-Confucianism in Korea*, ed. Wm. Theodore de Barry and JaHyun Kim Haboush, 135–160. New York: Columbia University Press, 1985.

———. "Kwago System and Its Characteristics: Centering on the Koryŏ and Early Chosŏn Periods." *Korea Journal* 21, no. 7 (1981): 4–19.

Yi Song-mu et al. *Chosŏnhugi tangjaeng ŭi chonghapjŏk kŏmt'o* (A comprehensive review of factional strife in the late Chosŏn). Sŏngnam: Hanguk Chŏngsin Munhwa Yŏn'guwŏn, 1992.

Yi Su-gŏn. *Hanguk chungse sahoesa yŏn'gu* (A study of the history of the medieval Korean society). Seoul: Ilchokak, 1985.

———. *Yŏngnam sarimp'a ŭi hyŏngsŏng* (The formation of the Yŏngnam literati group). Kyŏngsan: Yŏngnam Taehakkyo Ch'ulp'anbu, 1979.

Yi T'ae-jin. *Chosŏn yugyo sahoesaron* (On the history of the Confucian society of Chosŏn). Seoul: Chisiksanŏpsa, 1989.

———. *Hanguk sahoesa yŏn'gu: Nong'ŏp kisul paltal kwa sahoe pyŏndong* (A study of Korean social history: Advances in agricultural technology and social change). P'aju: Chisiksanŏpsa, 2008.

Yi To-hun. *See* Lee Do-hun.

Yi U-sŏng. *Hanguk chungse sahoe yŏn'gu* (A study of medieval Korean society). Seoul: Ilchokak, 1991.

Yi Wŏn-sun (李元淳). "Chosŏn sirhak chisigin ŭi hanyŏk chirisŏ ihae" (An appreciation of the Chinese translation of [Western] geographical works by Chosŏn Sirhak literati). In *Hanguk ui chŏnt'ong chiri sasang* (Traditional geographic thought of Korea), ed. Hanguk Munhwayŏksa Chirihakhoe. Seoul: Minumsa, 1991.

Yi Wŏn-sun (李源順), ed. *Hwahae hwip'yŏn* (Collection of books on China and Korea). Kyujanggak collection, ko 4300 1A 00, 1805.

Yi Yong-bŏm. *Hanguk kwahak sasangsa yŏn'gu* (A study of scientific thought in Korea). Seoul: Tongguk Taehakkyo Ch'ulp'anbu. 1993.

Yim Yŏng-gŏl. *See* Rim Young-gul.

Yinfu Jing (Book of hidden code). Shanghai: Shanghai Guji Chubanshe, 1990.

Yoon, Hong-key. "Confucianism and the Practice of Geomancy." In Buswell, ed., *Religions of Korea in Practice*, 205–222.

———. *The Culture of Fengshui in Korea*. Lanham, MD: Lexington Books, 2006.

———. "Human Modification of Korean Landforms for Geomantic Purposes," *The Geographical Review* 101, no. 2 (2011): 243–260.

———. "The Nature and Origin of Chinese Geomancy." *Eratosthene-Sphragide* 1 (1986): 88–102.

———. "Representations of Koguryo Heritage in the Mythical Legends from *Koryŏsa Segye*." *International Review of Korean Studies* 10 (2013): 1–18.

———. "*T'aengniji*: A Classical Cultural Geography of the Korean Settlement." *Korea Journal* 16, no. 8 (1976): 4–12.

———. "*T'aengniji*: A Korean Settlement Geography." Master's thesis, Brigham Young University, 1971.

Yoon, Inshil Choe. "Academic Relationship between Yi Ik and Yi Chung-hwan." In *Perspectives on Korea*, ed. Sang-Oak Lee and Duk-Soo Park, 164–171. Sydney: Wild Peony Pty Ltd., 1998.

———. "Early Period *T'aengniji* Manuscripts." *Korean Studies* 37 (2013): 225–249.

———. "An Examination of Geomancy (*P'ungsu*) as Employed in *T'aengniji*." *International Review of Korean Studies* 6, no. 1 (2009): 49–76.

———. "Geomantic Ideas in *T'aengniji* Manuscripts: An Examination of Changing Perceptions of *P'ungsu* during the Late Chosŏn Dynasty." In *"P'ungsu": A Study of Geomancy in Korea*, ed. Hong-key Yoon, 353–371. New York: State University of New York Press, 2017.

———. "A Study and Translation of *T'aengniji*." PhD diss., University of Auckland, 1996.

Yoon, Inshil Choe, and Yoon Hong-key. "Yi Chung-hwan (1690–1756)." In *Geographers Biobibliographical Studies* 21, ed. Patrick H. Armstrong and G. J. Martin, 123–130. London: Continuum, 2001.

Youn, Sa-Soon. "Main Stream of Korean Philosophy." *Korea Journal* 14, no. 6 (1974): 57–58.

———. *Tongyang sasang kwa hanguk sasang* (East Asian thought and Korean thought). Seoul: Ŭryu Munhwasa, 1985.

———. "Wŏn Buddhism and Practical Learning." *Korea Journal* 24, no. 6 (1984): 40–49.

Yu Chŏng-gi, ed. *Happon sasŏ samgyŏng* (Bound volumes of Four Books and Three Classics). Seoul: Hagyesa, 1976.

Yu Chung-nim. *Chŭngbo sallim kyŏngje* (Revised and enlarged farm management). Seoul National University, Kyujanggak collection, kyu 9100 7A.

Yu Sŏng-nyong. *Kugyŏk Sŏaejip* (Anthology of Sŏae). 2 vols. In vols. 122–123 of *Kojŏn Kugyŏk Ch'ongsŏ* (Korean translation classics series), ed. Minjok Munhwa Ch'ujinhoe. Seoul: Minmungo, 1989.

Yu Wŏn-dong. "Ch'ŏngdam Yi Chung-hwan." In *Hanguk sirhak kaeron* (Introduction to Korean Practical Learning) 127-144, Seoul: Chŏng'ŭm Munhwasa, 1983.

Yumahilsosŏlgyŏng (*Vimalakīrtinirdeśasūtra*). Koryŏdaejanggyŏng Yŏn'guso (Research Centre of Tripitaka Koreana), *Koryŏdaejanggyŏng Chirikbaeisŭ* (*Tripitaka Koreana Knowledgebase*). http://kb.sutra.re.kr/ritk/searchSimple/searchSimple.do.

Yun Hyu. *Paekhojip* (Collection of Paekho). In vol. 123 of *Hanguk munjip ch'onggan*, Seoul: Hanguk Kojŏn Pŏnyŏkwŏn, 2013.

Yun Kuk-il. *Kyŏngguk taejŏn yŏn'gu* (A study of the *National Code*). Ed. P'yŏngyang Kwahak Paekkwasajŏn Ch'ulp'ansa. Seoul: Yŏgang Ch'ulp'ansa, 1986.

Yun Sa-sun. *See* Youn Sa-Soon.

Glossary-Index

Page numbers in **boldface** type refer to maps or plates

About the Translator

Inshil Choe Yoon is a senior lecturer in the School of Languages, Cultures, and Linguistics at the University of Auckland. Her study of the *T'aengniji* has resulted in numerous publications. She is also the author of *Time for Korean*, which reflects her research interest in Korean-language education.

Korean Classics Library: Philosophy and Religion

Salvation through Dissent: Tonghak Heterodoxy and Early Modern Korea
George L. Kallander

Reflections of a Zen Buddhist Nun
Kim Iryŏp, translated by Jin Y. Park

A Handbook of Buddhist Zen Practice
translated by John Jorgensen

Korea's Great Buddhist-Confucian Debate: The Treatises of Chŏng Tojŏn (Sambong)
and Hamhŏ Tŭkt'ong (Kihwa)
translated and with an introduction by A. Charles Muller

A Korean Confucian Way of Life and Thought: The *Chasŏngnok* (Record of Self-
Reflection) by Yi Hwang (T'oegye)
translated, annotated, and with an introduction by Edward Y. J. Chung

Numinous Awareness Is Never Dark: The Korean Buddhist Master Chinul's *Excerpts*
on Zen Practice
translated, annotated, and with an introduction by Robert E. Buswell, Jr.

Doctrine and Practice in Medieval Korean Buddhism: The Collected Works of Ŭich'ŏn
translated, annotated, and with an introduction by Richard D. McBride II

The Foresight of Dark Knowing: *Chŏng Kam nok* and Insurrectionary Prognostication
in Pre-Modern Korea
translated, annotated, and with an introduction by John Jorgensen

A Place to Live: A New Translation of Yi Chung-hwan's *T'aengniji*, the Korean Classic
for Choosing Settlements
translated, annotated, and with an introduction by Inshil Choe Yoon

Korean Classics Library: Historical Materials

Imperatives of Culture: Selected Essays on Korean History, Literature, and Society
from the Japanese Colonial Era
edited by Christopher P. Hanscom, Walter K. Lew, and Youngju Ryu

A Chinese Traveler in Medieval Korea: Xu Jing's *Illustrated Account of the Xuanhe Em-
bassy to Koryŏ*
translated, annotated, and with an introduction by Sem Vermeersch

Seeking Order in a Tumultuous Age: The Writings of Chŏng Tojŏn, a Korean Neo-
Confucian
translated and with an introduction by David M. Robinson